A Longman Cultural Edition

BEOWULF

Translated by

Alan Sullivan and Timothy Murphy

Edited by

Sarah M. Anderson

PEARSON
Longman

OCM 53374794
New York   San Francisco   Boston
London   Toronto   Sydney   Tokyo   Singapore   Madrid
Mexico City   Munich   Paris   Cape Town   Hong Kong   Montreal

Vice President and Editor-in-Chief: Joseph P. Terry
Development Editor: Anne Brunell Ehrenworth
Senior Marketing Manager: Melanie Craig
Production Coordinator: Shafiena Ghani
Project Coordination, Text Design, and Electronic Page Makeup: Dianne Hall
Cover Designer/Manager: John Callahan
Cover Image: *The Claw of Grendel* by Alan Lee (1984)
Manufacturing Buyer: Roy L. Pickering
Printer and Binder: Courier Corporation
Cover Printer: Lehigh Press, Inc.

Library of Congress Cataloging-in-Publication Data

Beowulf / edited by Sarah M. Anderson; translated by Alan Sullivan and Timothy
Murphy.
    p. cm. — (A Longman cultural edition)
    Includes bibliographical references (pp. 229–34).
    ISBN 0-321-10720-9 (pbk.)
    1. Epic poetry, English (Old)—Modernized versions. 2. Scandinavia—Poetry.
3. Monsters—Poetry. 4. Dragons—Poetry. I. Anderson, Sarah M., 1950– .
II. Sullivan, Alan, 1948– . III. Murphy, Timothy, 1951– . IV. Series.
    PR1583.S75 2004
    829'.3—dc22

                                   2003065901

Please visit our website at http://www.ablongman.com

ISBN 0-321-10720-9

45678910—CRW—07

Contents

List of Illustrations

About Longman Cultural Editions

Reading always seems to vibrate with the transformation of the day—now, yesterday, and centuries ago, when the presses first put printed language into wide circulation. Correspondingly, literary culture has always been a matter of change: of new practices confronting established traditions; of texts transforming under the pressure of new techniques of reading and new perspectives of understanding; of canons shifting and expanding; of informing traditions getting reviewed and renewed, recast and reformed by emerging cultural interests and concerns; of culture, too, as a variable "text"—a reading. Inspired by the innovative *Longman Anthology of British Literature*, Longman Cultural Editions respond creatively to the changes, past and recent, by presenting key texts in contexts that illuminate the lively intersections of literature, tradition, and culture. A principal work is made more interesting by materials that place it in relation to its past, present, and future, enabling us to see how it may be reworking traditional debates and practices, how it appears amid the conversations and controversies of its own historical moment, how it gains new significances in subsequent eras of reading and reaction. Readers new to the work will discover attractive paths for exploration, while those more experienced will encounter fresh perspectives and provocative juxtapositions.

Longman Cultural Editions serve not only several kinds of readers but also (appropriately) their several contexts, from various courses of study to independent adventure. Handsomely produced and affordably priced, our volumes offer appealing companions to *The Longman Anthology of British Literature*, in some cases enriching and expanding units originally developed for the *Anthol-*

ogy, and in other cases presenting this wealth for the first time. The logic and composition of the contexts vary across the series. The constants are the complete text of an important literary work, reliably edited, headed by an inviting introduction, and supplemented by helpful annotation; a table of dates to track its composition, publication, and public reception in relation to biographical, cultural, and historical events; and a guide for further inquiry and study. With these common measures and uncommon assets, Longman Cultural Editions encourage your literary pleasures with resources for lively reflection and adventurous inquiry.

Susan J. Wolfson
General Editor
Professor of English
Princeton University

About This Edition

The anonymous 3,182-line Old English poem that we call *Beowulf* constitutes about one-tenth of the Old English poetry that survives from the Anglo-Saxon period and is the only epic poem of the period that has outlasted the accidents of time. The poem challenges us not only because of the complicated contextual and poetic problems it raises, but also because of our fascination with what the poem does not tell us, or tells us only incompletely. Though this is a deeply English poem—"English" in that it has become foundational for our reading of the history of English literature and in that it witnesses the construction of an English national identity—it features a Scandinavian hero and Scandinavian settings. Though it is touted as "great literature," it narrates rather indistinct conflicts in a time long, long ago and a place far, far away. Though it is generally agreed that the one manuscript that contains the poem was written c. 1000, no one agrees when it was composed, where, or for whom. No one knows who read it, or why, or what they thought of it. Of the many characters mentioned in the poem, often with maddeningly similar names, most are cited only once. And finally, for a poem that "put the monsters in the centre,"[1] in J. R. R. Tolkien's fine phrase, it is marked as much by talk, speeches, and rumination as it is by action.

Beowulf is not an easy poem, but, like all of our greatest works of literature, it repays the careful reader many times over. Tolkien was a lover of *Beowulf* and one of its best readers, and to read what he wrote about the poem enables one not only to understand Tolkien's own fictional responses to early literature, but also to hear

---

[1] Tolkien (1983, p. 25). Tolkien's famous 1936 address, "*Beowulf*: The Monsters and the Critics," ought to be read by any student of the poem. See *Further Reading*.

a knowing, impassioned voice describe the somber richness of *Beowulf*: "a drink dark and bitter: a solemn funeral-ale with the taste of death."[2] The dangers of the fierce world depicted in *Beowulf* are hair-raising—human, humanoid, and then the dragon. The unknown poet draws warriors up on their mettle, full of proud boasts or of beer, and then shows us these men as gobbets of gore, torn or cut into pieces, burned to ashes rising into the sky. *Beowulf* gives the reader bright flickers of heroic glory, and, all around and within this splendor, the grim grind of one's doom. Nothing suggests with such strength and such subtlety the problems of honor and fame as does *Beowulf*. The poem knows its fragile little world well.

But *Beowulf* is not just a sharp poem because of its sword edges. It is a poem of acute observations about the problems of remembering and of history, about the artistry of terror and of awe, a poem that demonstrates the astute inventiveness of traditional early poetry. This poem, although it observes neither the form of the classical epic nor the expectations of postmodern novel- and screen-reading audiences, tells a good story forcefully. And because it folds into itself the same experience told by several people, it is also a narrative that is very much about story-telling. Though the male hero commands attention, *Beowulf* keenly sees women too, a fact especially appreciated in the critical literature about the poem written after the 1970s. Woman speak in *Beowulf*: as voices arguing statecraft; as models of rulership, both good and bad; and as examples of the monster in a particularly troubling maternal manifestation. Finally, *Beowulf*, for all its vaunted qualities of massive balance—the Cyclopean architecture of its great half-lines, the rise and fall of a heroic life—is keen and quick. It has wit (and even humor); it queries every element it sets forth; its descriptions are deftly detailed, but also chillingly blank. To return to that part of the poem that Tolkien first turned us toward, this place of monsters and the anxiety about what makes the monstrous is constituted and examined at every turn in this canny poem.

This Longman Cultural Edition places *Beowulf* within several contexts, providing translations of ancillary works not readily available to first-time readers. The first context, defined by Latin texts bearing on *Beowulf* (*From the Latin*), includes se-

---

[2]Tolkien (1983, p. 49), from Tolkien's essay "On Translating *Beowulf*," which contains a succinct review of what a translation ought to accomplish and of the Old English metrical practices of the poem. See *Further Reading*.

lections from historians describing the origin and characteristics of the Germanic tribes in which *Beowulf* is interested. It highlights the poem's problems and themes: a fascination with the marvelous that may have put the poem into the manuscript anthology in which it is found, a concern with what makes a king and a nation, and the retrofitting of Germanic legendary cultures within a milieu of Christian Latinity. The second contextual section (*From the Old English*) takes up *Beowulf*'s analogues in the vernacular, giving examples from elegiac, heroic, wisdom, and religious literature whose topics and modes are allied with those of *Beowulf*. These selections are marked by the same Germanic legendary material to which *Beowulf* alludes; Old English religious poetry, too, reimagined its stories in comparable ways. A sub-section (*From the Old English—Reading Beowulf*) also takes up the problem of translating, a problem with which *Beowulf* is deeply engaged as it "carries over" the cultural materials of its continental European, non-Christian past into the newly constructed culture of an Anglo-Saxon England. By providing different translations of the poem's famous opening lines, this subsection gives the reader a chance to scrutinize two centuries of efforts to put this notoriously difficult poem into modern English. The third and final contextual unit (*From the Old Norse*) looks at analogues in Old Norse culture and literature, including cautionary maxims, tales of heroic determination, and Scandinavian poetry and prose featuring creatures that haunt the dark side of the human imagination.[3] Finally, genealogical charts, maps, a table of dates, a list of proper names, and suggestions for further reading are also included to aid the new reader. All of the contextual material included here is designed to help the reader follow Tolkien's lead in recognizing the poem in all its fullness.[4]

---

[3]Tolkien's "*Beowulf*: The Monsters and the Critics" has a great deal to say about the aptness of illuminating the Anglo-Saxon by the Icelandic. For example, he writes, in regards to the mythology of the two cultures, that it is "legitimate to suppose that in the matter of the position of the monsters in regard to men and gods the view was fundamentally the same [in pre-Christian English mythology] as in later Icelandic" (Tolkien 1983, pp. 24–25).

[4]"Nearly all the censure, and most of the praise, that has been bestowed on *The Beowulf* has been due either to the belief that it was something that it was *not* . . . or to disappointment at the discovery that it was itself and not something the scholar would have liked better. . . .", from "*Beowulf*: The Monsters and the Critics" (Tolkien 1983, p. 7).

Beowulf has been translated afresh by Alan Sullivan and Tim Murphy. This vivid new translation has its own pleasures, grasping the famously powerful beat and excitement of the original text. With this new translation and the material that supports it, it is hoped that readers will not only listen to *Beowulf*, as the poem commands us to do, but also hear the intensely stirring story and the song that it conveys.

I would like to thank Professor Susan J. Wolfson of Princeton University and General Editor of the Longman Cultural Editions for inviting me to participate in the series and for her support throughout the publishing of *Beowulf*. Anne Brunell Ehrenworth, Development Editor at Longman Publishers, was unstinting in her guidance, time, patience, and good humor during the long period of getting these pages to press, and she deserves kudos for her strenuous efforts. I would also like to thank my students of early literature at Princeton University, the Firestone Library at Princeton University, the Rare Books and Special Collections Division of Firestone Library, and my colleagues Lawrence Danson, U. C. Knoepflmacher, Jeff Nunokawa, and, most particularly, Claudia L. Johnson for discussions and assistance that made possible, and then sustained, my work on this subject.

Acknowledgments and thanks are due to the Board of The British Library for permission to reproduce a leaf from Cotton MS Vitellius A xv.; to Jesse L. Byock and the Penguin Group for permission to print excerpts from *The Saga of King Hrolf Kraki*; to Denton Fox, Hermann Pálsson, and The University of Toronto Press for permission to print excerpts from *Grettir's Saga*; to Charles W. Kennedy and Oxford University Press for permission to print his translations of *The Battle of Finnsburg* and *Waldere* from his *Anthology of Old English Poetry*; to the Estate of Ezra Pound and New Directions for permission to print his translation of *The Seafarer*; to Burton Raffel and Yale University Press for permission to print his translation of *The Wanderer* from *Poems and Prose from the Old English*; to Christopher Ricks and The University of California Press for permission to print *The Battle of Brunanburh* from *Tennyson: A Selected Edition*; to Tom A. Shippey and D. S. Brewer for permission to print his translation of *Vainglory* from *Poems of Wisdom and Learning in Old English*; to Patricia Terry and The University of Pennsylvania Press for permission to print excerpts from *Sayings of the High One* from her *Poems of the Elder Edda*; to the Estate of J. R. R. Tolkien and Oxford University

Press for permission to print excerpts from Professor Tolkien's translation of *Exodus* in *The Old English Exodus: Text, Translation, and Commentary. Edited by Joan Turville-Petre*; and to Craig Williamson and The University of Pennsylvania Press for permission to print a selection of riddles from *A Feast of Creatures: Anglo-Saxon Riddle Songs*.

In addition, I wish to thank the many thorough-going scholars who have made a work like this possible, particularly G. N. Garmonsway and Jacqueline Simpson for *Beowulf and Its Analogues* and Dorothy Whitelock for *English Historical Documents: c. 500–1042*, and the many extraordinary editors and readers of *Beowulf*, who have stimulated my teaching of the poem. Though I strive after their examples, the mistakes and omissions in the sections of this book that I contributed are my own.

Finally, I would like to express my warmest thanks and gratitude to L. Arthur and the late Anne Myers, who, a very long time ago, took me to Sutton Hoo, walked the mounds with me, and then made me tea.

Sarah M. Anderson
Princeton, New Jersey

Translators'
Introduction

Tim Murphy and I have come to *Beowulf* from very different angles. During his boyhood in Moorhead, Minnesota, Tim conceived a passion for the folk music of the Irish, the Scots, and their descendants in Canada and Appalachia. Later, when his voice crashed, he turned to the poetry of Frost and Yeats, but the Scottish Border ballads and Robert Burns have always remained dear to him. Meanwhile, in New York City, I was captivated by the work of J. R. R. Tolkien, author of the epic fantasy, *The Lord of the Rings*. Tolkien had derived his mythic realm from a boyhood passion of his own—he called it a vice—which undergirded all his subsequent fiction. He invented imaginary languages, drawing on his scholarship in Old English, Old Norse, and Old High German to shape his vocabularies and his runes.

As a student at Yale, Tim came under the tutelage of Robert Penn Warren, who pressed his pupil to memorize poetry until the young man's repertoire approached 30,000 lines. Not all those lines were Modern English. Some were Greek (the opening of *The Iliad*), and others were Old or Middle English (favorite passages from *Beowulf*, Chaucer, and various medieval lyrics). At the same time I was enrolled at Trinity College in Hartford, Connecticut, the city where Tim and I met in 1973. An indifferent student, I was cutting classes to write songs and play guitar when *Beowulf* was taught; but Tolkien had already given me a grounding in Old English, though I didn't realize it for nearly thirty years.

Our work began almost inadvertently, when Tim decided to try his hand on the passages he had memorized so long before. As Tim's long-time editor, I peered over his shoulder at Klaeber's scholarly edition of the text. Delving into Old English was a spooky experience for me. The language seemed almost uncannily familiar. Soon Tim trusted me to pursue the project on my own, though I kept good company. Donaldson's prose version, Alexander's crib, and Chickering's *en face* verse translation were all at hand. Although he was too busy to collaborate full-time, from the outset Tim had fastened on four principles for the translation. (1) It would be written in four-beat lines, like the original, though differing somewhat in metrical detail. (2) It would follow a loosened variant of the Scop's Rule, alliterating three times in most lines, but using other patterns of alliteration as well. (3) It would employ modern syntax, with some inversion for rhetorical effect. (4) Words of Germanic origin would be chosen preferentially.

Scholars argue over exactly how *Beowulf* might have sounded, but they agree broadly that Old English relied more than Modern English on *quantitative*, or time-based measure, while verse in Modern English is more *qualitative*, or stress-based. Because of this fundamental difference, the rhythm of *Beowulf* cannot be replicated in Modern English. The translator must employ a different metrical principle while attempting to recapture the force of the original. Our version is written in accentual tetrameter, with lines averaging nine or ten syllables. Some readers may think they hear trisyllabic feet of accentual-syllabic verse, but the translation cannot be scanned in this manner for more than a few lines at a time.

Homer and Virgil were impressively translated into iambic pentameter by Chapman, Dryden, Pope, and Fitzgerald. *Beowulf*'s poet has been less fortunate. He wrote in alliterative tetrameter, the standard form for Anglo-Saxon and Old Norse epics. Each line consists of two half-lines divided by a strong pause. Each half-line contains two principal stresses, highlighted by alliteration. A half line can be as simple as *"beortum byrnum"* or as complex as *"pat hio hyre hearmdagas."* While we cannot know just how *Beowulf* was spoken, sung, or chanted, we find that the translation fares well when read aloud with half lines given roughly the same duration.

Like rhyme, alliteration affords both mnemonic aid and aural pleasure. The Rule of the Scop's (performing bards), when followed strictly, requires that both stresses in half-line "a" alliterate with the first stress in half-line "b." As he began to work with the text, Tim altered the rule to fit the characteristics of Modern English.

There were three stressed alliterations in the majority of his lines, but he placed them in any of the four possible configurations (xxxy, xxyx, xyxx, yxxx), and sometimes he accepted alliteration on a secondary accent. Where there were only two alliterations, he usually bound them to others in a preceding or succeeding line. Often he used two pairs of alliterative words on the stress points of a line, arranged in one permutation or another: xxyy, xyyx, xyxy. In such cases he might also incorporate one or more x and/or y alliterations in adjoining lines. The objective was to weave a web of sound, not to follow a mechanical rule. And the *Beowulf*-poet himself indulged in such variations, though less frequently.

Syntax is a continual challenge for translators of *Beowulf*. Germanic languages do not use word order to indicate the parts of speech. Instead they are inflected: number, case, gender, tense, and voice are indicated by the spellings of words and the suffixes attached to them. Despite this superfluity of syllables, most translators have followed *Beowulf*'s line count, a practice that impels them to pad the poem. And few of them have dared meddle with the text enough to straighten out the syntax for modern readers. Groping our way toward a version that reads well in Modern English, we have striven to keep hold of the poem's sense. Though we change nouns to adjectives, and adjectives to adverbs, though we resequence clauses or omit conjunctions, we believe that such grammatical maneuvers need not alter materially what the poem *says*. Sometimes they enhance comprehension.

In vocabulary we have taken our cues from Tolkien, whose work helped familiarize a generation of readers with terms from the armories of old. To eschew such words would impoverish the text. *Beowulf* is full of artifacts, which Modern English cannot always name with terms that apply with perfect accuracy to equipage of the Anglo-Saxon era. Happily, our language remains rich in words with Nordic or Germanic roots—far more of them, in fact, than the *Beowulf*-poet employed, since the word-hoard of English has grown greatly over the centuries. Some are reasonably synonymous with words found in the poem, allowing us to imbue the translation with the sound and feel of an elder (sometimes an eldritch) tongue. At the same time we have avoided Latin and French derivatives as much as possible. More than 90 percent of words in our *Beowulf* come from the *losers* (Old English), not the *victors* (Latin) at the Battle of Hastings. Unfortunately, "triumph," "honor," "glory," and "fame" arrived with the Norman French. Modern English affords no synonyms of alternative derivation. However "hoard," "wrath," and "death" still sound exactly as they did in the mouths of Scops a millennium ago.

Alan Sullivan
Fargo, North Dakota
30 June 2003

A Summary
of Beowulf

I. Grendel (lines 1–870)

A compressed biography of Scyld Scefing, founder of the Danish royal dynasty the Scyldings, begins the poem. The Scyldings prosper until Hrothgar, the great grandson of Scyld, builds Heorot, the most splendid hall ever constructed, in the fiftieth year of his reign. The humanoid monster Grendel attacks the Danes ferociously and repeatedly, so that Hrothgar and his Danes cower in fear. After twelve years of these attacks, Beowulf the Geat, whose father was aided by Hrothgar, comes over the sea from Geatland with a band of men to kill the monster. Though the Dane Unferth challenges his credentials, Beowulf recounts his proven abilities to kill monsters and pledges to combat Grendel alone and unarmed. The Danes and Geats feast, then fall asleep in Heorot. Grendel enters the hall, tears one warrior to bits, and then seizes Beowulf. The two wrestle fiercely within Heorot, smashing its furnishings. The Geats try to help their leader, but discover that swords will not harm Grendel. Grendel tries to run from Beowulf, but the Geat won't let go of the monster's arm, and it is only by leaving the arm torn off in Beowulf's grip that Grendel is able to escape. The next day, Danes and Geats gaze in wonder at Grendel's clawlike limb, as it hangs from Heorot's roof, and then they follow Grendel's bloody trail to a small lake set in terrifying surroundings. The warriors, seeing the bloody waters of the lake, assume that Grendel is dead. They ride back to Heorot joyously, comparing Beowulf to Sigemund the dragon-slayer. Hrothgar thanks Beowulf, calling him as close as a son, and Beowulf responds graciously.

II. Grendel's Mother (lines 871–1939)

Heorot is cleaned, and then Hrothgar rewards Beowulf's deeds with many gifts. A great celebration is held in the hall. During it, a poet sings the tragic tale of Finn and Hildeburh. Wealhtheow serves the men, appealing to the warriors, and especially to Beowulf, to respect her sons' chances to succeed Hrothgar. The Danes and Geats fall asleep. Grendel's mother, seeking to avenge her son, enters Heorot, grabs a favorite advisor of Hrothgar, and escapes. Beowulf, who is revealed to have been sleeping elsewhere, is told of this new attack and sets off to get revenge. When the Danes and Geats reach the lake, they find the bloody head of the Danish advisor. The warriors kill some of the water-monsters in the lake from the shore. Borrowing Unferth's sword, Beowulf jumps into the waters. In his lengthy descent to the floor of the lake, he is attacked by water-monsters, but he prevails. Grendel's mother grabs the Geat, dragging him into the uncanny submarine hall where she has ruled for fifty years. They wrestle fiercely, and Beowulf finds that Unferth's sword does not harm Grendel's mother. Nearly overpowered, Beowulf miraculously is able to seize a giant sword that is hanging on the wall. With it, Beowulf kills Grendel's mother and beheads Grendel, whom he sees lying in the hall. The monsters' blood dissolves the sword blade. Above on the land, the waiting Danes and Geats again see blood in the water. The Danes, believing Beowulf dead, leave, but the Geats stay on. Carrying Grendel's head and the hilt of the giant sword, Beowulf swims to the surface, and his Geatish comrades joyfully accompany him to Heorot. Turning the spoils over to Hrothgar, Beowulf recounts his adventures to Hrothgar. Hrothgar mulls over the sword hilt and then delivers an address to Beowulf, citing his potential as a king and warning him of pride. Gifts are given to Beowulf and the Geats. The next day they bid the Danes farewell and sail back to Geatland. Beowulf tells his king, Hygelac, who is also his uncle, of his adventures and lays out the likelihood of political problems for Hrothgar when the king's daughter marries Ingeld. Hygelac and Beowulf exchange gifts.

III. The Dragon (lines 1940–2801)

The poem moves forward some fifty years: after Hygelac has been killed in a disastrous raid on the Franks, Beowulf has become king. Though offered the kingship by Hygd, Hygelac's widow, Beowulf supports the claim of Heardred, Hygelac's younger son, and serves him until he is killed in the recurring wars between the Geats and the Swedes. Beowulf has ruled for fifty years when he learns that a dragon harasses the Geatish kingdom. The dragon's wrath has been kindled because a cup has been stolen from its hoard, and the history of those treasures, hidden by the last of a people and found by the dragon three hundred years before, is told. Beowulf's career is set forth, with some important differences from other expositions of it in the poem. Beowulf decides to face the dragon alone, but with his armor, sword, and a specially forged iron shield. Accompanied by eleven of his warriors, Beowulf is guided to the dragon's barrow by the thief who took the cup. Before confronting the dragon, Beowulf considers the lives of Hrethel the Geat and Ongentheow the Swede, two other aged kings who met disastrous ends. Then Beowulf calls the dragon to do battle. The fight takes place in three stages, with Beowulf's need for help and probable defeat clearer at each stage. Though Beowulf's warriors are too frightened to aid their king, Wiglaf, a member of Beowulf's own tribe, the Waegmundings, enters the fight. With Wiglaf's help, Beowulf kills the dragon, though he is mortally wounded as a result. Wiglaf attends his dying king's wishes, fetching some of the dragon's treasure for the suffering king to see. Beowulf gives his kingdom to Wiglaf, instructs him about his funeral, and, while gazing at items from the hoard, dies. Wiglaf reproaches Beowulf's warriors severely. A messenger gives the news of Beowulf's death to the rest of the Geatish party and then envisions the terrible onslaughts that the Geats will suffer from the Swedes. The Geats come to the headland where the battle took place to honor their dead king; the dragon is pushed off a cliff into the sea. Wiglaf causes the dragon's hoard to be placed on Beowulf's pyre and the pyre burned. Beowulf is mourned by an old Geatish woman, who foretells briefly the dire future of the Geats. A grave-mound for Beowulf is made on the headland by the sea, and the dragon's hoard is placed within it along with Beowulf's ashes. The poem ends with Beowulf's warriors circling the mound and singing Beowulf's praises.

Glossary of Proper Names

ABEL: killed by Cain, his brother; see Genesis 4:1–16 for the story of Cain and Abel

AELFHERE: a kinsman of Wiglaf

AESCHERE: favored advisor to Hrothgar; killed by Grendel's mother

BEANSTAN: father of Breca

BEOW: a Danish king; son of Scyld and grandfather of Hrothgar

BEOWULF: son of Ecgtheow and maternal nephew of King Hygelac; later, king of the Geats

BRECA: a Bronding leader who, as a youth, was a companion of Beowulf

BRONDINGS: the name of a Germanic tribe that lived perhaps in southern Sweden or Norway

CAIN: slayer of Abel, his brother, and in this poem, ancestor of a race of monsters

DAEGHREFN: a Hugas champion killed by Beowulf, probably in the same battle in Frisia in which King Hygelac was killed

EADGILS: a Swedish prince who is the younger son of Ohthere and the brother of Eanmund; Beowulf aids him in winning the Swedish throne from Onela, his uncle, whom Eadgils kills

EANMUND: a Swedish prince who is the older son of Ohthere and the brother of Eadgils; slain by Weohstan, by order of Onela, his uncle

EARNANAESS: ("eagles' cape") a headland in Geatland near where the dragon fight takes place

ECGLAF: father of Unferth

ECGTHEOW: father of Beowulf and the son-in-law of King Hrethel; Hrothgar pays the wergeld on his behalf after Ecgtheow kills the Wylfing warrior Heatholaf

ECGWELA: an early Danish king

EOFOR: a Geatish warrior, son of Wonred and brother of Wulf; Eofor kills Ongentheow in battle, and Hygelac rewards Eofor by betrothing his daughter to him

EOMER: son of Offa and grandson of Garmund

EORMANRIC: a late fourth-century king of the East Goths and figure of Germanic legend

FINN: son of Folcwalda and king of the Frisians; married to Hnaef's sister Hildeburh; Finn and his men kill Hnaef at Finnsburg, but Finn is later defeated and killed by Hengest, Hnaef's successor (see also *The Battle of Finnsburg, Contexts, From the Old English*, pp. 148–150)

FITELA: both Sigemund's nephew and son

FRANKS: members of a Germanic tribe that conquered much of modern France and Germany and created an empire under Clovis (c. 465–511); the Franks became a confederation of tribes that included the Hetwares and the Hugas

FREAWARU: a Danish princess and daughter of Hrothgar; betrothed to Ingeld the Heathobard

FREYA: Norse goddess ("Freyja") and the owner of a famous necklace

FRISIA: a coastal region of northern Europe bordering the North Sea, south of modern Denmark

FRODA: a king of the Heathobards and father of Ingeld; killed fighting the Danes

GARMUND: father of the Anglian king Offa

GEATS: a tribe inhabiting southern Sweden

GIFTHAS: an East Germanic tribe

GRENDEL: a humanoid monster who harasses Heorot and is slain by Beowulf

GUTHLAF: a Danish warrior and companion of Hengest

HAERETH: father of Queen Hygd

HALGA: a Danish prince and son of Healfdene; Hrothgar's younger brother and the father of Hrothulf

HAMA: a protagonist of Gothic legend who stole the Brosing necklace from Eormanric

HAETHCYN: the second son of Hrethel; Haethcyn killed his brother Herebeald accidentally and is killed by King Ongentheow at the battle of Ravenswood

HEALFDENE: a Danish king; father of Heorogar, Halga, Hrothgar, and an unnamed daughter who marries Onela

HEARDRED: a son of Hygelac who briefly succeeds him as king of the Geats and is killed by Onela for aiding his rebellious nephews

HEATHOBARDS: a Germanic tribe that dwells on the south Baltic coast

HEATHOLAF: a Wylfing warrior killed by Ecgtheow

HEATHORAEM: a tribe living near the coast of southeastern Norway

HELMINGS: the family to which Queen Wealhtheow belonged, perhaps a part of the Wylfings

HEMMING: a kinsman of Offa and Eomer

HENGEST: successor to Hnaef and leader of the Danes; he avenges Hnaef by killing Finn

HEOROGAR: a Danish king and elder brother of Hrothgar

HEOROT: the hall of Hrothgar, king of the Danes

HEOROWEARD: son of the Danish king Heorogar

HEREBEALD: eldest son of the Geatish king Hrethel; killed accidentally by his brother Haethcyn

HEREMOD: an early king of the Danes, who serves here as a model of bad kingship

HERERIC: uncle of the Geatish king Heardred; probably the brother of Hygd

HETWARE: a Frankish tribe

HILDEBURH: a Danish princess and daughter of Hoc; sister of Hnaef and wife of Finn, king of the Frisians

HNAEF: a Danish leader and son of Hoc; brother of Hildeburh who visits Finn and is killed there by the Frisians

HOC: a Danish king; father of Hildeburh and Hnaef

HONDSCIOH: a Geatish warrior in Beowulf's band who is killed by Grendel

HREOSNA-BEORH: a hill in Geatland where the Swedes attack the Geats

HRETHEL: a king of the Geats; father of Hygelac, Herebeald, Haethcyn, and Beowulf's mother; thus, the maternal grandfather of Beowulf, whom he raises from an early age

HRETHRIC: elder son of Hrothgar and Wealhtheow

HRONESNAESS: ("whale's cape") the headland in Geatland where Beowulf is buried

HROTHGAR: king of the Danes during Grendel's raids on Heorot; son of Healfdene and brother of Heorogar, Halga, and an unnamed sister married to Onela; father of Hrethric, Hrothmund, and Freawaru

HROTHMUND: younger son of Hrothgar and Wealhtheow

HROTHULF: son of Halga and nephew of Hrothgar, who may have seized power after Hrothgar's death and, in turn, is killed by Heoroweard, his cousin

HRUNTING: the sword of Unferth, which he lends to Beowulf to use against Grendel's mother; the sword proves to be useless, and Beowulf later returns it to Unferth

HUGAS: the name of a tribe allied with the Franks

HUNLAF: a Danish warrior killed when Hnaef battles the Frisians

HYGD: daughter of Haereth and wife of Hygelac, king of the Geats; Beowulf gives her the neck ornament that Hrothgar gave him

HYGELAC: king of the Geats, husband of Hygd, and son of Hrethel; uncle of Beowulf, who gives Beowulf Hrethel's sword and is killed in action in Frisia by the Franks

INGELD: son of Froda and king of the Heathobards; betrothed to Freawaru

JUTES: allies of the Frisians, or perhaps another name for the Frisians

MEROVING: Franks

MODTHRYTH: queen of the Angles and wife of Offa; used here as an example of a bad queen and woman

NAEGLING: Beowulf's sword, which fails in the fight with the dragon

OFFA: a fourth-century king of the Angles of continental Europe and husband of Modthryth

OHTHERE: a Swedish king who is the elder son of Ongentheow and brother of Onela; father of Eanmund and Eadgils

ONELA: a Swedish king and younger son of Ongentheow; Onela marries Healfdene's daughter and usurps the Swedish throne from Eanmund and Eadgils, the heirs of his brother Ohthere, but Onela is killed by Eadgils, with Beowulf's support

ONGENTHEOW: a Swedish king; father of Onela and Ohthere; defeated by Hygelac and killed by Eofor

OSLAF: a Danish warrior; companion of Hengest

RAVENSWOOD: site of the battle between the Geats and the Swedes, where Ongentheow is slain

SCYLD SCEFING: a Danish king and the eponymous founder of the Scylding dynasty, to which Hrothgar belongs

SCYLDINGS: a Danish dynasty; or, Danes

SCYLFINGS: a Swedish dynasty; or, Swedes

SIGEMUND: son of Waels; a legendary Germanic hero, here famous as a dragon-slayer

SWERTING: either the maternal uncle or grandfather of Hygelac

UNFERTH: a ranking member of Hrothgar's court who lends *Beowulf* the sword Hrunting

WAEGMUNDING: the family to which Beowulf and Wiglaf belong

WAELS: father of Sigemund

WAELSING: the family descended from Waels; Old Norse "Völsung"

WEALHTHEOW: Hrothgar's queen; the mother of Hrethric and Hrothmund

WEDERS: another name for the Geats

WELAND: the famous smith of Germanic legend

WENDELS: a Germanic tribe, perhaps the Vandals

WEOHSTAN: father of Wiglaf; kills Eanmund when fighting on Onela's side against Onela's rebellious nephews

WIGLAF: son of Weohstan; Waegmunding kinsman of Beowulf who helps slay the dragon

WITHERGYLD: a Heathobard warrior slain by the Danes

WONRED: a Geat; father of Eofor and Wulf

WULF: a Geatish warrior; son of Wonred and brother of Eofor

WULFGAR: a Wendel attached to Hrothgar's court as an officer

WYLFINGS: a Germanic tribe living near the southern Baltic coast

YRMENLAF: a Dane, and Aeschere's younger brother

Table of Dates

Only one date found in Beowulf, *the death of Hygelac (Lat.* Chlochilaichus*) in c. 521, can be attested by an independent source. Dates from the seventh through the eleventh centuries have been suggested for the composition of the poem. This chronology lists some of the dates relevant to a reading of* Beowulf *in its broad historical context and its rediscovery in modern times. All dates are in the common era.*

43	Roman invasions of Britain under Claudius begin.
98	Tacitus writes *Germania*.
382	Jerome begins Latin version of the Bible (the "Vulgate") at the request of Pope Damasus.
410	Rome withdraws her remaining legions from Britain.
429	Germanus comes to Britain to convert the inhabitants to Christianity.
430	Patrick comes to Ireland to convert the inhabitants to Christianity.
449	Germanic tribes called Angles, Saxons, and Jutes by Bede invade British Isles.
c. 521	Hygelac, king of the Geats, is killed in battle in Frisia by the Franks; recorded by Gregory of Tours, *History of the Franks* (Book III, ch. 3).
524	Boethius writes *The Consolation of Philosophy.*
591	Gregory of Tours writes *History of the Franks.*
597	Pope Gregory I (590–604) sends Augustine (later archbishop of Canterbury) on a mission to convert and stabilize the Christian church in the British Isles.

c. 624	Raedwald, king of East Anglia, dies; he is perhaps the king interred in the ship burial at Mound I, Sutton Hoo.
627	Paulinus, bishop of York, baptizes Edwin, king of Northumbria.
664	Synod of Whitby accepts authority of Rome, ending dispute over hegemony of Irish or Roman Christianity in British Isles.
735	Bede, author of *An Ecclesiastical History of the English People*, dies.
757–96	Offa, king of Mercia, reigns.
766–814	Charles the Great, king of the Franks, reigns.
c. 780s	Vikings begin to attack England; First Viking Age, 780s–900.
793	Vikings sack the monastery at Lindisfarne.
804	May 19: Alcuin of York dies.
855	Parker version of the Anglo-Saxon Chronicle records that the Vikings overwinter in England for the first time.
865	"Great Army" of the Vikings, led by Ivar, Ubbi, and Halfdan, attacks England.
871–99	Alfred the Great, king of Wessex, reigns.
878	Alfred defeats Guthrum at Battle of Edington.
893	Asser names Alfred "king of the Anglo-Saxons" in his biography of the king.
937	Battle of Brunanburh takes place.
960–88	Benedictine monastic reforms occur in England.
c. 980–1066	Second Viking Age.
991	Battle of Maldon takes place.
c. 1000	Compilation of the four major extant poetic manuscripts of Old English poetry: the *Beowulf* manuscript, the Exeter Book, the Junius Book, and the Vercelli Book.

c. 1014   Wulfstan writes the *Sermon of the "Wolf" to the English*.

             Swein Forkbeard, king of Denmark (c. 987–1014) and of England (1013–14), dies.

1016–35   Cnut, king of England and Denmark and son of Swein Forkbeard, reigns.

1066   Late September: at the Battle of Stamford Bridge, Harold II Godwineson, king of England, defeats Earl Tostig and Harald Hardrada of Norway.

             October 14: at the Battle of Hastings, King Harold is defeated and killed by William the Bastard, later the Conqueror, duke of Normandy.

             December 25: William the Conqueror is crowned William I, king of England, at Westminster Abbey by Aldred, archbishop of York.

1154   The last entry in the Peterborough version of the Anglo-Saxon Chronicle is for this year.

1705   Humfrey Wanley (1672–1726) copies and describes part of the *Beowulf* manuscript for volume two of George Hickes's so-called *Thesaurus* ("Two Books of Ancient Northern Literature").

1731   October: fire destroys or damages over 200 manuscripts, including the *Beowulf* manuscript, in the collection of Sir Robert Bruce Cotton (1571–1631).

1786–89   Grímur Jónsson Thorkelin (1752–1829) commissions a transcript of *Beowulf* and makes a second transcript himself.

1815   Thorkelin publishes the first edition of *Beowulf* in Copenhagen; he believes the poem to be a Danish epic originally composed in Danish.

1845   Department of Manuscripts of The British Library conserves the *Beowulf* manuscript.

1 *The Danes*

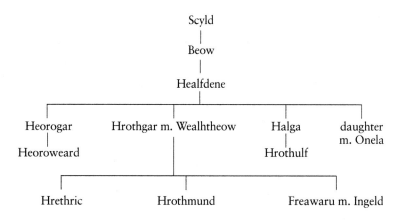

2 *The Geats*

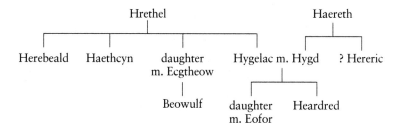

3 *The Half-Danes and the Frisians*

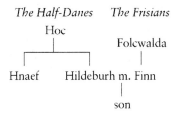

4 *The Heathobards*

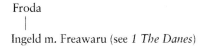

5 *The Swedes*

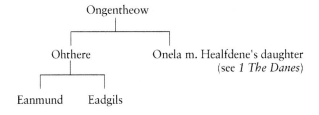

The Geography of Beowulf

Anglo-Saxon Englan∂

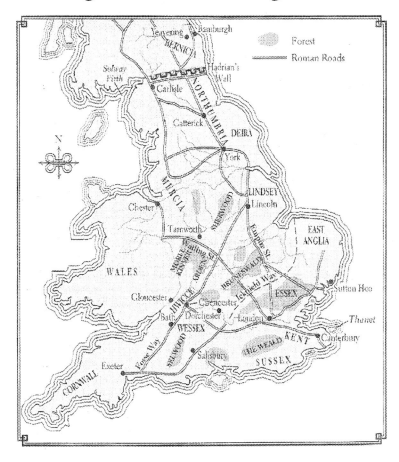

The English kingdoms at the beginning of the seventh century A.D. From Ralph Arnold, *A Social History of England.* Reprinted by permission of Penguin, Ltd. 1967, London.

BEOWULF

BEOWULF[1]

I. Grendel

So![2]   The Spear-Danes[3]   in days of old   1
were led by lords   famed for their forays.
We learned[4] of those princes'   power and prowess.

---

1 BEOWULF This modern English translation is by Alan Sullivan and Timothy Murphy
(2003). The poem is not titled in the single manuscript in which it is found, but it has
been known by the title *Beowulf* since John M. Kemble's (1807–57) edition *The Anglo-
Saxon Poems of Beowulf, The Traveller's Song and the Battle of Finnesburh*, which was
published in 1833 in London.   **2 So!** The first syllable of *Beowulf* sets forth the first of
the text's intriguing problems. The interjection *hwæt*, which occurs six other times in *Beowulf*, is written in the manuscript in capital letters, as is part of the first line of the poem
(through *WE GARDE*; see the facsimile of the manuscript leaf and the transcription of
it, pp. 124–25). Some scholars understand this interjection as a flat, unaccented start to
the poem. Others, however, read *hwæt* as a summons to attention—emphatic and extra-
metrical—noting its use at the beginning of other Old English poems and sermons (see
Mitchell and Robinson 1998, p. 45, n 1, and p. 315). The later explanation underscores
the poem's claim on recitation, whether the text as we have it is in some sense a "record-
ing" of a performance or evokes a deep understanding of itself as being enacted before
an audience.   **3 Spear-Danes** One of several epithets for Hrothgar's people found in the
poem. The Danes, also known by the patronymic Scyldings ("descendants of Scyld," see
note 5), are called the Bright-, East-, Half-, North-, Ring-, Spear-, and South-Danes in
Beowulf. The first line of the poem immediately puts us into the sixth-century aristocratic Scandinavian venue of the poem through this recollection of royal kingship "in
days of old."   **4 We learned** In his only use of the "we have heard" formula, translated
here as "we learned," the poet emphasizes that the stories of these "days of old" is
knowledge shared by the poet and his audience, identifying himself with them as recipi-
ents of this traditional lore. The Old English verb, "to learn of by asking" or "to hear
of," recollects the putatively oral delivery of the tales of the kingdom and its heroes. The
"I have heard" formula occurs several times in the poem; an example is found in line 56.

Often Scyld Scefing⁵   ambushed enemies,
took their mead-benches,⁶   mastered their troops,   5
though first he was found   forlorn and alone.⁷
His early sorrows   were swiftly consoled:
he grew under heaven,   grew to a greatness
renowned among men   of neighboring lands,
his rule recognized   over the whale-road,⁸   10
tribute⁹ granted him.   That was a good king!

Afterward God   gave him an heir,
a lad in the hall   to lighten all hearts.
The Lord had seen   how long and sorely
the people had languished   for lack of a leader.   15

5 **Scyld Scefing** The eponymous founder of the Danish royal house known as the Scyldings. The term "Scyldings" is also used in poetry to refer to the Danes generally. Scyld ("Scioldus," meaning "shield") is highly praised for his martial and noble qualities in the Latin history of Saxo Grammaticus, which, though itself later in date than *Beowulf*, points to the reputation of this figure in Northern Europe (for Saxo, see note 6 and *Contexts, From the Latin,* p. 118). "Scefing" has been taken as "son of Sceaf" (cf. the Old English poem *Widsith*, line 32, where "Sceafa" is named as a ruler of the Langobards, in *Contexts,* p. 160). "Scefing" has also been read as "with a sheaf," suggesting an association with a Germanic myth or legend in which a child floats ashore with a sheaf of grain at his head. If Scyld uncannily arrives by sea, note too that he mysteriously returns to it. For Scyld's status as an exiled orphan, see note 7.
6 **took their mead-benches** F. Klaeber, in his influential edition of *Beowulf* (1950), cites an analogue of this account of Scyld found in Saxo's *Deeds of the Danes.* "Mead-benches" is a metonymy for "hall" and also suggests the band of warriors needed to defend the hall.   7 **forlorn and alone** Scyld's arrival as a foundling without sponsors or protectors puts him in an acutely difficult position either in the imagined Scandinavian milieu in which the events of the poem occur or in the culture of the Anglo-Saxon audience of *Beowulf.* Compare Scyld's status with that of the protagonist in the Old English poem entitled *The Wanderer* in *Contexts,* pp. 138–41.
8 **whale-road** A kenning for "ocean." The kenning, a condensed figure of speech that is acutely observed, sometimes provocative, and frequently witty, is a staple of the Old English poetic grammar and is shared with the North Germanic poetic traditions as preserved in Old Norse. The ocean is elsewhere fancifully called "swan-road" (line 174) and "gannet's bath," translated here as "where the gannets bathe" (line 1650).
9 **tribute** The forced payment of money in the form of coins or ingots, treasure, and other goods to invaders in order to secure peace, even though these arrangements often collapsed, is a political commonplace during this period. The term "Danegeld" describes the tribute paid to bands of Scandinavians who harassed the British Isles; the first such payment is recorded in the Anglo-Saxon Chronicle for the year 865 (see *Contexts, From the Old English,* p. 186). Scandinavian runic stones contemporary with the Anglo-Saxon Chronicle commemorate raiders enriched by this tribute.

Beow[10] was blessed   with boldness and honor;
throughout the North   his name became known.
A soldierly son   should strive in his youth
to do great deeds,   give generous gifts
and defend his father.   Then in old age,   20
when strife besets him,   his comrades will stand
and his folk follow.   Through fair dealing
a prince shall prosper   in any kingdom.

Still hale on the day   ordained for his journey,
Scyld went to dwell   with the World's Warder.   25
His liegemen bore   his bier to the beach:
so he had willed   while wielding his words
as lord of the land,   beloved by all.
With frost on its fittings,   a lordly longboat
rode in the harbor,   ring-bowed and ready.   30
They placed their prince,   the gold-giver,
the famous man,   at the foot of the mast,
in the hollow hull   heaped with treasures
from far-off lands.   I have not heard another
ship ever sailed   more splendidly stocked   35
with war-weapons,   arms and armor.
About his breast   the booty was strewn,
keepsakes soon to be   claimed by the sea.
So he'd been sent   as a child chosen
to drift on the deep.   The Danes now returned   40
treasures no less   than those they had taken,
and last they hoisted   high overhead
a golden banner   as they gave the great one
back to the Baltic   with heavy hearts

---

10 **Beow** The manuscript reads "Beowulf" here (line 16; see *Contexts, Reading* Beowulf, p. 125) and once more when referring to this character (line 51). But this is not the poem's hero, Beowulf the Geat, who first introduces himself by name at line 307 in this translation. This first Beowulf is Beowulf the Dane ("Beowulf Scyldinga," or "Beowulf of the descendants of Scyld"), the son of Scyld and the grandfather of Hrothgar. Some editors emend the occurrences of Beowulf the Dane to "Beow," on the assumption that the copyist of the poem erred, anticipating the protagonist. Supporting such a change is also the evidence of a number of West Saxon genealogies that list a "Beow" in the ancestry of the royal house. The different nationalities of the two Beowulfs, however, seem sufficient to keep the characters distinct.

and mournful minds.   Though clever in council   45
or strong under sky,   men cannot say
or know for certain   who landed that shipload.[11]

But[12] the son of Scyld   was hailed in the strongholds
after the father   had fared far away,
and he long ruled   the lordly Scyldings.   50
A son was born   unto Beow also:
proud Healfdene,   who held his high seat,
battle-hardened   and bold in old age.
Four offspring   descended from Healfdene,
awake in the world: Heorogar, Hrothgar,   55
kindly Halga;[13]   I have heard that the fourth

11 **shipload** Scyld Scefing's funerary rites are paralleled by several European ship burials deposited over roughly the same period of time by similar cultures. Each example is a burial on land, however, and not at sea, as described here. Scyld's consignment to the sea may recall an actual funerary rite, but it may also be wholly or partly invented. Of special interest to *Beowulf* is Mound I at the East Anglian royal cemetery discovered at Sutton Hoo, near Woodbridge, Suffolk, England, which has been associated with Raedwald (fl. c. 604–24). Raedwald, the earliest king of the East Angles, is referred to once in the anonymous Whitby *Life of Gregory the Great* and four times in Bede's *Ecclesiastical History*. Bede claims that Raedwald maintained both Christian and pagan altars in a single temple (ii. 15), and the commingling of Christian and pagan grave goods is noteworthy at Sutton Hoo. The much later *Beowulf* raises afresh the problem of fusing Christian and other customs, and Scyld's funeral introduces the theme of mourning and funerary customs, so important to *Beowulf*, punctuating Scyld's paradigmatic biography with another sea trip.   12 **But** *Beowulf* is divided into sections called "fitts" by the Anglo-Saxons, as is much long Old English poetry. Each fitt is usually marked in this poem by a capital letter and by a Roman numeral in the margin indicating the fitt's number (one of the poem's two scribes habitually leaves a space between fitts as well and three fitts are marked only by a capital letter). The first marked fitt begins here, and thus the preceding section about Scyld Scefing may be considered a sort of prologue to the poem. Although the two scribes copying the poem may have introduced these divisions themselves as mechanical or incidental breaks, the meaningful way in which they segment the narrative suggests that the poet contributed them. An excellent summary of scholarly discussion of the fitts in this poem may be found in Mitchell and Robinson (1998, pp. 6–7).   13 **Halga** All three sons of Healfdene are mentioned in Scandinavian sources. Hrothgar, although not the first-born son of Healfdene, succeeded to the throne upon his elder brother Heorogar's apparently early death, despite the fact that Heorogar himself had a son. That Heorogar intended that line of succession is suggested by lines 1900 ff., where he is said to have given his mail-shirt to his brother Hrothgar rather than to his son. Of note too is the fact that Hrothgar and Wealhtheow raise Hrothulf, the child of the third brother, Halga, who also died young. An alliance between Hrothulf and Hrothgar is mentioned in *Widsith*, lines 45–49, and in *Beowulf*, lines 893 ff. and lines 1024 ff., the poet also hints of a darker event after the alliance: that Hrothulf will kill his first cousin Hrethric, the son of Hrothgar, in order to succeed to the Danish throne.

was Onela's queen[14]   and slept with the sovereign
of warlike Swedes.[15]
               Hrothgar was granted
swiftness for battle   and staunchness in strife,
so friends and kinfolk   followed him freely.   60
His band of young soldiers   swelled to a swarm.
In his mind he mulled   commanding a meadhall[16]
higher than humankind   ever had heard of,
and offering everyone,   young and old,
all he could give   that God had granted,   65
save common land   and commoners' lives.
Then, I am told,   he tackled that task,
raising the rafters   with craftsmen summoned
from many kingdoms   across middle-earth.[17]
They covered it quickly   as men count the time,   70
and he whose word   held the land whole
named it Heorot,[18]   highest of houses.
The prince did not fail   to fulfill his pledge:

---

14 Onela's queen See the Genealogies on pp. xxxvi–xxxvii for this marriage between Swedes and Danes. The union illustrates the attempt to create an alliance between competing kingdoms through marriage. From such strategies does a royal woman in this poem gain the poetic description "peace-weaver." The limited success of this strategy is pictured most fully in the narrative of the fight at Finnesburh (here, lines 936–1018; see also *Contexts, From the Old English*, p. 148). But alliances are always on the verge of dissolving in *Beowulf*. For instance, the "festering hatred" between Geats and Swedes is referred to at lines 2639 ff. in Wiglaf's evocation of the woes that will befall Beowulf's land after his death. In addition, failures in sense and meter in this line of the Old English poem show that something has been lost here, including the name of the woman alluded to as "Onela's queen." The line has been convincingly reconstructed to read "I heard that Yrse [i.e., Ursula] was Onela's queen." H. C. Matthes (*Anglia* 71, 165–80) suggests that an even longer passage has been dropped here. **15 Swedes** *Heaðo-Scylfings* in the Old English poem, where *heaðo-* means "war" or "battle." Like "Spear-Danes" for Danes at line 1, "Battle-Scylfings" is an epithet for Swedes, who are also called "Guð-Scylfings," where *guð-* is a synonym for "war." **16 meadhall** The hall functions as a major thematic and symbolic element in the poem. It is a place of safety and comfort, the locus for social and cultural rituals—a microcosmos for the aristocratic warriors in the poem. Recently excavated structures dating from the seventh and eighth centuries in the British Isles, such as the palace at Yeavering or at Cheddar, bear out many details of hall construction mentioned in *Beowulf*—the gabled roof, the iron door clasps, and the raised wooden floor. **17 middle-earth** A common Old English figure for the world that also reflects the position of our earth in the Anglo-Saxon cosmography. This compound word is the source for J. R. R. Tolkien's sub-created world of "middle-earth" as found in *The Silmarillion, The Hobbit*, and *The Lord of the Rings*. **18 Heorot** The name means "hart." The hart may have been a royal symbol or totem of the Danes, a conjecture that seems especially possible in light of the recovered Sutton Hoo scepter, a fine-grained whetstone topped by a bronze stag mounted on an iron ring and fitted by means of a bronze pedestal into the whetstone. Though its specific ceremonial uses are unknown, the object immediately claims a place among known Anglo-Saxon "emblems and instruments of royal power" (Bruce-Mitford 1979, p. 31). Hrothgar's hall, thus, may have had antlers or some representation of the royal animal affixed to its gables.

feasts were given,   favor and fortune.
The roof reared up;   the gables were great,   75
awaiting the flames   which would flare fiercely
when oaths were broken,   anger awakened;
but Heorot's ruin   was not yet at hand.[19]

Each day, one evil   dweller in darkness
spitefully suffered   the din from that hall   80
where Hrothgar's men   made merry with mead.
Harp-strings[20] would sound,   and the song of the scop
would recount the tales   told of time past:
whence mankind had come,   and how the Almighty
had fashioned flat land,   fair to behold,   85
surrounded with water.   The worker of wonders
lifted and lit   the sun and moon
for Earth's dwellers;   He filled the forests
with branches and blooms;   He breathed life
into all kinds of creatures.[21]   90
                           So the king's thanes
gathered in gladness;   then crime came calling,

---

19 at hand The fiery destruction of Heorot, which will take place outside of the frame of the poem after the alliance between the Danes and Swedes disintegrates, is alluded to in *Widsith*, line 49. Within the poem, the burning of the hall is intensified by the poet's allusions to the battle of Finnesburh, featured in the poet's description of Hildeburh's tragedy (lines 936–1018). The story of this battle is also found in the fragmentary Old English poem known as *The Battle of Finnsburg* (see *Contexts, From the Old English*, p. 148).   **20 Harp-strings** The Anglo-Saxon poet and performer ("scop") recited his songs accompanied by a small stringed instrument. The noun "scop" is derived from the Old English verb meaning to create or to make. The remains of a maple-wood instrument, decorated with two square gilt-bronze plaques with projecting birds' heads, were discovered in Mound I at Sutton Hoo. Of the type called the "round lyre," the approximately twenty-nine-inch instrument had been placed within a beaver-skin bag. The instrument was reconstructed using several fragmentary examples of lyres found in Northern Europe and by analogy with that pictured in the eighth-century *Vespasian Psalter*, which shows such a lyre in the hands of King David. This reference to the art of reciting poetry is one of several in the poem.   **21 creatures** A recitation of God's work of creation is found in Latin in the biblical book of Genesis and is paralleled by the short Old English poem *Caedmon's Hymn*, first recorded in Bede's (c. 673–735) eighth-century Latin *Ecclesiastical History* (for Bede, see *Contexts, From the Latin*, pp. 100–05), a history later translated into Old English during the reign of Alfred the Great (871–99). Bede relates how the illiterate cowherd Caedmon miraculously achieved the gift of poetry, reciting the creation of the world in the vernacular. Though he is often erroneously denominated the first English poet, Caedmon's nine-line work is nevertheless extraordinary. A "minor miracle of literary history," *Caedmon's Hymn* "demonstrated that the ancient heroic style was not incompatible with Christian doctrine and hence was worthy of preservation" (Mitchell and Robinson 2001, p. 220). But as Fred C. Robinson notes, this song of creation may be "a creation ascribed by the pagan Danes to whatever god they knew" (Mitchell and Robinson 1998, p. 34). The scop's poem about creation in *Beowulf* is artfully followed by the family history of Grendel and other malevolent creatures.

a horror from hell,   hideous Grendel,[22]
wrathful rover   of borders and moors,
holder of hollows,   haunter of fens.
He had lived long   in the homeland of horrors,   95
born to the band   whom God had banished
as kindred of Cain,   thereby requiting
the slayer of Abel.[23]   Many such sprang
from the first murderer: monsters and misfits,
elves and ill-spirits,   also those giants   100
whose wars with the Lord   earned them exile.

After nightfall   he nosed around Heorot,
saw how swordsmen   slept in the hall,
unwary and weary   with wine and feasting,
numb to the sorrows   suffered by men.   105
The cursed creature,   cruel and remorseless,
swiftly slipped in.   He seized thirty thanes[24]
asleep after supper,   shouldered away
what trophies he would,   and took to his lair
pleased with the plunder,   proud of his murders.   110

When daylight dawned   on the spoils of slaughter,
the strength of the fiend   was readily seen.
The feast was followed   by fits of weeping,
and cries of outrage   rose in the morning.
Hrothgar the strong   sank on his throne,   115
helpless and hopeless,   beholding the carnage,
the trail of the terror,   a trouble too wrathful,
a foe too ferocious,   too steadfast in rage,

---

22 Grendel The monster's habitat and descent are first described here and are then repeated when Grendel's mother is introduced (lines 1108 ff). The monsters in this description have analogues in Germanic and classical lore, but are related in this instance to evil creatures found in the Bible. But God has not utterly destroyed Grendel and his kin, as the poem suggests that the race of giants has been destroyed by the flood, an event represented on the sword hilt that Beowulf brings from the monsters' mere and gives to Hrothgar (see lines 1480–99).   **23 Abel** See Genesis 4:1–16 (*Contexts, From the Latin*, p. 92) for the story of how Cain killed his brother, Abel, and was exiled to the land of Nod for his crime.   **24 thanes** The retainers who protect the king and who are rewarded by him; compare the Old English verb *thegnian*, "to serve." These thanes are referred to as a "band of noblemen" (Old English, *aethelinga gedriht*), as distinct from the social class of "churls" (Old English, *ceorlas*), ordinary freemen. One measure of distinction between the two classes may be found in the laws of the Anglo-Saxon period, in which the wergeld (see note 26) for a thane was several times that for a churl.

ancient and evil.   The evening after
he murdered again   with no more remorse,   120
so fixed was his will   on that wicked feud.
Henceforth the fearful   were easily found
elsewhere, anywhere   far from the fiend,
bedding in barns,[25]   for the brutal hall-thane
was truly betokened   by terrible signs,   125
and those who escaped   stayed safer afar.

So wrath fought alone   against rule and right;
one routed many;   the mead-hall stood empty.
Strongest of Spear-Danes,   Hrothgar suffered
this fell affliction   for twelve winters' time.   130
As his woes became known   widely and well,
sad songs were sung   by the sons of men:
how season on season,   with ceaseless strife,
Grendel assailed   the Scyldings' sovereign.
The monster craved   no kinship with any,   135
no end to the evil   with wergeld[26] owed;
nor might a king's   council have reckoned
on quittance come   from the killer's hand.
The dark death-shadow[27]   daunted them all,
lying in ambush   for old and young,   140
secretly slinking   and stalking by night.
No man knows where   on the misty moor
the heathen keepers   of hell-runes[28] wander.

---

25 **bedding in barns** Hrothgar's main hall seems to have been surrounded by outbuildings in which there were sleeping quarters. (See, for instance, the reference to women's quarters outside of Heorot in lines 593–95 and the "queen's quarters" at line 816 from which Hrothgar makes his way back to Heorot.)   26 **wergeld** Literally, "man payment," a cash payment made to a victim's family to compensate for his death and thus the measure of one's legal worth. Amounts of wergeld to be paid for various members of society, excluding slaves, were set out in Anglo-Saxon laws beginning with those of the seventh century in Kent. Although it began as a payment to offset homicide, wergeld became a penalty for other sorts of offenses, including theft and desertion from the army. Grendel's status as monstrous is emphasized by his refusal to acknowledge this law, brutishly taking blood vengeance instead. Compare the actions recounted in lines 406–09, when Hrothgar reminds Beowulf that Hrothgar has paid the compensation for Heatholaf, a Wylfing warrior whom Beowulf's father, Ecgtheow, has killed.   27 **dark death-shadow** This phrase is an epithet for the devil in the Old English poem *Christ I*, line 257. But Chickering points out, "It seems fair to say that he [Grendel] is devilish, and about the Devil's business, though this may not necessarily entail his standing only for the Evil One." (Chickering 1977, p. 287)   28 **hell-runes** The Old English phrase means "ones skilled in the secrets of hell." This compound is almost certainly a kenning for "demons."

So over and over   the loathsome ogre
mortally menaced   mankind with his crimes.   145
Raiding by night,   he reigned in the hall,
and Heorot's high   adornments were his,
but God would not grant   throne-gifts[29] to gladden
a scourge who spurned   the Sovereign of Heaven.[30]

Stricken in spirit,   Hrothgar would often   150
closet his council   to ponder what plan
might be deemed best   by strong-minded men.
Sometimes the elders   swore before altars
of old war-idols,   offering prayers
for the soul-slayer[31]   to succor their people.[32]   155
Such was their habit,   the hope of heathens:
with hell in their hearts,   they were lost to the Lord.
Their inmost minds   knew not the Almighty;
they never would worship   the world's true protector.
Sorry is he   who sears his soul,   160
afflicted by flames   he freely embraced.
No cheer for the chastened!   No change in his fate!
But happy is he   whom heaven welcomes,
and after his death-day   he dwells with the Father.

So in his sorrow   the son of Healfdene[33]   165
endlessly weighed   how a wise warrior
might fend off harm.   The hardship this foe

---

29 throne-gifts The Old English compound word translated here is, literally, "gift-seat:" the place from which the king distributed gifts to reward his warriors. Thus, the word designates a throne.   **30 Heaven** Lines 146–49 are difficult to translate due to abrupt changes of subject and the ambiguity of several referents in the Old English poem. No less a scholar of *Beowulf* than Tolkien suggested that the lines were not authentic, but were a later retouching of the manuscript. Chickering (1977, pp. 287–88) states that "a wide variety of sentences can be composed from these different possibilities." As in this translation, most writers treat Grendel as the agent, but it is not clear if Grendel attacks only Hrothgar's throne—or, perhaps, God's.   **31 soul-slayer** The phrase *gast-bona* may be an epithet for devil, or it may suggest the pagan gods Woden or Tiw (also called Tig), both of whom seem to have been popular in the warrior cults of England and Scandinavia. Old English texts mention only Woden by name, although four pagan gods (Tiw, Woden, Thunor, and Frig or Freo) are commemorated in the days of the week and in English place-names.   **32 people** Because of their fear of Grendel, the Danes seem to resume heathen practices, and this rather vague account of their frightened backsliding into heathenism is in contrast to their apparently Christian beliefs elsewhere in the poem. See Klaeber (1950, p. 135, note to lines 175–88) who pointed out, citing evidence from Bede's *Ecclesiastical History*, that the Danes' behavior is similar to that of the Anglo-Saxons, who sometimes lapsed into paganism when menaced. **33 son of Healfdene** Hrothgar.

of his folk inflicted   was fierce and long-lasting,
most ruinous wrath   and wracking night-evil.

A thane of Hygelac[34]   heard in his homeland   170
of Grendel's deeds.   Great among Geats,
this man was more mighty   than any then living.
He summoned and stocked   a swift wave-courser,
and swore to sail   over the swan-road
as one warrior should   for another in need.   175
His elders could find   no fault with his offer,
and awed by the omens,   they urged him on.
He gathered the bravest   of Geatish guardsmen.
One of fifteen,   the skilled sailor
strode to his ship   at the ocean's edge.   180

He was keen to embark: his keel was beached
under the cliff   where sea-currents curled
surf against sand;   his soldiers were ready.
Over the bow   they boarded in armor,
bearing their burnished   weapons below,   185
their gilded war-gear   to the boat's bosom.
Other men shoved   the ship from the shore,
and off went the band,   their wood-braced vessel
bound for the venture   with wind on the waves
and foam under bow,   like a fulmar[35] in flight.   190

On the second day   their upswept prow
slid into sight   of steep hillsides,
bright cliffs, wide capes   at the close of their crossing,
the goal of their voyage   gained in good time.
Swiftly the sailors   steered for the shore,   195
moored their boat   and debarked on the berm.
Clad in corselets   of clattering mail,
they saluted the Lord   for their smooth sailing.

From the post he held   high on the headland,
a Scylding had spied   the strangers bearing   200

---

34 **A thane of Hygelac** That is, Beowulf, who is doing service as a retainer of Hygelac, his uncle and king. The first time that Beowulf is named directly is at line 307, when the hero himself declares his name.   35 **fulmar** A petrel-type sea bird with gray plumage, found in Arctic regions. The word may be of Old Norse origin.

bright bucklers   and battle-armor
over their gangplank.   Avid for answers
and minded to know   what men had come hence,
Hrothgar's thane   hastened on horseback
down to the beach   where he brusquely brandished   205
spear-haft in hand   while speaking stern words:

"What warriors are you,   wearers of armor,
bearers of weapons,   daring to bring
your lofty longboat   over the sea-lane?
Long have I looked   out on the ocean   210
so foreign foes   might never float hither
and harry our homeland   with hostile fleets.
No men have ever   more brazenly borne
shields to our shores,   nor have you sought
leave from our lords   to land in this place,   215
nor could you have known   my kin would consent.
I have never beheld   an earl on this earth
more mighty in arms   than one among you.
This is no hall-warmer,   handsome in harness,
showy with shield,   but the noblest of knights,   220
unless looks belie him.   Now let me know
who are your fathers   before you fare further
or spy on the Danes.   I say to you, sailors
far from your homes: hear me and hasten
to answer me well.   Whence have you wandered?   225
Why have you come?"
                              Wisest with words,
the eldest offered   an answer for all:
"From Geat-land we come;   we are Geatish men,
sharers of Hygelac's   hearth and hall.
My father was famous   among our folk   230
as a lordly leader   who lived many winters
before, full of years,   he departed our fastness.
His name was Ecgtheow.   All over earth
every wise man   remembers him well.
We have landed in friendship   to look for your lord,   235
the son of Healfdene,   sovereign of Scyldings.
Give us good guidance: a great errand
has driven us hence   to the holder of Danes.
Our purpose is open: this I promise;

but you could attest   if tales tell the truth.   240
They speak of some scourge,   none can say what,
secretly stalking   by night among Scyldings,
a shadowy shape   whose malice to men
is shown by a shameful   shower of corpses.
I offer Hrothgar,   with honest heart,   245
the means to make   an end to this menace.
Wise and good,   he will win his reward,
the scalding surges   of care will be cooled
if ever such awful   evil is vanquished.
So his sorrows   shall swiftly be soothed   250
or else his anguish   haunt him, unaltered,
as long as his house   holds on the hilltop."

Astride his steed,   the guard spoke again:
"A sharp-witted warrior   often must weigh
words against works   when judging their worth.   255
This I have learned: you honor our lord.
Thus you may come,   though clad in corselets
and weaponed for war.   I shall show you the way.
Meanwhile those thanes   who are mine to command
shall stand by the ship   you steered to our shore.   260
No thief will trouble   your newly-tarred[36] craft
before you return   and take to the tide.
A swan-necked bow   will bear you back
to your windward coast.   Most welcome of men,
may you be granted   good fortune in battle,   265
enduring unharmed   the deed you would do."

So they set out   while the ship sat at rest,
the broad-beamed vessel[37]   bound to the beach,

---

36 newly-tarred craft This ship is probably of the clinker-built variety instrumental to the martial and mercantile fortunes of Scandinavia and Anglo-Saxon England. Such ships are described in many sorts of texts, have been excavated in Scandinavia and England, and are illustrated on the Bayeux Tapestry (probably executed ca. 1075). A ship of this type was constructed of runs of planking fastened to keel, stem, and stern, so that the lower edge of each run was fixed by clench nails to the upper edge of the planking below it. This reference suggests that the planking was also tarred to further seal it in preparation for the approximately two-day journey to Hrothgar's kingdom.   **37 broad-beamed vessel** Like the one found in Mound I at Sutton Hoo, the ship in this poem presumably was broad across its widest point (the "beam") in order to carry the warriors and their gear. In other contexts, such ships could easily accommodate cattle, grain, and so forth.

lashed by its lines.   Lustrous boar-icons[38]
glinted on cheek-guards.   Adorned with gold,   270
the flame-hardened helms   defended their lives.
Glad of their mettle   while marching together,
the troop hastened   until they beheld
the highest of halls   raised under heaven,
most famed among folk   in foreign lands.   275
Sheathed with gold   and grandly gabled,
the roof of the ruler   lit up his realm.
The foremost warrior   waved them forward
and bade the band go   straight to that building,
court of the king   and his brave kinsmen.   280
Reining his steed,   he spoke a last word:
"It is time I returned.   May All-Ruling Father
favor your errand.   I fare to the ocean,
to watch and ward off   wrathful marauders."

The street was stone-paved;[39]   a straight path   285
guided the band.   Byrnies glittered,
jackets of chain-mail   whose jingling rings,
hard and hand-linked,   sang on harnesses.
Marshaled for battle,   they marched to the building.
Still sea-weary,   they set their broad-shields   290
of well-hardened wood   against Heorot's wall.
Their corselets clinked   as they bent to a bench
and stood their sturdy   spears in a row,

---

38 **boar-icons** In the areas settled by Germanic tribes, the boar represented a warrior's fe-
rocity and may have functioned as a protective amulet, as may perhaps be seen when Beowulf's helmet is described at lines 1284–90 before the hero plunges into the mere. Tacitus describes Germanic warriors who wore boar-images into battle (*Germania*, ch. 45;
for Tacitus, see *Contexts, From the Latin*, pp. 93–95). At a sixth- or seventh-century
Torslunda, Gotland, site, a die made for impressing a design on a small metal panel, like
the panels found on the parade dress helmet excavated at Sutton Hoo Mound I, was discovered that depicts two warriors wearing boar-crest helmets. Two Anglo-Saxon period
helmets, one recovered from a barrow in Benty Grange, Derbyshire, England, and the
other at Wollaston, Northamptonshire, England, are surmounted by boar-crests. Further,
an unmounted boar-crest has been identified from an older grave find in Guilden Morden, Cambridgeshire (Foster 1977). An eighth-century Anglo-Saxon manuscript shows a
defeated Goliath wearing a boar-crested helmet (Swanton 1980). Fighting men are sometimes called "boars" in *Beowulf*, showing the extent of the identification with the beast.
39 **stone-paved** Perhaps one of the roadways inherited from the Romans, such as Watling
Street, which ran from Dover past London. Though they clearly used the Roman routes,
the Anglo-Saxons also built roads themselves, as, for instance, the find of gravel ones in
seventh-century Hamwic, now Southampton, attests. The construction and maintenance
of these roads seems to have differed from those of the Roman period, which perhaps
makes this stone-paved street noteworthy.

gray from the ash grove,   ground to sharp points.
This was a war party   worthy of weapons.   295

Then a proud prince[40]   questioned their purpose:
"Where are you bringing   these burnished bosses,
these gray mail-shirts,   grimly-masked helms
and serried spears?   I am Hrothgar's
herald and door-ward.   I have never beheld   300
a band of wanderers   with bearings so brave.
I believe that boldness   has brought you to Hrothgar,
not banishment's shame."
                    The eldest answered,
hard and hardy   under his helmet,
a warlike prince   of the Weder people: 305
"We are Hygelac's   hearth-companions.
My name is Beowulf;   my purpose, to bear
unto Healfdene's son,   your lordly leader,
a message meant   for that noblest of men,
if he will allow us   leave to approach."   310

Wise Wulfgar,   man of the Wendels,
known to many   for boldness in battle,
stoutly spoke out: "I shall ask our sovereign,
well-wisher of Danes   and awarder of wealth,
about this boon   you have come to request   315
and bear you back,   as soon as may be,
whatever answer   the great man offers."

He went straightaway   where Hrothgar waited,
old and gray-haired,   with thanes gathered round.
Squarely he stood   for his king to assess him.   320
Such was the Scylding   custom at court,
and so Wulfgar spoke   to his sovereign and friend:
"Far-sailing Geats   have come to our kingdom
across the wide water.   These warriors call
their leader *Beowulf*   and bid me bring   325
their plea to our prince,   if it pleases him
to allow them entrance   and offer them audience.
I implore you to hear them,   princely Hrothgar,

40 **proud prince** Wulfgar, whom Beowulf addresses by name in line 311.

for I deem them worthy   of wearing their armor
and treating with earls.   Truly the elder   330
who led them hither   is a lord of some stature."

Helm of the Scyldings,   Hrothgar held forth:
"I knew him once.   He was only a lad.
His honored father,   old Ecgtheow,
received the sole   daughter of Hrethel.   335
The son now seeks us   solely from friendship.
Seamen have said,   after sailing hence
with gifts for the Geats,   that his hand-grip would match
the might and main   of thirty strong men.
The West-Danes have long   awaited God's grace.   340
Here is our hope   against Grendel's dread,
if I reckon rightly   the cause of his coming.
I shall give this brave man   boons for boldness.
Bring him in quickly.   The band of my kinsmen
is gathered together.   Welcome our guest   345
to the dwelling of Danes."
                     Then Wulfgar went[41]
through the hall's entry   with word from within:
"I am ordered to answer   that the lord of East-Danes
honors your father   and offers you welcome,
sailors who sought us   over the sea-waves,   350
bravely bent   on embarking hither.
Now you may march   in your mail and masks
to behold Hrothgar.   Here you must leave
war-shields and spears   sharpened for strife.
Your weapons can wait   for words to be spoken."   355

The mighty one rose   with many a man
marshaled about him,   though some were bidden
to stay with the weapons   and stand on watch.
Under Heorot's roof   the rest hastened
when Beowulf brought them   boldly before   360
the hearth of Hrothgar.   Helmed and hardy,
the war-chief shone   as he stood in skillfully
smithied chain-mail   and spoke to his host:

---

41 Then Wulfgar went Though there is no damage to the manuscript at this point, a half-line is missing here. An inoffensive phrase like the one the translators use is usually supplied.

"Hail to you, Hrothgar!   I am Hygelac's
kinsman and comrade,   esteemed by the king   365
for deeds I have done   in the years of youth.
I heard in my homeland   how Grendel grieves you.
Seafarers say   that your splendid hall
stands idle and useless   after the sun
sinks each evening   from heaven's height.   370
The most honored among us,   earls and elders,
have urged me to seek you,   certain my strength
would serve in your struggle.   They have seen me return
bloody from binding   brutish giants,
a family of five   destroyed in our strife;   375
by night in the sea   I have slain monsters.
Hardship I had,   but our harms were avenged,
our enemies mastered.   Now I shall match
my grip against Grendel's   and get you an end
to this feud with the fiend.   Therefore one favor   380
I ask from you, Hrothgar,   sovereign of Spear-Danes,
shelter of shield-bearers,   friend to your folk:
that I and my officers,   we and no others,
be offered the honor   of purging your hall.
I have also heard   that the rash thing reckons   385
the thrust of a weapon   no threat to his thews,[42]
so I shall grab   and grapple with Grendel.
Let my lord Hygelac   hear and be glad
that I foreswore.   My sword and strong shield
when I fought for life   with that fearsome foe.   390
Whomever death takes,   his doom is doubtless
decreed by the Lord.   If I let the creature
best me when battle   begins in this building,
he will freely feast   as he often has fed
on men of much mettle.   My corpse will require   395
no covering cloth.[43]   He will carry away
a crushed carcass   clotted with gore,
the fiend's fodder   gleefully eaten,
smearing his lonesome   lair on the moor.
No need to worry   who buries my body   400

---

42 **thews** Well-developed sinew or muscle.   43 **no covering cloth** Alluding to a Germanic funerary custom, Beowulf dourly observes that if Grendel devours him, there will be nothing left of him for a funeral.

if battle takes me.   Send back to my sovereign
this best of shirts   which has shielded my breast,
this choice chain-mail,   Hrethel's heirloom
and Weland's work.[44]   Fate[45] goes as it will."

Helm of the Scyldings,   Hrothgar answered: 405
"It is fair that you seek   to defend us, my friend,
in return for the favor   offered your father[46]
when a killing fanned   the fiercest of feuds
after he felled   the Wylfing, Heatholaf.
Wary of war,   the Weder-Geats wanted   410
Ecgtheow elsewhere,   so over the sea-swells
he sought the South-Danes,   strong Scyldings.
I had lately become   king of my kinsmen,
a youth ruling   this jewel of a realm,
this store-house of heroes,   with Heorogar gone,   415
my brother and better,   born of Healfdene.
I calmed your father's   quarrel with wergeld
sent over sea   straight to the Wylfings,
an ancient heirloom;   and Ecgtheow's oath
I took in return.
              It pains me to tell   420
what grief Grendel   has given me since,
what harm in Heorot,   hatred and shame
at his sudden onset.   My circle is shrunken;

---

44 **Weland's work** Weland is the preeminent blacksmith of the gods in Germanic legends. For Beowulf to attribute this "best of shirts" to Weland's craft is to construct a peerless ancestry for his armor and to match his achievements to his wargear. The front panel of the Franks Casket contains a scene depicting Weland's revenge. The legend is also memorialized in England in the place-name Wayland's Smithy, a Neolithic long barrow known by that name since the tenth century, found just off the prehistoric track called the Ridgeway on the Berkshire Downs. Somewhere among these Downs, King Alfred defeated the Danes at the Battle of Ashdown in 871, and Professor J. R. R. Tolkien took his family on weekend outings. 45 **Fate** Used for the first time in the poem in what seems to be a proverbial expression, the Old English *wyrd* stands for a pre-Christian idea of destiny or fate. Etymologically related to the Old English verb *weorðan*, which means what will come about or happen, *wyrd* is not a fully personified divine power like the classical Fates or the goddess Fortuna. In Christian literature of the Anglo-Saxon period, *wyrd* seems to be under the control of the Christian God. The concept of *wyrd* developed in interesting ways in the Anglo-Saxon period; for example, King Alfred opposes *wyrd* to Providence in his translation of the influential *Consolation of Philosophy (De consolatione Philosophiae)* by Boethius (c. 475–525) from Latin into the vernacular. 46 **father** Because Hrothgar pays the wergeld for Heatholaf, the man whom Beowulf's father, Ecgtheow, has killed, Ecgtheow swears an oath of loyalty to Hrothgar. It is this oath between Ecgtheow and Hrothgar that Hrothgar declares that Beowulf fulfills.

my guardsmen are gone,   gathered by fate
into Grendel's grip.   How simply the Sovereign   425
of Heaven could hinder   deeds of this hell-fiend!
Beer-swollen boasters,   brave in their ale-cups,
often have sworn   to stay with their swords
drawn in the dark,   to strike down the demon.
Then in the morning   the mead-hall was drenched,   430
blood on the bench-boards,   blood on the floor,
the highest of houses   a horror at dawn.
Fewer were left   to keep faith with their lord
since those dear retainers   were taken by death.
But sit now to sup   and afterward speak   435
of soldierly pride,   if the spirit prompts you."

A bench was then cleared   there in the beer-hall,
so all of the Geats   could sit together,
sturdy soldiers,   proud and stout-hearted.
A dutiful Dane   brought them bright ale-cups   440
and poured sweet mead   while the scop was singing
high-voiced in Heorot.   That host of warriors,
Weders and Scyldings,   shared in the wassails.

But envious Unferth,[47]   Ecglaf's son,
spat out his spite   from the seat he took   445
at his sovereign's feet.   The seafarer's quest
grieved him greatly,   for he would not grant
any man ever,   in all middle-earth,
more fame under heaven   than he himself had:

"Are you that Beowulf   Breca bested   450
when both of you bet   on swimming the straits,
daring the deep   in a dire struggle,
risking your lives   after rash boasting?
Though friend or foe,   no man could deflect
your foolhardy foray.   Arms flailing,   455
you each embraced   the billowing stream,

---

47 Unferth Unferth may be a sort of spokesman in Hrothgar's court, which his place
at the king's feet suggests, though his exact status is unclear. Considering his dramatic
function in the poem, his name, which means either "un-peace" or "un-reason," may
be significant.

spanned the sea-lane   with swift-dipping hands
and wended over   the warring ocean.
Winter-like waves   were roiling the waters
as the two of you toiled   in the tumult of combers.   460
For seven nights   you strove to outswim him,
but he was the stronger   and saw at sunrise
the sea had swept him   to Heathoraem shores.
Breca went back   to his own homeland,
his burg on the bluff,   stronghold of Brondings,   465
a fair realm and wealthy.   The wager was won;
Beanstan's son   had brought off his boast.
However you fared   in onslaughts elsewhere,
I doubt you will live   the length of a night
if you dare to linger   so near Grendel."   470

Then Beowulf spoke,   son of Ecgtheow:
"Listen, Unferth,   my fuddled friend
brimful of beer,   you blabber too much
about Breca's venture.   I tell you the truth:
my force in the flood   is more than a match   475
for any man   who wrestles the waves.
Boys that we were,   brash in our youth
and reckless of risk,   both of us boasted
that each one could swim   the open ocean.
So we set forth,   stroking together   480
sturdily seaward   with swords drawn
hard in our hands   to ward off whale-fish.
No swifter was he   in those heaving seas;
each of us kept   close to the other,
floating together   those first five nights.   485
Then the storm-surges   swept us apart:
winter-cold weather   and warring winds
drove from the north   in deepening darkness.
Rough waves rose   and sea-beasts raged,
but my breast was bound   in a woven mail-shirt.   490
Hard and hand-linked,   hemmed with gold,
it kept those creatures   from causing me harm.
I was drawn to the depths,   held fast by the foe,
grim in his grasp;   yet granted a stab,
I stuck in my sword-point,   struck down the horror.   495
The mighty sea-monster   met death by my hand.

"Often afterward   snatchers of swimmers
snapped at my heels.   With my strong sword
I served them fitly.   I would fatten no foes,
feed no man-banes   munching their morsels   500
when setting to feast   on the floor of the sea.
Instead at sunrise   the sword-stricken
washed up in windrows   to lie lifelessly,
lodged by the tide-line,   and nevermore trouble
sailors crossing   the steep-cliffed straits.   505
As God's beacon   brightened the East,
I spied a cape   across calming seas,
a windward wall.   So I was spared,
for fate often favors   an unmarked man
if he keeps his courage.   My sword was the slayer   510
of nine monsters.   I've not heard of many
who fended off   a more fearsome assault
while hurled by the waves   under heaven's vault.
Yet I broke the beasts' grip   and got off alive,
weary of warfare.   Swiftly surging   515
after the storm,   the sea-current swept me
to Finland's coast.
                    Such close combat
or stark sword-strokes   you have not seen,
you or Breca.   No tale has told
how either of you two   ever attempted   520
so bold a deed   done with bright sword,
though I would not claim   a brother's bane[48]
if the killing of kin   were all I'd accomplished.
For that you are certain   to suffer in Hell,
doomed with the damned   despite your swift wit.   525
I say straight out,   son of Ecglaf,
that ghastly Grendel,   however gruesome,
would never have done   such dreadful deeds,
harming your lord   here in his hall,
if your spirit were stern,   your will, warlike,   530
as you have affirmed.   The foe has found

---

48 **brother's bane** Unferth's fratricide not only further discredits him, but also brings up
one of the deepest problems in *Beowulf*: the slaying of one's kin. The webs of loyalty and
revenge may indeed have pitted family members against each other in this era. But fratricide is a particularly potent version of this problem, alluding to Grendel's descent from
Cain, the murderer of his brother Abel (see note 23).

that he need not reckon   with wrathful swords
or look with alarm   on the likes of you,
Scylding victor.[49]   He takes his tribute,
sparing no man,   snatching and supping   535
whenever he wishes   with wicked delight,
expecting no strife   with spear-bearing Danes.
But soon, very soon,   I shall show him the strength
and boldness of Geats   giving him battle.
When morning comes   to light up the land,   540
you may go again   and gladly get mead
as the bright sun   beams in the South
and starts a new day   for the sons of men."

Gray-haired Hrothgar,   giver of hoard-wealth,
was happy to hear   Beowulf bolster   545
hope for his folk   with forthright avowal.
About the Bright-Danes'   battle-leader
rang warriors' laughter   and winsome words.
The queen, Wealhtheow,[50]   by custom courteous,
greeted the party   aglitter with gold   550
and bore the full cup   first to her lord,
the keeper of East-Danes,   dear to his people,
bidding him drink   and be glad of his beer.
That soldierly sovereign   quaffed and supped
while his Helming princess   passed through the hall   555
offering everyone,   young men and old,
the dole he was due.   Adorned with rings,
she bore the burnished   mead-bowl to Beowulf,
last of them all,   and honored the Geat
with gracious words,   firm in her wisdom   560
and grateful to God   for granting her wish.
Here was the prayed-for   prince who would help
to end the ill deeds.   He emptied the cup
Wealhtheow offered;   then the willing warrior,

---

49 Scylding victor This conventional phrase of praise, when used by Beowulf of Hrothgar at this point in the narrative, may be a rather intemperate sarcasm. **50 Wealhtheow** The Queen's name means "foreign slave." The reference to her in line 555 using the patronymic Helming recalls her father's name, Helm. The Helmings seem to belong to the Wylfing tribe. Carefully constructing her delicate speeches to remind those in Heorot to protect her sons, Wealhtheow is fated to see both her sons killed by their cousin Hrothulf after the death of her husband Hrothgar.

Ecgtheow's son,   spoke as one ready   565
for strife and slaughter:
                "When I set my ship
to sail on the sea   and steered her hence
with my squadron of swords,   I swore to fulfill
the will of the Scyldings   or die in the deed,
fall with the slain,   held fast by the foe,   570
my last day lived out   here in your hall."

The wife was well-pleased   with Beowulf's words,
this oath from the Geat;   and glinting with gold
the queen, Wealhtheow,   went to her king.
Boasts were bandied   once more in the beer-hall,   575
the hearty speech   of a hopeful household,
forceful fighters.   But soon the sovereign,
son of Healfdene,   hankered for sleep.
He knew his enemy   brooded on battle
all day from dawn   until deepening dusk.   580
Covered by darkness,   the creature would come,
a shade under shadows.   The company stood.
One man to another,   Hrothgar hailed
brave Beowulf,   wishing him well
and granting him leave   to guard the wine-hall: 585

"So long as my hand   has hefted a shield,
I never have yielded   the Danes' mansion
to any man else,   whatever his mettle.
Now you shall hold   this highest of houses.
Be mindful of fame;   make your might known;   590
but beware of the brute.   You will want no boon
if you tackle this task   and live to request it."

Hrothgar and his princes   departed the hall;
the warder of Danes   went to his woman,
couched with his queen.   The King of Glory[51]   595
had granted a guard   against Grendel's wrath,
as all had now learned.   One man had offered
to take on this task   and watch for the terror.

---

51 **King of Glory** The phrase in Old English could also be construed as "glorious king,"
that is, Hrothgar.

The leader of Geats   would gladly trust
the force of God's favor.   He flung off his mail-shirt,   600
then handed his helmet   and inlaid sword
to the steward assigned   safe-keeping of iron
and gilded war-gear.   Again the bold
Beowulf boasted   while bound for his bed:

"I am no weaker   in works of war,   605
no less a grappler   than Grendel himself.
Soon I shall sink him   into his death-sleep,
not with my sword   but solely by strength.
He is unschooled in skills   to strike against me,
to shatter my shield,   though feared for his fierceness.   610
So I shall bear   no blade in the night
if he sees fit   to fight without weapons.
May God in His wisdom   grant whom He wills
blessing in battle."
             The brave soldier
stretched out for sleep,   and a bolster pillowed   615
his proud cheekbone.   About him were sprawled
the strong sea-warriors,   each one wondering
whether he ever   would walk once again
his beloved land,   or find his own folk
from childhood's time   in an untroubled town.   620
All had been told   how often before
dreadful death   had swept up the Danes
who lay in this hall.   But the Lord lent them
aid in their anguish,   weaving their war-luck,[52]
for one man alone   had the might and main   625
to fight off the fiend,   crush him in combat,
proving who ruled   the races of men,
then and forever: God, the Almighty.[53]

Cunningly creeping,   a spectral stalker
slunk through the gloom.   The bowmen were sleeping   630
who ought to have held   the high-horned house,

---

52 **weaving their war-luck** The figure of a man's web of luck seems to refer to a Germanic belief in supernatural women who spin one's web of destiny, thus paralleling the three classical goddesses known in Latin as the *Fata* or *Parcae*, who supervised the course of human life at one's birth by spinning its thread, determining its length, and cutting it off. 53 **God, the Almighty** The force of this assertion here is to affirm for the poem's audience God's omnipotence, more powerful than either man's strength or luck.

all except one,   for the Lord's will
now became known: no more would the murderer
drag under darkness   whomever he wished.
Anger was wakeful,   watching the enemy;   635
hot-hearted Beowulf   was bent upon battle.

Then from the moor   under misty hillsides,
Grendel came gliding   girt with God's anger.
The man-scather sought   someone to snatch
from the high hall.   He crept under clouds   640
until he caught sight   of the king's court
whose gilded gables   he knew at a glance.
He often had haunted   Hrothgar's house;
but he never found,   before or after,
hardier hall-thanes   or harder luck.   645
The joyless giant   drew near the door,
which swiftly swung back   at the touch of his hand
though bound and fastened   with forge-bent bars.
The building's mouth   had been broken open,
and Grendel entered   with ill intent.   650
Swollen with fury,   he stalked over flagstones
and looked round the manse   where many men lay.
An unlovely light   most like a flame
flashed from his eyes,   flared through the hall
at young soldiers dozing   shoulder to shoulder,   655
comradely kindred.   The cruel creature laughed
in his murderous mind,   thinking how many
now living would die   before the day dawned,
how glutted with gore   he would guzzle his fill.
It was not his fate   to finish the feast   660
he foresaw that night.
                         Soon the Stalwart,
Hygelac's kinsman,   beheld how the horror,
not one to be idle,   went about evil.
For his first feat   he suddenly seized
a sleeping soldier,   slashed at the flesh,   665
bit through bones   and lapped up the blood
that gushed from veins   as he gorged on gobbets.
Swiftly he swallowed   those lifeless limbs,
hands and feet whole;   then he headed forward
with open palm   to plunder the prone.   670

One man angled[54]   up on his elbow:
the fiend soon found   he was facing a foe
whose hand-grip was harder   than any other
he ever had met   in all middle-earth.
Cravenly cringing,   coward at heart,   675
he longed for a swift   escape to his lair,
his bevy of devils.   He never had known
from his earliest days   such awful anguish.

The captain, recalling   his speech to the king,
straightaway stood   and hardened his hold.   680
Fingers fractured.   The fiend spun round;
the soldier stepped closer.   Grendel sought
somehow to slip   that grasp and escape,
flee to the fens;   but his fingers were caught
in too fierce a grip.   His foray had failed;   685
the harm-wreaker rued   his raid on Heorot.
From the hall of the Danes   a hellish din
beset every soldier   outside the stronghold,
louder than laughter   of ale-sodden earls.
A wonder it was   the wine-hall withstood   690
this forceful affray   without falling to earth.
That beautiful building   was firmly bonded
by iron bands   forged with forethought
inside and out.   As some have told it,
the struggle swept on   and slammed to the floor   695
many mead-benches   massive with gold.
No Scylding elders   ever imagined
that any would harm   their elk-horned hall,
raze what they wrought,   unless flames arose
to enfold and consume it.   Frightful new sounds   700
burst from the building,   unnerved the North-Danes,
each one and all   who heard those outcries
outside the walls.   Wailing in anguish,
the hellish horror,   hateful to God,
sang his dismay,   seized by the grip   705
of a man more mighty   than any then living.

---

54 **One man angled** Though each of the actions of the combatants is clear as the contest begins, the Old English text does not make completely lucid which fighter does what, thus imitating poetically the struggle in the dark hall.

That shielder of men　　meant by no means
to let the death-dealer　　leave with his life,
a life worthless　　to anyone elsewhere.
Then the young soldiers　　swung their old swords　　710
again and again　　to save their guardian,
their kingly comrade,　　however they could.
Engaging with Grendel　　and hoping to hew him
from every side,　　they scarcely suspected
that blades wielded　　by worthy warriors　　715
never would cut　　to the criminal's quick.
The spell was spun　　so strongly about him
that the finest iron　　of any on earth,
the sharpest sword-edge　　left him unscathed.
Still he was soon　　to be stripped of his life　　720
and sent on a sore　　sojourn to Hell.
The strength of his sinews　　would serve him no more;
no more would he menace　　mankind with his crimes,
his grudge against God,　　for the high-hearted kinsman
of King Hygelac　　had hold of his hand.　　725
Each found the other　　loathsome in life;
but the murderous man-bane　　got a great wound
as tendons were torn,　　shoulder shorn open,
and bone-locks broken.　　Beowulf gained
glory in war;　　and Grendel went off　　730
bloody and bent　　to the boggy hills,
sorrowfully seeking　　his dreary dwelling.
Surely he sensed　　his life-span was spent,
his days upon days;　　but the Danes were grateful:
their wish was fulfilled　　after fearsome warfare.　　735

Wise and strong-willed,　　the one from afar
had cleansed Heorot,　　hall of Hrothgar.
Great among Geats,　　he was glad of his night-work
ending the evil,　　his fame-winning feat,
fulfilling his oath　　to aid the East-Danes,　　740
easing their anguish,　　healing the horror
they suffered so long,　　no small distress.
As token of triumph,　　the troop-leader hung
the shorn-off shoulder　　and arm by its hand:
the grip of Grendel　　swung from the gable!　　745

Many a warrior   met in the morning
around Hrothgar's hall,   so I have heard.
Folk-leaders fared   from near and far
over wide lands   to look on the wonder,
the track of the terror,   glad he had taken   750
leave of his life   when they looked on footprints
wending away   to the mere of monsters.
Weary and weak,   defeated in war,
he dripped his blood-trail   down to dark water,
tinting the terrible   tide where he sank,   755
spilling his lifeblood   to swirl in the surge.
There the doomed one   dropped into death
where he long had lurked   in his joyless lair,
and Hell received   his heathen soul.

Many went hence: young men and old   760
mounted white mares   and rode to the mere,
a joyous journey   on brave battle-steeds.
There Beowulf's   prowess was praised
and approved by all.   Everyone said
that over the Earth   and under bright sky,   765
from north to south   between sea and sea,[55]
no other man   was more worthy of wearing
corselet or crown,   though no one denied
the grace of Hrothgar: that was a good king.

Sometimes they galloped   great-hearted bays;   770
races were run   where roads were smooth
on open upland.   Meanwhile a man
skilled as a singer,   versed in old stories,
wove a new lay   of truly-linked words.[56]
So the scop started   his song of Beowulf's   775
wisdom and strength,   setting his spell

---

55 **between sea and sea** The two seas referred to may be the North and the Baltic, although neither of those bodies of water is named in the Old English text. This expression, parallel to "from north to south," emphasizes the extent of Beowulf's fame and
perhaps suggests the cultural currency of *Beowulf*. 56 **truly-linked words** This sentence
refers to a scop's practice of adapting "old stories" to new occasions, in this case, the
praise of Beowulf's deeds by means of a "new lay." To "link" words is a figure of speech
that represents the poetic work of structural alliteration.

with subtle staves.   Of Sigemund[57] also
he said what he knew: many marvels,
deeds of daring   and distant journeys,
the wars of Waels' son,[58]   his wildness, his sins,   780
unsung among men   save by Fitela,[59]
Sigemund's nephew,   who knew his secrets
and aided his uncle   in every conflict
as comrade-at-need.   A whole clan of ogres
was slain by the Waelsing[60]   wielding his sword.   785
No small esteem   sprang up for Sigemund
after his death-day.   Dauntless in war,
he struck down a serpent   under gray stone
where it held its hoard.   He fared alone
on this fearsome foray,   not with Fitela;   790
but fate allowed him   to lunge with his blade,
spitting the scaly   worm to the wall.
His pluck repaid,   Sigemund was pleased
to take his pick   of the piled-up treasure
and load bright arms   in his longboat's breast   795
while the molten worm   melted away.

Thus that wayfarer   famed far and wide
among nations of men,   that mighty war-maker,
shelter of shield-bearers,   outshone another:

---

57 **Sigemund** Hrothgar's scop relates a summary of the legend of Sigemund, a champion
known for his monster-slaying, and thus compares Beowulf to him. This version of Sigemund's story may differ from those found in the Old Norse *Saga of the Volsungs (Völ-
sunga saga)*, which gives the fullest extant account, or the Middle High German *Nibe-
lungenlied*, and, significantly, it is unclear whether the Old English audience would
have known all elements of the story, including that of the curse on the treasure that
the hero wins from the worm. In the Old English poem, Sigemund may slay the dragon,
rather than Siegfried, his son, as in all other accounts. Lines 886 and 888 of the Old
English text of *Beowulf*, however, may allude to an unnamed son of Sigemund, who
slays the dragon (and the discrepancy among the witnesses to the event). In either case,
a hero is victorious in his youthful adventure against the monster. But a mature Beowulf, though triumphant over Grendel and Grendel's mother, will die as a result of his
dragon-fight, making this digression an artful and ironic anticipation of the reversal to
come.   58 **Waels' son** Sigemund, whose father is Waels.   59 **Fitela** In the Old Norse
Saga of the Volsungs, Fitela is Sigmundr's son by his own sister, Signý. To call Fitela
Sigemund's "nephew" here may be to use a euphemism for bastard, perhaps of a piece
with the Old English poem's omission of the themes of revenge and incest in the Sigemund story (see Chickering 1977, p. 316).   60 **Waelsing** Sigemund (cf. Old Norse
"Völsung").

unhappy Heremod,[61]   king of the Danes,   800
whose strength, spirit,   and courage were spent.
He fell among foes,   was taken by traitors
and swiftly dispatched.   So his sorrows
ended at last.   Too long had lords
and commoners suffered,   scourged by their king,   805
who ought to have honored   his father's office,
defending his homeland,   his hoard and stronghold.
Evil had entered him.[62]   Dearer to Danes
and all humankind   was Hygelac's kinsman.[63]

Still running heats,   the horses hurtled   810
on sandy lanes.   The light of morning
had swung to the south,   and many men sped,
keen to behold   the hall of the king,
the strange sights inside.   Hrothgar himself,
keeper of treasures   and leader of troops,   815
came from the queen's   quarters to march
with measured tread   the track to his mead-hall;
the queen and her maidens   also came forth.
He stopped on the stairs   and gazed at the gable,
glinting with gold   behind Grendel's hand: 820

"My thanks for this sight   go straight to heaven!
Grendel has given me   grief and grievance;
but God often works   wonders on wonders.
Not long ago   I had no hope at all
of living to see   relief from my sorrows   825
while slaughter stained   the highest of houses,
wide-spilling woes   the wisest advisors
despaired of stanching.   None of them knew
how to fend off our foes: the ghosts and ghasts
afflicting our folk   here in our fastness.   830
Now, praise heaven,   a prince has proven
this deed could be done   that daunted us all.

---

61 **Heremod** An earlier king of the Danes whose rule became tyrannical and who is
finally killed, Heremod exemplifies the unjust and unwise leader. This negative example
of a king is paired with the positive example of Sigemund the successful champion, and
Beowulf's behavior and fortune become a middle term between the two.   **62 him**
Heremod. Evil or sin is imagined as an external power that can take a man over.
63 Hygelac's kinsman Beowulf.

Indeed the mother   who bore this young man
among mankind   may certainly say,
if she still is living,   that the Lord of Old   835
blessed her child-bearing.   Henceforth, Beowulf,
best of the brave,   I shall hold you in heart
as close as a son.   Keep our new kinship,
and I shall award you   whatever you wish
that is mine to command.   Many a time   840
I have lavished wealth   on lesser warriors,
slighter in strife.   You have earned your esteem.
May the All-Wielder   reward you always,
just as He gives you   these goods today."

Beowulf spoke,   son of Ecgtheow: 845
"We gladly engaged   in this work of war
and freely faced   the unknowable foe,
but I greatly regret   that you were not granted
the sight of him broken,   slathered with blood.
I sought to grip him   swiftly and strongly,   850
wrestle him down   to writhe on his death-bed
as life left him,   unless he broke loose.
It was not my fate   to fasten the man-bane
firmly enough.   The fiend was so fierce
he secured his escape   by leaving this limb   855
to ransom his life,   though little the wretch
has gained for his hurt,   held in the grip
of a dire wound,   awaiting death
as a savage man,   besmirched by his sins,
might wait to learn   what the Lord wills."   860

Unferth was silent.   He spoke no more boasts
about works of war   when warriors gazed
at the hand hanging   from Heorot's roof,
the fiend's fingers   jutting in front,
each nail intact,   those terrible talons   865
like spikes of steel.   Everyone said
that the strongest sword   from smithies of old,
the hardest iron   edge ever forged,
would never have harmed   that monstrous mauler,
those bloody claws   crooked for combat.   870

II. Grendel's Mother

Inside Heorot   many hands hastened
at Hrothgar's command: men and women
washed out the wine-hall,   unfurled on the walls
gold-woven hangings[1]   to gladden their guests,
each of whom gazed   wide-eyed in wonder.   875
Though bound with iron,   the bright building
was badly battered,   its hinges broken.
Only the roof   had escaped unscathed
before the fell creature   cringed and fled,
stained by his sin   and despairing of life.   880
Flee it who will,   a well-earned fate
is not often altered,   for every earth-dweller
and soul-bearing son   must seek out a spot
to lay down his body,   lie on his death-bed,
sleep after feasting.
                So came the season   885
for Healfdene's son   to stride through his hall:
the king himself   would sup with his kin.
I have never heard   in any nation
of such a great host   so graciously gathered,
arrayed on benches   around their ruler,   890
glad of his fame   and glad for the feast.
Many a mead-cup   those masterful kinsmen
Hrothgar and Hrothulf   raised in the hall.
All were then friends   who filled Heorot,
treason and treachery   not yet contrived.[2]   895

Crowning his conquest,   the King of the Danes
bestowed on the soldier   a battle-standard

---

1 **gold-woven hangings** The tapestries that were a feature of Heorot's decoration. Little evidence of these decorations has remained for archaeology to uncover, but Mound I at Sutton Hoo did yield remnants of textiles, some of which could be interpreted as wall hangings, though they had been reduced over time to pads of woven material (Carver 1998, pp. 30, 36–37). **2 contrived** Other sources suggest that following Hrothgar's death, his nephew Hrothulf, and not his son Hrethric, ruled the Danes. If a fuller account of this allusion were known to the poem's audience, as is supposed, these lines would allude to treacherous plots in the future and make Wealhtheow's addresses particularly poignant.

embroidered with gold,   a helmet, mail-shirt,
and unblemished blade   borne out while ranks
of warriors watched.   Then Beowulf drank   900
a flagon before them: he would feel no shame
facing bold spearmen   with boons such as these.
Not many men   on mead benches
have given another   four golden gifts
in friendlier fashion.   The head-guard was flanged   905
with windings of wire.   Facing forward,
it warded off harm   when the wearer in war
was obliged to bear shield   against enemy blades
that were hammer-hardened   and honed by files.
The sovereign ordered   eight swift steeds   910
brought to the court   on braided bridles.
One bore a saddle   studded with gems
and glinting gold-work: there the great king,
son of Healfdene,   would sit during sword-strife,
never faltering,   fierce at the front,   915
working his will   while the wounded fell.
Then Hrothgar awarded   horses and weapons
both to Beowulf,   bade that he keep them
and wield them well.   So from his hoard
he paid the hero   a princely reward   920
of heirlooms and arms   for braving the battle;
no man could fairly   or truthfully fault them.

That lord also lavished   gifts on the Geats
whom Beowulf brought   over broad seas,
and wergeld he gave   for the one Grendel   925
had wickedly killed,   though the creature would surely
have murdered more   had God in his wisdom,
man in his strength   failed to forestall it.
So the Almighty   has always moved men;
yet man must consistently   strive to discern   930
good from evil,   evil from good
while drunk with days   he dwells in this world.

Music and story   now sounded together
as Hrothgar's scop   sang for the hall-fest
a tale often told   when harp was held: 935

how Finn's followers,[3]   faithless Jutes,
fell to fighting   friends in his fortress;
how Hnaef the Half-Dane,   hero of Scyldings,
was fated to fall   in Frisian warfare;
how by shield-swagger   harmless Hildeburh,   940
faithful to Finn   though daughter of Danes,
lost her beloved   brother and son
who were both born   to be struck by spears.
Not without cause   did Hoc's daughter
bewail the Lord's will   when morning awoke: 945
she who had known   nothing but happiness
beheld under heaven   the horror of kin-strife.

War had taken   its toll of attackers;
few men remained   for Finn to muster,
too few to force   the fight against Hengest,   950
a dutiful thane   who had rallied the Danes.
As tokens of truce   Finn offered these terms:
a haven wholly   emptied of foes,
hall and high seat,   with an equal share
in gifts given   his own gathered kin.   955
Each time he treated   his sons to treasures
plated with gold,   a portion would go
to sweeten Hengest's   stay in his hall.
The two sides swore   a strict treaty;
and Finn freely   affirmed to Hengest   960
that all would honor   this oath to the Danes,
as his council decreed,   and further declared
no Frisian would ever,   by word or work,

---

3 **Finn's followers** The following episode is one of the most difficult in *Beowulf*. Hnaef and Hildeburh are children of an earlier Danish king, Hoc. As a strategy of alliance to settle a bloodfeud between the two kingdoms, Hildeburh is sent to marry Finn, the son of Folcwalda and the king of the Frisians. When Hnaef goes to visit his sister and her husband, Hnaef is treacherously ambushed by one of Finn's men and killed. During the fight, Hildeburh's son by Finn is also killed, avenging the death of her brother. Thus, Hildeburh, the putative "peace-weaver," is rent by conflicting loyalties to her brother and her husband. The situation parallels that of Hrothgar's daughter Freawaru, who is to marry Ingeld, king of the Heathobards, and that of Wealhtheow, who may be betrayed by the Danes (through Hrothulf's usurpation of the throne), as was Hildeburh by the Frisians. A fragmentary Old English poem, called *The Battle of Finnsburg* (see *Contexts, From the Old English*, p. 148) and known only from a transcript of a now-lost manuscript leaf, tells a short portion of the same story, but with the fast-moving pace of a lay about a battle, rather than the slow elegiac tone of its recital in *Beowulf*. The story of the battle is also alluded to in the Old English poem *Widsith*.

challenge the peace   or mention with malice
the plight of survivors   deprived of their prince   965
and wintered-in   at the slayer's stronghold.
Should any Frisian   enter in anger,
the sword's edge   would settle the quarrel.

That oath[4] offered,   the hoard was opened
for gold to array   the greatest of War-Danes.   970
Iron-hard guardians   gilded with gold,
bloody mail-shirts   and boar-tusked helms
were heaped on his bier,   awaiting the balefire.
Many a warrior,   weakened by wounds,
had faltered and fallen   with foes he had slain.   975
Hildeburh ordered   her own dear son
be placed on the pyre,   the prince and his uncle
shoulder to shoulder.   Their bodies were burned
while the stricken lady   sang out her sorrow.
Streamers of smoke   burst from the bier   980
as corpses kindled   with cruelest of flames.
Faces withered,   wounded flesh yawned,
and blood boiled out   as the blaze swallowed
with hateful hunger   those whom warfare
had borne away,   the best of both houses.   985
Their glory was gone.
                        The Frisians were fewer
heading for home;   their high stronghold
was empty of allies.   For Hengest also
that winter was woeful,   walled up in Frisia,
brooding on bloodshed   and longing to leave,   990
though knowing his vessel   never[5] could breast
the wind-darkened swells   of a wide ocean
seething with storms,   or break the ice-bindings
that barred his bow   from the bitter waters.
Constrained to wait   for kindlier weather,   995
he watched until spring,   season of sunlight,
dawned on men's dwellings   as ever it did

---

4 **oath** The manuscript reading is emended here by some editors to "pyre"; thus "the
funeral pyre was made ready" (Mitchell and Robinson 1998, note to line 1107, p. 85).
5 **never** Though this negation is not present in the manuscript, editors usually add it to
make sense of the following passage, which explains why Hengest did not sail home.

and still does today.   Winter withdrew
and Earth blossomed.

                          Though the exile was eager
to end his visit,   he ached for vengeance   1000
before sailing home.   Loathe to foreswear
the way of this world,   he schemed to assail
the sons of slayers.   So Hengest heeded
Hunlaf's son,[6]   who laid on his lap
the sword War-Flame,   feared by all foes,   1005
asking its edge   be offered the Jutes.
His heart was hot;   he could hold back no more.
Gladly he answered   Guthlaf and Oslaf,
who wrathfully spoke   of the wrong they suffered,
the shame of Scyldings   sharing their plight.   1010
Then fierce-hearted Finn   fell in his turn,
stricken by swords   in his own stronghold.
The building was bloody   with bodies of foemen:
the king lay slain,   likewise his kin;
and the queen was captured.   Scyldings carried   1015
off in their ship   all of the chattels
found in Finn's fortress,   gemstones and jewels.
The lady was borne   to the land of her birth.

So that story   was sung to its end,
then mirth mounted   once more in Heorot.   1020
Revelry rang   as wine-bearers brought
finely-wrought flagons   filled to the brim.
Wearing her circlet,   Wealhtheow walked
where uncle and nephew,   Hrothgar and Hrothulf,
were sitting in peace,   two soldiers together,   1025
each still believing   the other was loyal.
Likewise the officer,[7]   Unferth, was honored
to sit at the feet   of the Scylding sovereign.
Everyone thought him   honest and trustworthy,
blameless and brave,   though his blade had unjustly   1030
stricken a kinsman.

---

6 **Hunlaf's son** It is not clear who or what this refers to. It may be to one of the Danish
warriors named in this passage, but some scholars have argued that it is the name of a
sword placed in Hengest's lap to remind him of the duty of vengeance.   7 **officer** The
Old English word *thyle* is twice used in the poem to refer to Unferth. The word may
mean an official spokesman for Hrothgar, but others have argued that the word means
some sort of court jester.

So the queen spoke:
"Receive this cup,   sovereign of Scyldings,
giver of gold;   drink and be glad;
greet the Geats mildly   as well a man might,
mindful of gifts   graciously given   1035
from near and far,   now in your keeping.
They say you would name   that knight as a son
for purging the ring-hall.   Employ as you please
wealth and rewards,   but bequeath to your kin
rule of this realm   when the Ruler of All   1040
holds that you must.   I know that Hrothulf
will honor our trust   and treat these youths well
if you have to leave   this life before him.
I am counting on him   to recall our kindness
when he was a child   and repay our children   1045
for presents we gave   and pleasures we granted."

She turned to the bench   where her sons were seated,
Hrethric and Hrothmund.   Between the two brothers
Beowulf sat;   and the cup-bearer brought him
words of welcome,   willingly gave him   1050
as tokens of favor   two braided arm-bands,
jerkin, corselet,   and jeweled collar[8]
grander than any   other on Earth.
I have heard under heaven   of no higher treasure
hoarded by heroes   since Hama stole off   1055
to his fair fortress   with Freya's necklace,[9]
shining with stones   set by the Fire-Dwarves.
So Hama[10] earned   Eormanric's[11] anger,

---

8 **collar** Wealhtheow's gift to Beowulf introduces an episode that tells a history of great
neck-rings, and the poet uses this rich decorative collar as a figure to bind together several events that occur at chronologically different times in the poem.   9 **Freya's necklace**
As known from Old Norse mythological poetry, the neck-ring of the Brosings is worn by
the goddess Freyja (Freya). She gained it by sleeping with the dwarves who made it, but
the neck-ring was stolen by Loki and later regained by the god Heimdall.   10 **Hama**
Known from *The Saga of Thidrek of Bern (þiðreks saga af Bern)* (chs. 288 and 429),
where he is called Heimir, and mentioned twice in the Old English poem *Widsith*, Hama
is a figure about whom little is certain. In the saga narrative, Heimir sides with Thidrek
against his uncle King Jörmunrekkr (Eormanric/Erminrekr), whose wrath Heimir flees by
entering a monastery. Though he leaves the monks his riches and his armor to atone for
his sins, neither the saga nor the Old English poem mentions a neck-ring.   11 **Eormanric's**
This king is known from Latin chronicles, the Old English poems *Widsith* and *Deor*, and
from Old Norse literature as Jörmunrekkr (Erminrekr).

and fame for himself.   Foolhardy Hygelac,[12]
grandson of Swerting   and sovereign of Geats,   1060
would wear it one day   on his final foray.
He fell in the fray   defending his treasure,
the spoils he bore   with his battle-standard.
Recklessly raiding   the realm of Frisia,
the prince in his pride   had prompted misfortune   1065
by crossing the sea   while clad in that collar.[13]
He fell under shield,   fell to the Franks,
weaker warriors   stripping the slain
of armor and spoil   after the slaughter.
Hygelac held   the graveyard of Geats.   1070

The hall approved   the princely prize
bestowed by the queen,   and Wealhtheow spoke
for the host to hear: "Keep this collar,
beloved Beowulf.   Bear this armor,
wealth of our realm.   May it ward you well.   1075
Swear that your strength   and kindly counsel
will aid these youngsters,   and I shall reward you.
Now your renown   will range near and far;
your fame will wax wide,   as wide as the water
hemming our hills,   homes of the wind.   1080
Be blessed, Beowulf,   with abundant treasures
as long as you live;   and be mild to my sons,
a model admired.   Here men are courtly,
honest and true,   each to the other,
all to their ruler;   and after the revels,   1085
bolstered with beer,   they do as I bid."

The lady left him   and sat on her seat.
The feast went on;   fine wine was flowing.
Men could not know   what fate would befall them,
what evil of old   was decreed to come   1090
for the earls that evening.   As always, Hrothgar

---

12 **Foolhardy Hygelac** This reference is the first of several to the rash raid of Hygelac against the Frisians, during which he was killed.   13 **that collar** Here the narrative moves to a point beyond Beowulf's return home to the Geats. Later we will learn that Beowulf gave to Hygd, the wife of his uncle Hygelac, the neck-ring that Wealhtheow had presented to Beowulf (see lines 1916–19). Hygd apparently lends the neck-ring to Hygelac to wear on his final reckless foray, an attack on the Frisians in which he is killed (see lines 1059–63). The neck-ring then becomes the plunder of the Franks (see lines 1067–70).

headed for home,   where the ruler rested.
A great many others   remained in the hall,
bearing bright benches   and rolling out beds
while one drunkard,   doomed and death-ripened,   1095
sprawled into sleep.   They set at their heads
round war-shields,   well-adorned wood.
Above them on boards,   their battle-helms rested,
ringed mail-shirts   and mighty spear-shafts
waiting for strife.   Such was their wont   1100
at home or afield,   wherever they fared,
in case their king   should call them to arms.
Those were stern people.
                          They sank into slumber,
but one paid sorely   for sleep that evening,
as often had happened   when grim Grendel   1105
held the gold-hall,   wreaking his wrongs
straight to the end: death after sins.
It would soon be perceived   plainly by all
that one ill-wisher   still was alive,
maddened by grief: Grendel's mother,   1110
a fearsome female   bitterly brooding
alone in her lair   deep in dread waters
and cold currents   since Cain had killed
the only brother   born of his father.
Marked by murder,   he fled from mankind   1115
and went to the wastes.   Doomed evil-doers
issued from him.   Grendel was one,
but the hateful Hell-walker   found a warrior
wakefully watching   for combat in Heorot.
The monster met there   a man who remembered   1120
strength would serve him,   the great gift of God,
faith in the All-Wielder's   favor and aid.
By that he mastered   the ghastly ghoul;
routed, wretched,   the hell-fiend fled,
forlornly drew near   his dreary death-place.   1125
Enraged and ravenous,   Grendel's mother
swiftly set out   on a sorrowful journey
to settle the score   for her son's demise.

She slipped into Heorot,   hall of the Ring-Danes,
where sleeping soldiers   soon would endure   1130

an awful reversal.   Her onslaught was less
by as much as a woman's   mettle in war
is less than a man's   wielding his weapon:[14]
the banded blade   hammered to hardness,
a blood-stained sword   whose bitter stroke   1135
slashes a boar-helm   borne into battle.
In the hall, sword-edge   sprang from scabbard;
broadshield was swung   swiftly off bench,
held firmly in hand.   None thought of helmet
or sturdy mail-shirt   when terror assailed him.   1140

Out she hastened,   out and away,
keen to keep living   when caught in the act.
She fastened on one,   then fled to her fen.
He was Hrothgar's   highest counselor,
boon companion   and brave shield-bearer,   1145
slain in his bed.[15]   Beowulf slept
elsewhere that evening,   for after the feast
the Geat had been given   a different dwelling.
A din of dismay   mounted in Heorot:
the gory hand   was gone from the gable.   1150
Dread had retaken   the Danes' dwelling.
That bargain was bad   for both barterers,
costing each one   a close comrade.

It was grim for the sovereign,   the grizzled soldier,
to learn his old thane   was no longer living,   1155
to know such a dear one   was suddenly dead.
Swiftly he sent   servants to fetch
battle-blessed Beowulf   early from bed,
together with all   the great-hearted Geats.
He marched in their midst,   went where the wise one   1160
was wondering whether   the All-Wielder
ever would alter   this spell of ill-fortune.
That much-honored man   marched up the floor,
and timbers dinned   with the tread of his troop.

---

14 weapon Beowulf's battle with Grendel's mother will turn out to be much tougher
than his struggle with her son, making it difficult to weigh the tone of the *Beowulf*-poet
here. Many Old Norse sagas contain contests between a hero and a ferocious she-
monster who very nearly bests him (see, e.g., *Grettir's Saga* in *Contexts, From the Old
Norse*, p. 201).   **15 slain in his bed** The victim is Aeschere, named by Hrothgar in line
1169.

He spoke soberly   after the summons,   1165
asking how soundly   the sovereign had slept.

Hrothgar answered,   head of his house:
"Ask not about ease!   Anguish has wakened
again for the Danes.   Aeschere is dead.
He was Yrmenlaf's   elder brother,   1170
my rune-reader   and keeper of counsel,
my shoulder's shielder,   warder in war
when swordsmen struck   at boar-headed helms.
Whatever an honored   earl ought to be,
such was Aeschere.   A sleepless evil   1175
has slipped into Heorot,   seized and strangled.
No one knows where   she will wander now,
glad of the gory   trophy she takes,
her fine fodder.   So she requites
her kinsman's killer   for yesterday's deed,   1180
when you grabbed Grendel   hard in your hand-grip.
He plagued and plundered   my people too long.
His life forfeit,   he fell in the fray;
but now a second   mighty man-scather
comes to carry   the feud further,   1185
as many a thane   must mournfully think,
seeing his sovereign   stricken with grief
at the slaying of one   who served so well.

I have heard spokesmen   speak in my hall,
country-folk saying   they sometimes spotted   1190
a pair of prodigies   prowling the moors,
evil outcasts,   walkers of wastelands.
One, they descried,   had the semblance of woman;
the other, ill-shapen,   an aspect of man
trudging his track,   ever an exile,   1195
though superhuman   in stature and strength.
In bygone days   the border-dwellers
called him Grendel.   What creature begot him,
what nameless spirit,   no one could say.
The two of them trekked   untraveled country: 1200
wolf-haunted heights   and windy headlands,
the frightening fen-path   where falling torrents
dive into darkness,   stream beneath stone

amid folded mountains.   That mere[16] is not far,
as miles are measured.   About it there broods   1205
a forest of fir trees   frosted with mist.
Hedges of wood-roots   hem in the water
where each evening   fire-glow flickers
forth on the flood,   a sinister sight.
That pool is unplumbed   by wits of the wise;   1210
but the heath-striding hart   hunted by hounds,
the strong-antlered stag   seeking a thicket,
running for cover,   would rather be killed
at bay on the bank   before hiding its head
under that welter.   It is no peaceful place   1215
where water-struck waves   whipped into clouds,
surge and storm,   swept by the winds,
so the heights are hidden   and heaven weeps.
Now you alone   can relieve our anguish:
look, if you will,   at the lay of the land;   1220
and seek, if you dare,   that dreadful dale
where the she-demon dwells.   Finish this feud,
and I shall reward you   with age-old wealth,
twisted-gold treasures,   if you return."

Beowulf spoke,   son of Ecgtheow: 1225
"Grieve not, good man.   It is better to go
and avenge your friend   than mourn overmuch.
We all must abide   an end on this earth,
but a warrior's works   may win him renown
as long as he lives   and after life leaves him.   1230
Rise now, ruler;   let us ride together
and seek out the signs   of Grendel's mother.
I swear to you this: she[17] shall not escape
in chasm or cave,   in cliff-climbing thicket

---

16 mere A small lake. A similar description of this terrible lake is found in an Old
English vision of Hell recorded in the tenth-century *Blickling Homilies* (Sermon 17)
(see *Contexts, From the Old English,* p. 192). In the apocryphal *Vision of St. Paul,*
which is the source of the allusion in the sermon, Paul visits Hell under the protection
of the archangel Michael and sees a frozen venue remarkably similar to that depicted in
Beowulf. Another frequently mentioned analogue to the mere is the noxious black lake in
the *Aeneid* (VI, 237–42). Similar fights pitting a champion against a monster in a watery
venue occur in Old Norse sagas, though the setting there is a waterfall with a cave beyond it. Hrothgar's frightening depiction of Grendel's mere is underscored and amplified
by the poet's description of Hrothgar's reaction to it, beginning at line 1249.   **17 she**
Corrected from the Old English masculine pronoun *he* found in the manuscript.

or bog's bottom,   wherever she bides.   1235
Suffer your sorrow   this one day only;
I wish you to wait,   wait and be patient."

The elder leapt up   and offered his thanks
to God Almighty,   Master of all,
for such hopeful speech.   Then Hrothgar's horse,   1240
a steed with mane braided,   was brought on its bridle.
The sage sovereign   set out in splendor
with shield-bearing soldiers   striding beside him.
Tracks on the trail   were easy to trace:
they went from woodland   out to the open,   1245
heading through heather   and murky moors
where the best of thanes   was borne off unbreathing.
He would live no longer   in Hrothgar's house.
Crossing the moorland,   the king mounted
a stony path   up steepening slopes.   1250
With a squad of scouts   in single file,
he rode through regions   none of them knew,
mountains and hollows   that hid many monsters.
The sovereign himself,   son of great forebears,
suddenly spotted   a forest of fir-trees   1255
rooted on rock,   their trunks tipping
over a tarn   of turbulent eddies.
Danes were downcast,   and Geats, grim;
every soldier   was stricken at heart
to behold on that height   Aeschere's head.   1260

As they looked on the lake,   blood still lingered,
welled to the surface.   A war-horn sounded
its bold battle-cry,[18]   and the band halted.
Strange sea-dragons   swam in the depths;
sinuous serpents   slid to and fro.   1265
At the base of the bluff   water-beasts lay,
much like monsters   that rise in the morning
when seafarers sail   on strenuous journeys.
Hearing the horn's   high-pitched challenge,
they puffed up with rage   and plunged in the pool.   1270
One Geatish lad   lifted his bow

---

18 **battle-cry** As in a hunt on land, the horn is sounded to flush out the sea-beasts.

and loosing an arrow,   ended the life
of a wondrous wave-piercer.   War-shaft jutting
hard in its heart,   the swimmer slowed
as death seized it.   With startling speed   1275
the waters were torn   by terrible tuskers.
They heaved the hideous   hulk to the shore
with spear-hooked heads   as warriors watched.

Undaunted, Beowulf   donned battle armor.
His woven war-corselet,   wide and ornate,   1280
would safeguard his heart   as he searched underwater.
It knew how to armor   the breast of its bearer
if an angry grappler   grasped him in battle.
The bright war-helm   would hold his head
when he sought the seafloor   in swirling flood.   1285
A weapon-smith   had skillfully worked
its gilding of gold   in bygone days
and royally ringed it.   He added afterward
figures of boars   so blades of foemen
would fail to bite.   One further aid   1290
Beowulf borrowed: Unferth offered
the hilt of Hrunting,   his princely sword,
a poisoned war-fang   with iron-edged blade,
blood-hardened   in battles of old.
It never had failed   in any man's grasp   1295
if he dared to fare   on a dreadful foray
to fields of foes.   This was not the first time
it was forced to perform   a desperate deed.

Though strong and sly,   the son of Ecglaf[19]
had somehow forgotten   the slander he spoke,   1300
bleary with beer.   He loaned his blade
to a better bearer,   a doer of deeds
that he would not dare.   His head never dipped
under wild waves,   and his fame waned
when bravery failed him   as battle beckoned.   1305
Not so, the other,   armed and eager.

19 son of Ecglaf Unferth.

Beowulf spoke,   son of Ecgtheow:
"Remember, wise master,   mover of men
and giver of gold,   since now I begin
this foray full-willing,   how once before   1310
you pledged to fill   the place of a father
if I should be killed   acquitting your cause.
Guard these young aides,   my partners in arms,
if death takes me.   The treasures you dealt,
Hrothgar, my lord,   I leave to Hygelac.   1315
Let the king of Geats   gaze on the gold
and see that I found   a fair bestower,
a generous host   to help while I could.
Let Unferth have back   his heirloom, Hrunting,
this wonderful weapon,   wavy-skinned sword[20]   1320
renowned among men.   Now I shall conquer
or die in the deed."
                      So saying, he dived,
high-hearted and hasty,   awaiting no answer.
The waters swallowed   that stout soldier.
He swam a half-day   before seeing sea-floor.   1325
Straightaway someone   spied him as well:
she that had hidden   a hundred half-years
in the void's vastness.   Grim and greedy,
she glimpsed a creature   come from above
and crept up to catch him,   clutch him, crush him.   1330
Quickly she learned   his life was secure;
he was hale and whole,   held in the ring-mail.
Linked and locked,   his life-shielding shirt[21]
was wrapped around him,   and wrathful fingers
failed to rip open   the armor he wore.   1335
The wolf of the waters   dragged him away
to her den in the deep,   where weapons of war,

---

20 **wavy-skinned sword** A sword produced by the difficult process of "pattern-welding"
consisted of several bars of metal twisted together and forged into a single strong and
flexible blade. Such a blade would have had distinctive sinuous patterns on its surface.
21 **life-shielding shirt** Beowulf's mail-shirt, which protects him effectively from the she-
monster's claws. Its special efficacy may suggest an analogy with the magical shirts woven by elvish women to protect heroes mentioned in Old Norse sagas. On the other
hand, the mail-shirt, which seems so rare in this period that it has been identified for certain only once—as part of the wargear of the well-equipped ruler memorialized at Sutton
Hoo, Mound I—may simply have been an exceptional item of defensive armor and thus
worth mentioning. Somewhat later, the mail-shirt seems to have been commoner, and it
is depicted on infantrymen in the Bayeux Tapestry.

though bravely wielded,   were worthless against her.
Many a mere-beast   banded about him,
brandishing tusks   to tear at his shirt.   1340

The soldier now saw   a high-roofed hall:
unharmed, he beheld   the foe's fastness
beyond the reach   of the roiling flood.
Fire-light flared;   a blaze shone brightly.
The lordly one looked   on the hellish hag,   1345
the mighty mere-wife.   He swung his sword
for a swift stroke,   not staying his hand;
and the whorled blade   whistled its war-song.
But the battle-flame   failed to bite her;
its edge was unable   to end her life,   1350
though Hrunting had often   hacked through helmets
and slashed mail-shirts   in hand-to-hand strife.
For the first time   the famous blade faltered.

Resolve unshaken,   courage rekindled,
Hygelac's kinsman   was keen for conquest.   1355
In a fit of fury,   he flung down the sword.
Steely and strong,   the ring-banded blade
rang on the stones.   He would trust in the strength
of his mighty hand-grip.   Thus should a man,
unmindful of life,   win lasting renown.   1360
Grabbing the tresses   of Grendel's mother,
the Geats' battle-chief,   bursting with wrath,
wrestled her down: no deed to regret
but a favor repaid   as fast as she fell.
With her grim grasp   she grappled him still.   1365
Weary, the warrior   stumbled and slipped;
the strongest foot-soldier   fell to the foe.
Astraddle the hall-guest,[22]   she drew her dagger,
broad and bright-bladed,   bent on avenging
her only offspring.   His mail-shirt shielded   1370
shoulder and breast.   Barring the entry
of edge or point,   the woven war-shirt

22 **Astraddle the hall-guest** The Old English verb *ofsæt* may mean "charged" or "set upon," rather than "sat atop" (Mitchell and Robinson 1998, note to lines 1545–46a, p. 99). But the themes of gender that play across Grendel's mother in the poem are intensified in this translation.

saved him from harm.   Ecgtheow's son,
the leader of Geats,   would have lost his life
under Earth's arch   but for his armor   1375
and heaven's favor   furnishing help.
The Ruler of All   readily aided
the righteous man   when he rose once more.

He beheld in a hoard   of ancient arms
a battle-blessed sword   with strong-edged blade,   1380
a marvelous weapon   men might admire
though over-heavy   for any to heft
when finely forged   by giants of old.^{23}
The Scyldings' shielder   took hold of the hilt
and swung up the sword,   though despairing of life.   1385
He struck savagely,   hit her hard neck
and broke the bone-rings,   cleaving clean through
her fated flesh.   She fell to the floor;
the sword sweated;   the soldier rejoiced.

The blaze brightened,   shining through shadows   1390
as clearly as heaven's   candle on high.
Grim and angry,   Hygelac's guardsman
glanced round the room   and went toward the wall
with his weapon raised,   holding it hard
by the inlaid hilt.   Its edge was ideal   1395
for quickly requiting   the killings of Grendel.
Too many times   he had warred on the West-Danes.
He had slain Hrothgar's   hearth-mates in sleep,
eagerly eaten   fifteen of those folk
and as many more borne   for his monstrous booty.   1400
He paid their price   to the fierce prince,
who looked on the ground   where Grendel lay limp,
wound-weary,   defeated in war.
The lifeless one lurched   at the stroke of the sword
that cleaved his corpse   and cut off his head.^{24} 1405

23 **by giants of old** Excellent weapons or any awe-provoking work is often praised as
having been made by giants. An example is found in the Old English poem *The Ruin*,
where the great wasted buildings are described as the work of giants (see *Contexts, From
the Old English*, p. 146).   24 **cut off his head** Perhaps as a repayment for the dismem-
berment of Aeschere, whose head the warriors discover at line 1260, or perhaps the appropriate act of the victor in this sort of desperate struggle of man and monster.

At once the wise men   waiting with Hrothgar
and watching the waters   saw the waves seethe
with streaks of gore.   Gray-haired and glum,
age around honor,   they offered their counsel,
convinced that no victor   would ever emerge   1410
and seek out the sovereign.   All were certain
the mere-wolf had mauled him.   It was mid-afternoon,
and the proud Danes   departed the dale;
generous Hrothgar   headed for home.
The Geats lingered   and looked on the lake   1415
with sorrowful souls,   wistfully wishing
they still might see   their beloved leader.

The sword shrank   from battle-shed blood;
its blade began melting,   a marvel to watch,
that war-icicle   waning away   1420
like a rope of water   unwound by the Ruler
when Father releases   fetters of frost,
the true Sovereign   of seasons and times.
The Weders' warlord   took only two treasures
from all he beheld: the head and the hilt,   1425
studded with gems.   The sword had melted.
Its banded blade   was burnt by the blood,
so hot was the horror,   so acid the evil
that ended thereon.   Soon he was swimming:
the strife-survivor   drove up from the deep   1430
when his foe had fallen.   The foaming waves,
the wide waters   were everywhere cleansed;
that alien evil   had ended her life-days,
left the loaned world.   Landward he swam;
the strong-minded savior   of sea-faring men   1435
was glad of his burden,   the booty he brought.
Grateful to God,   the band of brave thanes
hastened gladly   to greet their chieftain,
astonished to see him   whole and unharmed.
His helm and chain-mail   were swiftly unstrapped.   1440
Calm under clouds,   the lake lay quietly,
stained by the slain.   They found the foot-path
and marched manfully,   making their way
back through the barrens.   Proud as princes,

they hauled the head   far from the highland,   1445
an effort for each   of the four who ferried it
slung from spear-shafts.   They bore their booty
straight to the gold-hall.   Battle-hardened,
all fourteen strode   from the field outside,
a bold band of Geats   gathered about   1450
their leader and lord,   the war-worthy man,
peerless in prowess   and daring in deeds.
He hailed Hrothgar   as Grendel's head
was dragged by the hair,   drawn through the hall
where earls were drinking.   All were awe-stricken: 1455
women and warriors   watched in wonder.

Beowulf spoke,   son of Ecgtheow:
"Hail, Hrothgar,   Healfdene's son.
Look on this token   we took from the lake,
this glorious booty   we bring you gladly.   1460
The struggle was stark;   the danger, dreadful.
My foe would have won   our war underwater
had the Lord not looked   after my life.
Hrunting failed me,   though finely fashioned;
but God vouchsafed me   a glimpse of a great-sword,   1465
ancient and huge,   hung from the wall.
All-Father often   fosters the friendless.
Wielding this weapon,   I struck down and slew
the cavern's keeper   as soon as I could.
My banded war-blade   was burned away   1470
when blood burst forth   in the heat of battle.
I bore the hilt here,   wrested from raiders.
Thus I avenged   the deaths among Danes
as it was fitting,   and this I assure you:
henceforth in Heorot   heroes shall sleep   1475
untroubled by terror.   Your warrior troop,
all of your thanes,   young men and old,
need fear no further   evil befalling,
not from that quarter,   king of the Scyldings."

He gave the gold hilt   to the good old man;   1480
the hoary war-chief   held in his hand
an ancient artifact   forged by giants.
At the devils' downfall,   this wondrous work

went to the Danes.   The dark-hearted demon,
hater of humans,   heaven's enemy,   1485
committer of murders,   and likewise his mother,
departed this Earth.   Their power passed
to the wisest world-king   who ever awarded
treasure in Denmark   between the two seas.

Hrothgar spoke   as he studied the hilt,   1490
that aged heirloom   inscribed[25] long ago
with a story of strife: how the Flood swallowed
the race of giants   with onrushing ocean.
Defiant kindred,   they fared cruelly,
condemned for their deeds   to death by water.   1495
Such were the staves   graven in gold-plate,
runes rightly set,   saying for whom
the serpent-ribbed sword[26]   and raddled hilt
were once fashioned   of finest iron.
When the wise one spoke,   all were silent:[27]   1500

"Truth may be told   by the homeland's holder
and keeper of kinfolk,   who rightly recalls
the past for his people: this prince was born
bravest of fighters.   My friend, Beowulf,
your fame shall flourish   in far countries,   1505
everywhere honored.   Your strength is sustained
by patience and judgment.   Just as I promised,
our friendship is firmed,   a lasting alliance.
So you shall be   a boon to your brethren,
unlike Heremod   who ought to have helped   1510
Ecgwela's sons,   the Honor-Scyldings.
He grew up to grief   and grim slaughter,

---

25 inscribed Presumably the story of the flood was cut into the hilt of the sword in runic
letters, but considering how limited an area a sword hilt presents, we may imagine the
story to have been represented by a combination of runic captions and drawings. Such a
combination of visual and textual representation is found on the panels of the Franks
Casket, an eighth-century Anglo-Saxon whalebone box that combines relief carving of
Biblical and legendary scenes with descriptive texts in Old English, written in runes, and
Latin texts, written in the Roman alphabet (see Webster 1982, pp. 20–32; Webster
1999, pp. 227–46).   **26 serpent-ribbed sword** Here the "pattern-welded" blade is
thought of as animated. Scandinavian swords are also described as stinging or biting
like snakes.   **27 silent** The advice that old King Hrothgar gives to the young hero
Beowulf are often referred to as "Hrothgar's Sermon." (See, for example, Kaske 1958,
in which the speech is used to set out the "controlling theme" of *sapientia et fortitudo*
["wisdom and courage"] in the poem.)

doling out death   to the Danish nation.
Hot-tempered at table,   he cut down comrades,
slew his own soldiers   and spurned humankind,   1515
alone and unloved,   an infamous prince,
though mighty God   had given him greatness
and raised him in rank   over all other men.
Hidden wrath   took root in his heart,
bloodthirsty thoughts.   He would give no gifts   1520
to honor others.   Loveless, he lived,
a lasting affliction   endured by the Danes
in sorrow and strife.   Consider him well,
his life and lesson.
                Wise with winters,
I tell you this tale   as I mull and marvel   1525
how the Almighty   metes to mankind
the blessings of reason,   rule and realm.
He arranges it all.   For a time He allows
the mind of a man   to linger in love
with earthly honors.   He offers him homeland   1530
to hold and enjoy,   a fort full of fighters,
men to command   and might in the world,
wide kingdoms   won to his will.
In his folly, the fool   imagines no ending.
He dwells in delight   without thought of his lot.   1535
Illness, old age,   anguish or envy:
none of these gnaw   by night at his mind.
Nowhere are swords   brandished in anger;
for him the whole world   wends as he wishes.
He knows nothing worse   till his portion of pride   1540
waxes within him.   His soul is asleep;
his gate, unguarded.   He slumbers too soundly,
sunk in small cares.   The slayer creeps close[28]
and shoots a shaft   from the baneful bow.
The bitter arrow   bites through his armor,   1545
piercing the heart   he neglected to guard
from crooked counsel   and evil impulse.
Too little seems all   he has long possessed.
Suspicious and stingy,   withholding his hoard

28 **The slayer creeps close** Hrothgar's advice to Beowulf includes developing a martial figure of stealthy attack, with sin as the slayer of the soul whose guardian, reason or prudence, sleeps.

of gold-plated gifts,   he forgets or ignores   1550
what fate awaits him,   for the world's Wielder
surely has granted   his share of glory.
But the end-rune   is already written:
the loaned life-home   collapses in ruin;
some other usurps   and openly offers   1555
the hoarded wealth,   heedless of worry.

Beloved Beowulf,   best of defenders,
guard against anger   and gain for yourself
perpetual profit.   Put aside pride,
worthiest warrior.   Now for awhile   1560
your force flowers,   yet soon it shall fail.
Sickness or age   will strip you of strength,
or the fangs of flame,   or flood-surges,
the sword's bite   or the spear's flight,
or fearful frailty   as bright eyes fade,   1565
dimming to darkness.   Afterward death
will sweep you away,   strongest of war-chiefs.

I ruled the Ring-Danes   a hundred half-years,
stern under clouds   with sword and spear
that I wielded in war   against many nations   1570
across middle-earth,   until none remained
beneath spacious skies   to reckon as rivals.
Recompense happened   here in my homeland,
grief after gladness   when Grendel came,
when the ancient enemy   cunningly entered.   1575
Thereafter I suffered   constant sorrows
and cruelest cares.   But God has given me
long enough life   to look at this head
with my own eyes,   as enmity ends
spattered with gore.   Sit and be glad,   1580
war-worthy one: the feast is forthcoming,
and many gifts   will be granted tomorrow."

Gladly the Geat   sought out his seat
as the old man asked.   Hall-guests were given
a second feast   as fine as the first.   1585
The helm of heaven   darkened with dusk,
and the elders arose.   The oldest of Scyldings

was ready to rest   his hoary-haired head
at peace on his pillow.   Peerless with shield,
the leader of Geats   was equally eager   1590
to lie down at last.   A thane was appointed
to serve as his esquire.   Such was the courtesy
shown in those days   to weary wayfarers,
soldiers sojourning   over the ocean.

Beneath golden gables   the great-hearted guest   1595
dozed until dawn   in the high-roofed hall,
when the black raven[29]   blithely foretold
joy under heaven.   Daybreak hastened,
sun after shadow.   The soldiers were ardent,
the earls eager   to hurry homeward;   1600
the stern-minded man   would make for his ship,
fare back to his folk.   But first he bade
that Hrunting be sent   to the son of Ecglaf,[30]
a treasure returned   with thanks for the loan
of precious iron.   He ordered the owner   1605
be told he considered   the sword a fine friend,
blameless in battle.   That man was gallant![31]
Keen for the crossing,   his weapons secure,
the warrior went   to the worthy Dane;
the thane sought the throne   where a sovereign sat,   1610
that steadfast hero,   Hrothgar the Great.

Beowulf spoke,   son of Ecgtheow:
"Now we must say   as far-sailing seamen,
we wish to make way   homeward to Hygelac.
Here we were well   and warmly received.   1615
If anything further   would earn your favor,
some deed of war   that remains to be done
for the master of men,   I shall always be ready.
Should word ever wend   over wide ocean
that nearby nations   menace your marches,   1620

---

29 black raven The raven makes an ironic bearer of joyful news. The Old English adjective modifying the bird could be either *blæc*, "black," or *blāc*, "shining," which conveys the quality of the raven's glossy feathers. Brightness and luster seem to be an integral part of the comprehension of color in Old English.   **30 son of Ecglaf** Unferth.
31 gallant The poet here contrasts Beowulf's restrained, noble treatment of Unferth, despite the failure of the weapon he lent Beowulf, with Unferth's earlier sarcasms about Beowulf's heroic status.

as those who detest you   sometimes have tried,
I shall summon a thousand   thanes to your aid.
I know Hygelac,   though newly-anointed
the nation's shepherd,   will surely consent
to honor my offer   in word and action.   1625
If you ever need men,   I shall muster at once
a thicket of spears   and support you in strength.
Should Hrethric, your son,   sail overseas,
he shall find friends   in the fort of the Geats.
It is well for the worthy   to fare in far countries."   1630

Hrothgar offered   these answering words:
"Heaven's Sovereign   has set in your heart
this vow you have voiced.   I never have known
someone so young   to speak more wisely.
You are peerless in strength,   princely in spirit,   1635
straightforward in speech.   If a spear fells
Hrethel's son,[32]   if a hostile sword-stroke
kills him in combat   or after, with illness,
slays your leader   while you still live,
the Sea-Geats surely   could name no better   1640
to serve as their king   and keeper of treasure,
should you wish to wield   rule in your realm.
I sensed your spirit   the instant I saw you,
precious Beowulf,   bringer of peace
for both our peoples: War-Danes and Weders,   1645
so often sundered   by strife in the past.
While I wield the rule   of this wide realm,
men will exchange   many more greetings
and riches will ride   in ring-bowed ships
bearing their gifts   where the gannets bathe.   1650
I know your countrymen   keep to old ways,
fast in friendship,   and war as well."

Then the hall's holder,   Healfdene's son,
gave his protector   twelve more treasures,
bidding he bear   these tokens safely   1655
home to his kin,   and quickly return.

---

32 Hrethel's son Hygelac.

That hoary-haired king   held and kissed him,
clasping his neck.   The noble Scylding
was too well aware   with the wisdom of age
that he never might meet   the young man again   1660
coming to council.   So close had they grown,
so strong in esteem,   he could scarcely endure
the surfeit of sorrow   that surged in his heart;
the flame of affection   burned in his blood.
But Beowulf walked   away with his wealth;   1665
proud of his prizes,   he trod on the turf.
Standing at anchor,   his sea-courser
chafed for its captain.   All the way home
Hrothgar's gifts   were often honored.
That was a king   accorded respect   1670
until age unmanned him,   like many another.

High-hearted,   the troop of young soldiers
strode to the sea,   wrapped in their ring-mesh,
linked and locked shirts.   The land-watcher spied
the fighters faring,   just as before.   1675
He called no taunts   from the top of the cliff
but galloped to greet them   and tell them the Geats
would always be welcome,   armored warriors
borne on their ship.   The broad-beamed boat
lay by the beach,   laden with chain-mail,   1680
chargers and treasures   behind its tall prow.
The mast soared high   over Hrothgar's hoard.

The boat-guard was given   a gold-bound sword;
thereafter that man   had honor enhanced,
bearing an heirloom   to Heorot's mead-bench.   1685
They boarded their vessel,   breasted the deep,
left Denmark behind.   A halyard hoisted
the sea-wind's shroud;   the sail was sheeted,
bound to the mast,   and the beams moaned
as a fair wind wafted   the wave-rider forward.   1690
Foamy-throated,   the longboat bounded,
swept on the swells   of the swift sea-stream
until welcoming capes   were sighted ahead,
the cliffs of Geat-land.   The keel grounded
as wind-lift thrust it   straight onto sand.   1695

The harbor-guard hastened   hence from his post.
He had looked long   on an empty ocean
and waited to meet   the much-missed men.
He moored the broad-beamed   bow to the beach
with woven lines   lest the backwash of waves   1700
bear off the boat.   Then Beowulf ordered
treasures unloaded,   the lordly trappings,
gold that was going   to Hygelac's hall,
close to the cliff-edge,   where the ring-giver kept
his comrades about him.
               That building was bold   1705
at the hill's crown;   and queenly Hygd,[33]
Haereth's daughter,   dwelt there as well.
Wise and refined,   though her winters were few,
she housed in the stronghold.   Open-handed,
she granted generous   gifts to the Geats,   1710
most unlike Modthryth,[34]   a maiden so fierce
that none but her father   dared venture near.
The brave man who gazed   at Modthryth by day
might reckon a death-rope   already twisted,
might count himself quickly   captured and killed,   1715
the stroke of a sword   prescribed for his trespass.
Such is no style   for a queen to proclaim:
though peerless, a woman   ought to weave peace,[35]
not snatch away life   for illusory slights.

Modthryth's temper   was tamed by marriage.   1720
Ale-drinkers say   her ill-deeds ended

---

33 Hygd Hygelac's queen. **34 Modthryth** A difficult section of the poem that has provoked several interpretations. As it is understood in this translation, both elements of this
compound word are read as a single proper name, a rather sudden introduction of a new
character in the brief biography of Hygd. Or, Hygd may be condemned here for her own
earlier arrogance, if the Old English *mod thrytho* is understood as a compound, not
found elsewhere, that means "arrogance." The Old English compound *mod thrytho* also
yields "the pride / arrogance / mood of Thryth," in which case Queen Hygd considers
here the flawed character of another queen, Thryth. Mitchell and Robinson (1998, p.
112) suggest further that this parallels Hrothgar's advice to Beowulf to avoid the model
furnished by Heremod (see lines "1509–24). The story of (Mod)thryth's murderous rejec-
tion of marriage parallels that found in the "maiden-king" tales, in which a bloodthirsty
woman is naturalized through marriage, well-known in northern Europe; cf. also the motif of the "taming of the shrew." **35 to weave peace** A frequently found description of
women in the poem, the epithet "peace-weaver" refers to the practice of settling wars between tribes by marrying the daughter of one chieftain to the son of another. The sometimes tragic results of this strategy are explored elsewhere in the poem.

once she was given   in garlands of gold
to Hemming's kinsman.[36]   She came to his hall
over pale seas,   accepted that prince,
a fine young heir,   at her father's behest.   1725
Thenceforth on the throne,   she was famed for fairness,
making the most   of her lot in life,
sustained by loving   her lordly sovereign.
That king, Offa,   was called by all men
the ablest of any   ruling a realm   1730
between two seas,   so I am told.
Gifted in war,   a wise gift-giver
everywhere honored,   the spear-bold soldier
held his homeland   and also fathered
help for the heroes   of Hemming's kindred: 1735
war-worthy Eomer,   grandson of Garmund.

Brave Beowulf   marched with his band,
strode up the sands   of the broad beach
while the sun in the south   beamed like a beacon.
The earls went eagerly   up to the keep   1740
where the strong sovereign,   Ongentheow's slayer,[37]
the young war-king   doled out gold rings.
Beowulf's coming   was quickly proclaimed.
Hygelac heard   that his shoulder-shielder
had entered the hall,   whole and unharmed   1745
by bouts of battle.   The ruler made room
for the foot-guests crossing   the floor before him.

Saluting his lord   with a loyal speech
earnestly worded,   the winner in war
sat facing the king,   kinsman with kinsman.   1750
A mead-vessel moved   from table to table
as Haereth's daughter,[38]   heedful of heroes,

---

36 **Hemming's kinsman** Offa I, a king of the continental Angles in the fourth century.
It has been argued that the poem here lauds Offa II, a king of Mercia in the British Isles
in the eighth century, thus suggesting that the composition of the poem was sponsored
within the rich and powerful kingdom of Mercia at a time of its greatest influence and
ambitions. Though an attractive speculation, little direct evidence supports this thesis.
37 **Ongentheow's slayer** Hygelac, by means of his men's actions acting on his behalf. The
slaying of the Swedish king by Hygelac's retainers Wulf and Eofor is related in lines
2608–21. 38 **Haereth's daughter** Hygd.

bore the wine-beaker   from hand to hand.[39]
Keen to elicit   his comrade's account
in the high-roofed hall,   Hygelac graciously   1755
asked how the Sea-Geats   fared on their foray:

"Say what befell   from your sudden resolve
to seek out strife   over salt waters,
to struggle in Heorot.   Have you helped Hrothgar
ward off the well-known   cares of his kingdom?   1760
You have cost me disquiet,   angst and anguish.
Doubting the outcome,   dearest of men,
for anyone meeting   that murderous demon,
I sought to dissuade you   from starting the venture.[40]
The South-Danes themselves   should have settled their feud   1765
with ghastly Grendel.   Now I thank God
that I see you again,   safe and sound."

Beowulf spoke,   son of Ecgtheow:
"For a great many men   our meeting's issue
is hardly hidden,   my lord Hygelac.   1770
What a fine fracas   passed in that place
when both of us battled   where Grendel had brought
sore sorrow   on scores of War-Scyldings!
I avenged every one,   so that none of his kin
anywhere need   exult at our night-bout,   1775
however long   the loathsome race lives,
covered with crime.   When Hrothgar came
and heard what had happened   there in the ring-hall,
he sat me at once   with his own two sons.

The whole of his host   gathered in gladness;   1780
all my life long   I never have known
such joy in a hall   beneath heaven's vault.
The acclaimed queen,   her kindred's peace-pledge,

---

39 from hand to hand Part of a word in the manuscript has been erased (see Klaeber 1950, line 1983a), and so this phrase is often emended. Klaeber prefers the phrase "to the hands of heroes," retained by Michael Alexander (1995). Mitchell and Robinson (1998) emend it "to the hands of heathens," which Liuzza (2000, p. 113n) remarks "makes sense." This translation charts a third tack around the problem. **40 dissuade . . . venture** As Klaeber (1950, p. 201) and others have noted, Hygelac's dissuasion of Beowulf is not found elsewhere in the poem.

would sometimes circle   the seated youths,
lavishing rings   on delighted young lords.   1785
Hrothgar's daughter   handed the elders
ale-cups aplenty,   pouring for each
old trooper in turn.   I heard the hall-sitters
call her Freawaru   after she proffered
the studded flagon.   To Froda's fair son[41]   1790
that maiden is sworn.   This match seems meet
to the lord of Scyldings,   who looks to settle
his Heathobard feud.   Yet the best of brides
seldom has stilled   the spears of slaughter
so swiftly after   a sovereign was stricken.   1795

Ingeld and all   his earls will be rankled,
watching that woman   walk in their hall
with high-born Danes   doing her bidding.
Her escorts will wear   ancient heirlooms:
Heathobard swords   with braided steel blades,   1800
weapons once wielded   and lost in war
along with the lives   of friends in the fray.
Eyeing the ring-hilts,   an old ash-warrior[42]
will brood in his beer   and bitterly pine
for the stark reminders   of men slain in strife.   1805
He will grimly begin   to goad a young soldier,
testing and tempting   a troubled heart,
his whispered words   waking war-evil:

'My friend, have you spotted   the battle-sword
that your father bore   on his final foray?   1810
Wearing his war-mask,   Withergyld[43] fell
when foemen seized   the field of slaughter.
His priceless blade   became battle-plunder.
Today a son   of the Scylding who slew him
struts on our floor,   flaunting his trophy,   1815
an heirloom that you   should rightfully own.'

41 Froda's fair son Ingeld, prince of the Heathobards. At lines 75–78, the poem alludes to his unsuccessful attack on Hrothgar's Danes, also mentioned in the Old English poem *Widsith*.   **42 an old ash-warrior** With economy and force Beowulf describes the reaction of a veteran Heathobard warrior as he observes the Danes displaying weapons plundered from his dead companions. The scene enforces too the duty to revenge such an injury. "Ash" refers to the wood used in the shaft of a spear.   **43 Withergyld** A Heathobard warrior.

He will prick and pique   with pointed words
time after time   till the challenge is taken,
the maiden's attendant   is murdered in turn,
blade-bitten   to sleep in his blood,   1820
forfeit his life   for his father's feat.
Another will run,   knowing the road.
So on both sides   oaths will be broken;
and afterward Ingeld's   anger will grow
hotter, unchecked,   as he chills toward his wife.   1825
Hence I would hold   the Heathobards likely
to prove unpeaceable   partners for Danes.

Now I shall speak   of my strife with Grendel,
further acquainting   the kingdom's keeper
with all that befell   when our fight began.   1830
Heaven's gem   had gone overhead;
in darkness the dire   demon stalked us
while we stood guard   unharmed in Heorot.
Hondscioh[44] was doomed   to die with the onslaught,
first to succumb,   though clad for combat   1835
when grabbed by Grendel,   who gobbled him whole.
That beloved young thane   was eaten alive.
Not one to leave   the hall empty-handed,
the bloody-toothed terror   intended to try
his might upon me.   A curious creel[45]   1840
hung from his hand,   cunningly clasped
and strangely sewn   with devilish skill
from skin of a dragon.   The demon would stuff me,
sinless, inside   like so many others;
but rising in wrath,   I stood upright.   1845

---

44 **Hondscioh** Killed by Grendel in lines 664–70, but unnamed until Beowulf recounts
his Danish adventures to Hygelac. The noun *hondscioh* means "glove" (cf. Modern
German *Handschuh*), and Orchard (2003, p. 122) observes that the conjunction of
naming the devoured Geat with the mention of Grendel's "glove" (here translated
"creel") is "evidently another example of the *Beowulf*-poet's tendency to etymologise
names." (See further Orchard 2003, pp. 122, 172–73, 223–24.) Beowulf's report to
Hygelac (lines 1769–1896) is marked by many differences when compared with the
events narrated earlier in the poem as they occur or when Beowulf briefly reports
them to Hrothgar. As Klaeber (1950, p. 201) and others have noted, these differences
include the omission of some details, a change in emphasis, the introduction of
Freawaru's story, the naming of Hondscioh and Withergyld, and a description of
Grendel's dragon-skin bag.   45 **creel** Grendel's "glove," perhaps a kind of pouch,
such as that carried by trolls in Old Norse narratives. The pouch is not referred to in
the earlier accounts of Grendel's attacks.

It is too long a tale,   how the people's plaguer
paid for his crimes   with proper requital;
but the feat reflected   finely, my lord,
on the land you lead.   Though the foe fled
to live awhile longer,   he left behind him   1850
as sign of the strife   a hand in Heorot.
Humbled, he fell   to the floor of the mere.

The warder of Scyldings   rewarded my warfare
with much treasure   when morning arrived,
and we sat for a feast   with songs and sagas.   1855
He told many tales   he learned in his lifetime.
Sometimes a soldier   struck the glad harp,
the sounding wood;   sometimes strange stories
were spoken like spells,   tragic and true,
rightly related.   The large-hearted lord   1860
sometimes would start   to speak of his youth,
his might in war.   His memories welled;
ancient in winters,   he weighed them all.

So we delighted   the livelong day
until darkness drew   once more upon men.   1865
Then Grendel's mother,   mourning her son,
swiftly set out   in search of revenge
against warlike Geats.   The grisly woman
wantonly slew   a Scylding warrior:
aged Aeschere,   the king's counselor,   1870
relinquished his life.   Nor in the morning
might death-weary Danes   bear off his body
to burn on a bier,   for the creature clutching him
fled to her fastness   under a waterfall.
This was the sorest   of sorrows that Hrothgar   1875
suffered as king.   Distraught, he beseeched me
to do in your name   a notable deed.
If I dived in the deep,   heedless of danger,
to war underwater,   he would reward me.

Under I went,   as now is well-known;   1880
and I found the hideous   haunter of fens.
For a time we two   contested our hand-strength;
then I struck off her head   with a huge sword

that her battle-hall held,   and her hot blood
boiled in the lake.   Leaving that place   1885
was no easy feat,   but fate let me live.
Again I was granted   gifts that the guardian,
Healfdene's son,   had sworn to bestow.
The king of that people   kept his promise,
allotting me all   he had earlier offered: 1890
meed for my might,   with more treasures,
my choice from the hoard   of Healfdene's son.
These, my lord,   I deliver to you,
as proof of fealty.   My future depends
wholly on you.   I have in this world   1895
few close kin   but my king, Hygelac."

He bade the boar-banner   now be brought in,
the high helmet,   hard mail-shirt,
and splendid sword,   describing them thus:
"When Hrothgar gave me   this hoarded gear,   1900
the sage sovereign   entreated I tell
the tale of his gift: this treasure was held
by Heorogar,[46] king,   who long was the lord
of Scylding people.   It should have passed
to armor the breast   of bold Heoroweard,   1905
the father's favorite,   faithful and brave;
but he willed it elsewhere,   so use it well."

I have heard how horses   followed that hoard,
four dappled mounts,   matching and fleet.
He gave up his gifts,   gold and horses.   1910
Kinsmen should always   act with honor,
not spin one another   in snares of spite
or secretly scheme   to kill close comrades.
Always the nephew   had aided his uncle;
each held the other's   welfare at heart.   1915
He gave to Queen Hygd   the golden collar,
wondrously wrought,   Wealhtheow's token,
and also three steeds,   sleek and bright-saddled.
Thereafter her breast   was graced by the gift.

---

46 **Heorogar** Hrothgar's eldest brother.

So Ecgtheow's son   won his repute   1920
as a man of mettle,   acting with honor,
yet mild-hearted   toward hearth-companions,
harming no one   when muddled with mead.
Bold in battle,   he guarded the guerdon
that God had granted,   the greatest strength   1925
of all humankind,   though once he was thought
weak and unworthy,   a sluggardly sloucher,[47]
mocked for meekness   by men on the mead-bench,
and given no gifts   by the lord of the Geats.
Every trouble   untwined in time   1930
for the glory-blessed man.
                 A blade was brought
at the king's request,   Hrethel's heirloom
glinting with gold.   No greater treasure,
no nobler sword   was held in his hoard.
He lay that brand   on Beowulf's lap   1935
and also bestowed   a spacious estate,
hall and high seat.   When land and lordship
were left to them both,   by birthright and law,
he who ranked higher   ruled the wide realm.

III. The Dragon

It happened long after,   with Hygelac dead,   1940
that war-swords slew   Heardred, his son,
when Battle-Scylfings   broke his shield-wall
and hurtled headlong   at Hereric's nephew.
So Beowulf came   to rule the broad realm.
For fifty winters   he fostered it well;   1945
then the old king,   keeper of kinfolk,
heard of a dragon   drawn from the darkness.
He had long lain   in his lofty fastness,

---

47 **sloucher** Although not developed in the poem, Beowulf's unpromising youth parallels
that of many an Old Norse hero of the "coal-biter" type, an epithet earned by the young-
ster's slouching about the hearth, rather than undertaking heroic adventures. Grettir is
an example of this sort of slack, ill-tempered prankster.

the steep stone-barrow,   guarding his gold;
but a path pierced it,   known to no person   1950
save him who found it   and followed it forward.
That stranger seized   a singular treasure.
He bore it in hand   from the heathen hoard:
a finely-worked flagon   he filched from the lair
where the dragon dozed.   Enraged at the robber,   1955
the sneaking thief   who struck while he slept,
the guardian woke   glowing with wrath,
as his nearest neighbors   were soon to discern.

It was not by choice   that the wretch raided
the wondrous worm-hoard.   The one who offended   1960
was stricken himself,   sorely mistreated,
the son of a warrior   sold as a slave.
Escaped and seeking   a safe refuge,
he guiltily groped   his way below ground.
There the intruder,   trembling with terror,   1965
sensed an ancient   evil asleep.
His fate was to find   as fear unmanned him
his fingers feeling   a filigreed cup.

Many such goblets   had gone to the earth-house,
legacies left   by a lordly people.   1970
In an earlier age   someone unknown
had cleverly covered   those costly treasures.
That thane held the hoard   for the lifetime allowed him,
but gold could not gladden   a man in mourning.
Newly-built   near the breaking waves,   1975
a barrow stood   at the base of a bluff,
its entrance sculpted   by secret arts.
Earthward the warrior   bore the hoard-worthy
portion of plate,   the golden craftwork.
The ringkeeper spoke   these words as he went: 1980

"Hold now, Earth,   what men may not,
the hoard of the heroes,   earth-gotten wealth
when it first was won.   War-death has felled them,
an evil befalling   each of my people.
The household is mirthless   when men are lifeless.   1985
I have none to wear sword,   none to bear wine

or polish the precious   vessels and plates.
Gone are the brethren   who braved many battles.
From the hard helmet   the hand-wrought gilding
drops in the dust.   Asleep are the smiths   1990
who knew how to burnish   the war-chief's mask
or mend the mail-shirts   mangled in battle.
Shields and mail-shirts   molder with warriors
and follow no foes   to faraway fields.
No harp rejoices   to herald the heroes,   1995
no hand-fed hawk   swoops through the hall,
no stallion stamps   in the stronghold's courtyard.
Death has undone   many kindreds of men."

Stricken in spirit,   he spoke of his sorrow
as last of his line,   drearily drifting   2000
through day and dark   until death's flood-tide
stilled his heart.   The old night-scather
was happy to glimpse   the unguarded hoard.
Balefully burning,   he seeks out barrows.
Naked and hateful   in a raiment of flame,   2005
the dragon dreaded   by outland dwellers
must gather and guard   the heathen gold,[1]
no better for wealth   but wise with his winters.

For three hundred winters   the waster of nations
held that mighty   hoard in his earth-hall   2010
till one man wronged him,   arousing his wrath.
The wretched robber   ransomed his life
with the prize he pilfered,   the plated flagon.
Beholding that marvel   men of old made,
his fief-lord forgave   the skulker's offense.   2015
One treasure taken   had tainted the rest.
Waking in wrath,   the worm reared up
and slid over stones.   Stark-hearted,
he spotted the footprints   where someone had stepped,
stealthily creeping   close to his head.   2020
The fortunate man   slips swiftly and safely

---

1 gold The dragon, characteristically sitting on its hoard of treasure, is a monster found widely in Germanic sources. This reference underscores the theme of worldly wealth in the poem.

through the worst dangers   if the World's Warder
grants him that grace.[2]
                Eager and angry,
the hoard-guard hunted   the thief who had haunted
his hall while he slept.   He circled the stone-house,   2025
but out in that wasteland   the one man he wanted
was not to be found.   How fearsome he felt,
how fit for battle!   Back in his barrow
he tracked the intruder   who dared to tamper
with glorious gold.   Fierce and fretful,   2030
the dragon waited   for dusk and darkness.
The rage-swollen holder   of headland and hoard
was plotting reprisal: flames for his flagon.
Then day withdrew,   and the dragon, delighted,
would linger no longer   but flare up and fly.   2035
His onset was awful   for all on the land,
and a cruel ending   soon came for their king.

When the ghastly specter   scattered his sparks
and set their buildings   brightly burning,
flowing with flames   as householders fled,   2040
he meant to leave   not one man alive.
That wreaker of havoc   hated and harried
the Geatish folk   fleeing his flames.
Far and wide   his warfare was watched
until night waned,   and the worm went winging   2045
back to the hall   where his hoard lay hidden,
sure of his stronghold,   his walls and his war,
sure of himself,   deceived by his pride.

Then terrible tidings   were taken to Beowulf:
how swiftly his own   stronghold was stricken,   2050
that best of buildings   bursting with flames
and his throne melting.   The hero was heart-sore;
the wise man wondered   what wrong he had wrought
and how he transgressed   against old law,
the Lord Everlasting,   Ruler of All.   2055
His grief was great,   and grim thoughts

---

2 grace Compare this comment made by the narrator to the maxim Beowulf voices at
lines 509–10.

boiled in his breast   as never before.
The fiery foe   had flown to his coastlands,
had sacked and seared   his keep by the sea.
For that the war-king   required requital.   2060
He ordered a broad-shield   fashioned of iron,
better for breasting   baleful blazes
than the linden-wood   that warded his warriors.
Little was left   of the time lent him
for life in the world;   and the worm as well,   2065
who had haughtily held   his hoard for so long.
Scorning to follow   the far-flying foe
with his whole host,   the ring-giver reckoned
the wrath of a dragon   unworthy of dread.
Fearless and forceful,   he often had faced   2070
the straits of struggle   blessed with success.
Beowulf braved   many a battle,
after ridding Hrothgar's   hall of its horrors
and grappling with Grendel's   gruesome kin.

Not least of his clashes   had come when the king   2075
Hygelac fell   while fighting the Frisians
in hand-to-hand combat.   His friend and fief-lord,
the son of Hrethel,   was slain in the onslaught,
stricken to death   by a blood-drinking blade.
Beowulf battled   back to the beach   2080
where he proved his strength   with skillful swimming,
for he took to the tide   bearing the trophies
of thirty warriors   won on the field.
None of the Hetware[3]   needed to boast
how they fared on foot,   flaunting their shields   2085
against that fierce fighter,   for few remained
after the battle   to bear the tale home.

Over wide waters   the lone swimmer went,
the son of Ecgtheow   swept on the sea-waves
back to his homeland,   forlorn with his loss,   2090
and hence to Hygd   who offered her hoard:
rings and a realm,   a throne for the thane.

---

3 **Hetware** A Frankish tribe, allies of the Frisians according to this passage.

With Hygelac dead   she doubted her son[4]
could guard the Geats   from foreigners' forays.
Refusing her boon,   Beowulf bade   2095
the leaderless lords   to hail the lad
as their rightful ruler.   He chose not to reign
by thwarting his cousin   but to counsel the king
and guide with good will   until Heardred grew older.

It was Heardred who held   the Weder-Geats' hall   2100
when outcast Scylfings[5]   came seeking its safety:
Eanmund and Eadgils,   nephews of Onela.
That strong sea-king[6]   and spender of treasures
sailed from Sweden   pursuing the rebels
who challenged his right   to rule their realm.   2105
For lending them haven,   Hygelac's son[7]
suffered the sword-stroke   that spilled out his life.
The Swede headed home   when Heardred lay dead,
leaving Beowulf   lordship of Geats.
That was a good king,   keeping the gift-seat;   2110
yet Heardred's death   dwelled in his thoughts.
A long time later   he offered his aid
to end the exile   of destitute Eadgils.
He summoned an army,   and Ohthere's son,[8]
cold in his cares,   went over wide waters   2115
with weapons and warriors   to kill off a king.

Such were the struggles   and tests of strength
the son of Ecgtheow   saw and survived.
His pluck was proven   in perilous onslaughts
till that fateful day   when he fought the dragon.   2120
As leader of twelve[9]   trailing that terror,

4 son Heardred, the son of Hygelac and Hygd whose regency Beowulf supports and who
is killed by Onela for aiding Onela's nephews, Eanmund and Eadgils, in their rebellion
against their uncle. (See note 6.)   5 outcast Scylfings Eanmund and Eadgils, the sons of
Ohthere and nephews of Onela.   6 sea-king Onela, a son of Ongentheow, who displaces
his brother Ohthere after Ohthere had succeeded following their father's death. It is
Onela who forces Eanmund and Eadgils into exile at the Geatish court (lines 2100–02),
which results in the Geatish ruler Heardred being killed by Onela (lines 2106–07). Eanmund is killed by Weohstan (lines 2305–08), while Eadgils becomes king, supported by
Beowulf (lines 2112–16), and finally kills Onela (line 2116).   7 Hygelac's son Heardred.
8 Ohthere's son Eadgils, whom Beowulf aids in killing Onela.   9 twelve The party hunting the dragon consists of Beowulf, Wiglaf, and ten men, who are mentioned later in the
dragon episode for deserting Beowulf when he needs their help. The thief is the thirteenth
man (see line 2130).

the greatest of Geats   glowered with rage
when he looked on the lair   where the worm lurked.
By now he had found   how the feud flared,
this fell affliction   befalling his kingdom,   2125
for the kingly cup   had come to his hand
from the hand of him   who raided the hoard.
That sorry slave   had started the strife,
and against his will   he went with the warriors,
a thirteenth man   bringing the band   2130
to the barrow's brink   which he alone knew.
Hard by the surge   of the seething sea
gaped a cavern   glutted with golden
medallions and chains.   The murderous man-bane,
hidden within,   hungered for warfare.   2135
No taker would touch   his treasures cheaply:
the hoard's holder   would drive a hard bargain.

The proud war-king   paused on the sea-point
to lighten the hearts   of his hearth-companions,
though his heart was heavy   and hankered for death.   2140
It was nearing him now.   That taker of treasure
would sunder the soul   from his old bones and flesh.
So Beowulf spoke,   the son of Ecgtheow,
recalling the life   he was loathe to lose:

"From boyhood I bore   battles and bloodshed,   2145
struggles and strife: I still see them all.
I was given at seven   to house with King Hrethel,[10]
my mother's father   and friend of our folk.
He kept me fairly   with feasts and fine gifts.
I fared no worse   than one of his sons: 2150
Herebeald, Haethcyn,   or princely Hygelac
who was later my lord.   The eldest, Herebeald,
unwittingly went   to a wrongful death
when Haethcyn's horn-bow   hurled an arrow.
Missing the mark,   it murdered the kinsman;   2155

---

10 **Hrethel** Beowulf refers to the custom of noble fosterage, frequently through a maternal relation of the child. As line 2148 indicates, Hrethel is Beowulf's maternal grandfather, and Beowulf has been brought up with Hrethel's three sons, Herebeald, Haethcyn,
and Hygelac.

a brother was shot   by the blood-stained shaft.[11]
This blow to the heart   was brutal and baffling.
A prince had fallen.   The felon went free.

So it is sore   for an old man to suffer
his son swinging   young on the gallows,   2160
gladdening ravens.   He groans in his grief
and loudly laments   the lad he has lost.
No help is at hand   from hard-won wisdom
or the march of years.   Each morning reminds him
his heir is elsewhere,   and he has no heart   2165
to wait for a second   son in his stronghold
when death has finished   the deeds of the first.
He ceaselessly sees   his son's dwelling,
the desolate wine-hall,   the windswept grave-sward
where swift riders   and swordsmen slumber.   2170
No harp-string sounds,   no song in the courtyard.
He goes to his bed   sighing with sorrow,
one soul for another.   His home is hollow;
his field, fallow.[12]
                         So Hrethel suffered,
hopeless and heart-sore   with Herebeald gone.   2175
He would do no deed   to wound the death-dealer
or harrow his household   with hatred and anger;
but bitter bloodshed   had stolen his bliss,
and he quit his life   for the light of the Lord.
Like a luckier man,   he could leave his land   2180
in the hands of a son,   though he loved him no longer.

---

11 **shaft** The resemblance between Haethcyn's accidental slaying of his brother Herebeald and that of the inadvertent killing of the Old Norse god Baldr by his brother Höðr as recorded in the Old Icelandic *Edda* of Snorri Sturluson (see Faulkes 1987, pp. 48–51) has frequently been noted (see, e.g., Harris 1994). This analogy suggests that Hrethel is a type of Óðinn, the Norse god who is the father of Baldr and Höðr and who is associated with ritual death by hanging accompanied by the marking of the victim with a spear. Orchard (2003, p. 118) also notes that the "'bloody shaft', literally 'bloody spear' . . . seems inappropriate for an 'arrow from a horn-bow'"(line 2154 in this translation). Another analogue is found in *Ynglinga saga* (*Contexts, From the Old Norse*, p. 218), which contains a legendary tale regarding King Hugleikr's (Old English, Hygelac) rule, in which one princely brother kills the other in a hunting accident.   12 **fallow** Perhaps an epic simile in which the sorrow of Hrethel over the death of his son, whose death he cannot avenge, is compared with the sorrow of an old, unnamed man, whose son has been hanged as a criminal (a judicial execution with the custom of vengeance (see Whitelock 1939). Clover (2002, p. 32) also notes the resemblance between Hrethel's grief over his son's death and that of the Old Icelandic warrior-poet Egill Skallagrímsson, who composes the poem, *On the Loss of a Son, (Sonatorrek)* after his son is killed.

Then strife and struggle   of Geats and Swedes
crossed the wide water.   Warfare wounded
both sides in battle   when Hrethel lay buried.
Ongentheow's sons,   fierce and unfriendly,   2185
suddenly struck   at Hreosna-Beorh[13]
and bloodied the bluff   with baneful slaughter.
Our foes in this feud   soon felt the wrath
of my kinsman the king   claiming our due,[14]
though the counterblow   cost his own life.   2190
Haethcyn was killed,   his kingship cut short.
The slayer himself   was slain in the morning.[15]
I have heard how Eofor[16]   struck the old Scylfing.
Sword-ashen,   Ongentheow sank
with his helm split: heedful of harm,   2195
to kinsman and king,   the hand would not halt
the death-blow it dealt.
                  My own sword-arm
repaid my prince   for the gifts he granted.
He[17] gave me a fiefdom,   the land I have loved.
He never had need   to seek among Spear-Danes,   2200
Gifthas[18] or Swedes   and get with his gifts
a worse warrior.   I wielded my sword
at the head of our host;   so shall I hold
this blade that I bear   boldly in battle
as long as life lasts.   It has worn well   2205
since the day when Daeghrefn[19]   died by my hand,

---

13 Hreosna-Beorh A Geatish place-name that is the site of a Swedish attack on the Geats. W. J. Sedgefield, in his 1910 edition of *Beowulf*, suggested that the first element of this place-name should be emended to Hrefna- ("ravens"). Orchard (2003, p. 172), citing evidenced scribal confusion between *s* and *f*, also records the temptation to emend "the otherwise meaningless Geatish place-name" to *Hrefnaburh* or "ravens' stronghold." This change brings the place-name closer to the style of other presumably fictive places in the poem, like the two Swedish place-names found in the poem called "Ravenswood" or "-holt." The raven is frequently associated with battle and death (see line 2161), as well as with Óðinn (see note 11).   **14 due** Their vengeance is exacted at the battle of Ravenswood, apparently in Sweden, and referred to once more by name in this translation at line 2574.   **15 morning** Ongentheow kills Haethcyn but will himself be killed the next day.   **16 Eofor** Hygelac, who arrives later to the battle, thus revenges the killing of his brother Haethcyn by Ongentheow through Eofor's killing of Ongentheow.   **17 He** Hygelac.   **18 Gifthas** This tribe is apparently named in the Old English poem *Widsith* (line 60, *Gefthas*) and known from Latin sources as *Gepidae*.   **19 Daeghrefn** Beowulf may refer here to events that occurred in the battle in which Hygelac was killed. The killing of Daeghrefn, like that of Grendel, is accomplished by a weaponless Beowulf who, as his vivid account makes clear, crushes his opponent with a bear-like hug (see lines 2210–14).

the Frankish foe   who fought for the Frisians,
bearing their banner.   He broke in my grip,
never to barter   the necklace[20] he robbed
from Hygelac's corpse.   I crushed that killer;   2210
his bones snapped,   and his life-blood spilled.
I slew him by strength,   not by the sword.
Now I shall bear   his brand into battle:
hand and hard sword   will fight for the hoard."

Now Beowulf spoke   his last battle-boast: 2215
"In boyhood I braved   bitter clashes;
still in old age   I would seek out strife
and gain glory   guarding my people,
if the man-bane comes   from his cave to meet me."

Then he turned to his troop   for the final time,   2220
bidding farewell   to bold helmet-bearers,
fast in friendship: "I would wear no sword,
no weapon at all   to ward off the worm,
if I knew how to fight   this fiendish foe
as I grappled with Grendel   one bygone night.   2225
But here I shall find   fierce battle-fire
and breath envenomed;   therefore I bear
this mail-coat and shield.   I shall not shy
from standing my ground   when I greet the guardian,
follow what will   at the foot of his wall.   2230
I shall face the fiend   with a firm heart.
Let the Ruler of men   reckon my fate:
words are worthless   against the war-flyer.
Bide by the barrow,   safe in your byrnies,
and watch, my warriors,   which of us two   2235
will better bear   the brunt of our clash.
This war is not yours;   it is meted to me,
matching my strength,   man against monster.
I shall do this deed   undaunted by death
and get you gold   or else get my ending,   2240
borne off in battle,   the bane of your lord."

---

20 **necklace** Probably the same "jeweled collar" mentioned at line 1052 and equaled only
by Freya's necklace.

The hero arose,   helmed and hardy,
a war-king clad   in shield and corselet.
He strode strongly   under the stone-cliff:
no faint-hearted man,   to face it unflinching!   2245
Stalwart soldier   of so many marches,
unshaken when shields   were crushed in the clash,
he saw between stiles   an archway[21] where steam
burst like a boiling   tide from the barrow,
woeful for one   close to the worm-hoard.   2250
He would not linger long   unburned by the lurker
or safely slip   through the searing lair.
Then a battle-cry broke   from Beowulf's breast
as his rightful wrath   was roused for the reckoning.
His challenge sounded   under stark stone   2255
where the hateful hoard-guard   heard in his hollow
the clear-voiced call   of a man coming.

No quarter was claimed;   no quarter given.
First the beast's breath   blew hot from the barrow
as battle-bellows   boomed underground.   2260
The stone-house stormer   swung up his shield
at the ghastly guardian.   Then the dragon's grim heart
kindled for conflict.   Uncoiling, he came
seeking the swordsman   who'd already drawn
the keen-edged blade[22]   bequeathed him for combat.   2265
Each foe confronted   the other with fear.
His will unbroken,   the warlord waited
behind his tall shield,   helm and armor.
With fitful twistings   the fire-drake hastened
fatefully forward.   His defense held high,   2270
Beowulf felt   the blaze blister through
hotter and sooner   than he had foreseen.
So for the first time   fortune was failing
the mighty man   in the midst of a struggle.
Wielding his sword,   he struck at the worm   2275
and his fabled blade   bit to the bone

---

21 archway The dragon's barrow, with its defamiliarized stone vaulting, may recall the architecture of a megalithic chambered tomb. See also lines 2401–04. **22 blade** The sword Naegling, named in line 2369.

through blazoned hide: bit and bounced back,
no match for the foe   in this moment of need.

The peerless prince   was hard-pressed in response,
for his bootless blow   had maddened the monster   2280
and fatal flames   shot further than ever,
lighting the land.   The blade he bared
failed in the fray,   though forged from iron.
No easy end   for the son of Ecgtheow:
against his will   he would leave this world   2285
to dwell elsewhere,   as every man must
when his days are done.   Swiftly the death-dealer
moved to meet him.   From the murderous breast
bellows of breath   belched fresh flames.
Enfolded in fire,   he who formerly   2290
ruled a whole realm   had no one to help him
hold off the heat,   for his hand-picked band
of princelings had fled,   fearing to face
the foe with their lord.   Loving honor
less than their lives,   they hid in the holt.   2295
But one among them   grieved for the Geats
and balked at the thought   of quitting a kinsman.

This one was Wiglaf,[23]   son of Weohstan,
kinsman of Aelfhere,   earl among Scylfings.
Seeing his liege-lord   suffering sorely   2300
with war-mask scorched   by the searing onslaught,
the thankful thane   thought of the boons
his sovereign bestowed: the splendid homestead
and folk-rights his father   formerly held.
No shirker could stop him   from seizing his shield   2305
of yellow linden   and lifting the blade
Weohstan won   when he slew Eanmund,
son of Ohthere.   Spoils of that struggle,
sword and scabbard,   smithwork of giants,
a byrnie of ring-mail   and bright burnished helm   2310
were granted as gifts,   a thane's war-garb,

---

23 **Wiglaf** Though Wiglaf's father, Weohstan, fought with the Swedes against the Geats,
Wiglaf also owes allegiance to the Waegmundings, as does Beowulf (see lines 2483–85)
and seems to be not just one of Beowulf's "hand-picked band"(line 2292), but also a
relation (lines 2299 and 2394).

for Onela never   acknowledged his nephews,
but struck against both   of his brother's sons.
When Eadgils avenged   Eanmund's death,
Weohstan fled.   Woeful and friendless,   2315
he[24] saved that gear   for seasons of strife,
foreseeing his son   someday might crave
sword and corselet.   He came to his kinsman,
the prince of the Geats,   and passed on his heirlooms,
hoping Wiglaf   would wear them with honor.   2320
Old then, and wise,   he went from the world.

This war was the first   young Wiglaf would fight
helping the king.   His heart would not quail
nor weapon fail   as the foe would find
going against him;   but he made his grim mood   2325
known to the men: "I remember the time
when taking our mead   in the mighty hall,
all of us offered   oaths to our liege-lord.
We promised to pay   for princely trappings
by staunchly wielding   sword-blades in war,   2330
if need should arise.   Now we are needed
by him who chose,   from the whole of his host,
twelve for this trial,   trusting our claims
as warriors worthy   of wearing our blades,
bearing keen spears.   Our king has come here   2335
bent on battling   the man-bane alone,
because among warriors   one keeper of kinfolk
has done, undaunted,   the most deeds of daring.
But this day our lord   needs dauntless defenders
so long as the frightful   fires keep flaring.   2340
God knows I would gladly   give my own body
for flames to enfold   with the gold-giver.
Shameful, to shoulder   our shields homeward!
First we must fell   this fearsome foe
and protect the life   of our people's lord.   2345
It is wrong that one man   be wrathfully racked
for his former feats   and fall in this fight,
guarding the Geats.   We shall share our war-gear:
shield and battle-shirt,   helm and hard sword."

24 **he** Weohstan.

So speaking, he stormed   through the reek of smoke,   2350
with helmet on head,   to help his lord.
"Beloved Beowulf,   bear up your blade.
You pledged in your youth,   powerful prince,
never to let   your luster lessen
while life was left you.   Now summon your strength.   2355
Stand steadfast.   I shall stand with you."

After these words   the worm was enraged.
For a second time   the spiteful specter
flew at his foe,   and he wreathed in flames
the hated human   he hungered to harm.   2360
His dreadful fire-wind   drove in a wave,
charring young Wiglaf's   shield to the boss,
nor might a mail-shirt   bar that breath
from burning the brave   spear-bearer's breast.
Wiglaf took cover   close to his kinsman,   2365
shielded by iron   when linden[25] was cinder.
Then the war-king,   recalling past conquests,
struck with full strength   straight at the head.
His battle-sword, Naegling,   stuck there and split,
shattered in combat,   so sharp was the shock   2370
to Beowulf's great   gray-banded blade.
He never was granted   the gift of a sword
as hard and strong   as the hand that held it.
I have heard that he broke   blood-hardened brands,
so the weapon-bearer   was none the better.   2375

The fearful fire-drake,   scather of strongholds,
flung himself forward   a final time,
wild with wounds   yet wily and sly.
In the heat of the fray,   he hurtled headlong
to fasten his fangs   in the foe's throat.   2380
Beowulf's life-blood   came bursting forth
on those terrible tusks.   Just then, I am told,
the second warrior[26]   sprang from his side,
a man born for battle   proving his mettle,
keen to strengthen   his kinsman in combat.   2385
He took no heed   of the hideous head

---

25 **linden** Wiglaf's shield was made of linden-wood.   26 **the second warrior** Wiglaf.

scorching his hand   as he hit lower down.
The sword sank in,   patterned and plated;
the flames of the foe   faltered, faded.
Quick-witted still,   the king unsheathed   2390
the keen killing-blade   he kept in his corselet.
Then the Geats' guardian   gutted the dragon,
felling that fiend   with the help of his friend,
two kinsmen together   besting the terror.
So should a thane   succor his sovereign.   2395

That deed was the king's   crowning conquest;
Beowulf's work   in the world was done.
He soon felt his wound   swelling and stinging
where fell fangs   had fastened upon him,
and evil venom   enveloped his heart.[27]   2400
Wisely he sought   a seat by the stone-wall,
and his gaze dwelled   on the dark doorway
delved in the dolmen,   the straight stiles
and sturdy archway   sculpted by giants.
With wonderful kindness   Wiglaf washed   2405
the clotting blood   from his king and kinsman;
his hands loosened   the lord's high helm.
Though banefully bitten,   Beowulf spoke,
for he knew his lifetime   would last no longer.
The count of his days   had come to a close.   2410
His joys were done.   Death drew near him:

"Now I would wish   to will my son
these weapons of war,   had I been awarded
an heir of my own,   holder of heirlooms.
I fathered the Weders   for fifty winters.   2415
No warlike lord   of neighboring lands
dared to assail us   or daunt us with dread.
A watchful warden,   I waited on fate
while keeping our people   clear of quarrels.
I swore many oaths;   not one was wrongful.   2420

27 **enveloped his heart** Beowulf is not mortally wounded by the dragon's bites, but dies
as a result of the poison in the dragon's fangs that festers in his wounds. This element of
the dragon fight is similar to the Norse god Thor's struggle with the ferocious Midgard-
serpent (found in the eddic poem *Völuspá* and in Snorri Sturluson's thirteenth-century
Edda). Though Thor kills the monster, it also spits venom at the god, causing Thor to
stagger back for nine paces before falling dead (see Dronke 1969).

So I rejoice,   though sick with my death-wound,
that God may not blame me   for baseless bloodshed
or killing of kin   when breath quits my body.
Hurry below   and look on the hoard,
beloved Wiglaf.   The worm lies sleeping   2425
under gray stone,   sorely stricken
and stripped of his gold.   Go swiftly and seize it.
Get me giltwork   and glittering gems:
I would set my sight   on that store of wealth.
Loath would I be   to leave for less   2430
the life and lordship   I held for so long."

I have heard how swiftly   the son of Weohstan
hastened to heed   his wounded and weakening
war-lord's behest.   In his woven mail-shirt,
his bright byrnie,   he entered the barrow;   2435
and passing its threshold,   proud and princely,
he glimpsed all the gold   piled on the ground,
the walled-in wealth   won by the worm,
that fierce night-flyer.   Flagons were standing,
embossed wine-beakers   lying unburnished,   2440
their inlays loosened.   There were lofty helmets
and twisted arm-rings   rotting and rusting.
Gold below ground   may betray into grief
any who hold it: heed me who will!

Wiglaf saw also   a gold-woven standard,   2445
a wonder of handiwork,   skillfully filigreed,
high above ground.   It gave off a glow
that let him behold   the whole of the hoard.
I am told he took   from that trove of giants
goblets and platters   pressed to his breastplate,   2450
and the golden banner   glinting brightly.
He spotted no sign   of the stricken dragon.
The iron-edged brand   old Beowulf bore
had mortally wounded   the warder of wealth
and fiery foe   whose flames in the night   2455
welled so fiercely   before he was felled.

Bent with his burden,   the messenger hastened
back to his master,   burning to know

whether the brave   but wound-weakened
lord of the Weders   was lost to the living.   2460
Setting his spoils   by the storied prince
whose lifeblood blackened   the ground with gore,
Wiglaf wakened   the war-lord with water,
and these words thrust   like spears through his breast[28]
as the ancient one grimly   gazed on the gold: 2465

"I offer my thanks   to the Almighty Master,
the King of Glory,   for granting my kindred
these precious things   I look upon last.
Losing my life,   I have bought this boon
to lighten my leave-day.   Look to our people,   2470
for you shall be leader;   I lead no longer.
Gather my guard   and raise me a grave-mound
housing my ashes   at Hronesnaess,
reminding my kin   to recall their king
after his pyre   has flared on the point.   2475
Seafarers passing   shall say when they see it
'Beowulf's Barrow'   as bright longboats
drive over darkness,   daring the flood."

So the stern prince   bestowed on his sword-thane
and keen spear-wielder   the kingly collar,   2480
his gold-plated helm   and hammered armor.
He told him to bear them   bravely in battle:
"Farewell, Wiglaf,   last Waegmunding.
I follow our fathers,   foredestined to die,
swept off by fate,   though strong and steadfast."   2485
These heartfelt words   were the warrior's last
before his body   burned in the bale-fire
and his soul sought   the doom of the truthful.[29]

---

28 breast A half-line or more is missing from the manuscript here (Old English, line 2792b), as a defect in the meter shows. **29 truthful** Following Mitchell and Robinson (1998, p. 147, note to line 2820), this difficult half-line (literally, "the judgment of the truth-fast") suggests two alternatives: either that Beowulf's soul will be judged as a righteous soul ought to be judged ("judgment passed on those who are firm in truth") or that it will be judged by the "truthful" ("judgment by those speaking the truth"). Liuzza (2000, p. 139, note to line 2820) observes that in the first instance, Beowulf's soul will "go to Heaven" and in the second "to Hell as an unbaptized pagan."

Smitten with sorrow,   the young man saw
the old lord he loved   lying in pain   2490
as life left him.   Slain and slayer
died there together: the dread earth-dragon,
deprived of his life,   no longer would lurk
coiled on the hoard.   Hard-hammered swords
had felled the far-flyer   in front of his lair.   2495
No more would he sport   on the midnight sky,
proud of his wealth,   his power and pomp.
He sprawled on stone   where the war-chief slew him.
Though deeds of daring   were done in that land,
I have heard of no man   whose might would suffice   2500
to face the fire-drake's   fuming breath
or help him escape   if he handled the hoard
once he had woken   its warder from sleep.
Beowulf paid   for that lode with his life;
his loan of days   was lost to the dragon.   2505

Before long the laggards   limped from the woods,
ten cowards together,   the troth-breakers
who had failed to bare   their blades in battle
at the moment their master   needed them most.
In shame they shouldered   their shields and spears.   2510
Armored for war,   they went to Wiglaf
who sorrowfully sat   at their sovereign's shoulder.
Laving his leader,   the foot-soldier failed
to waken the fallen   fighter one whit,
nor could he will   his lord back to life.   2515
The World's Warden   decided what deeds
men might achieve   in those days and these.

A hard answer   was easily offered
by young Wiglaf,   Weohstan's son.
With little love   he looked on the shirkers: 2520
"I tell you in truth,   takers of treasure,
bench-sitting boasters   brave in the hall:
Beowulf gave you   the gear that you wear,
the most finely fashioned   found near or far
for a prince to proffer   his thankless thanes;   2525
but he wasted his wealth   on a worthless troop
who cast off their king   at the coming of war.

Our lord had no need   to laud his liege-men;
yet God, giver   of glory and vengeance,
granted him strength   to stand with his sword.   2530
I could do little   to lengthen his life
facing that foe,   but I fought nonetheless:
beyond my power   I propped up my prince.
The fire-drake faltered   after I struck him,
and his fuming jaws   flamed less fiercely,   2535
but too few friends   flew to our king
when evil beset him.   Now sword-bestowing
and gold-getting   shall cease for the Geats.
You shall have no joy   in the homeland you love.
Your farms shall be forfeit,   and each man fare   2540
alone and landless   when foreign lords
learn of your flight,   your failure of faith.
Better to die   than dwell in disgrace."

Then Wiglaf bade   that the battle-tidings
be sent to the camp   over the sea-cliff   2545
where warriors waited   with shields unslung,
sadly sitting   from dawn until noon
to learn if their lord   and beloved leader
had seen his last sunrise   or soon would return.
The herald would leave them   little to doubt;   2550
he sped up the headland   and spoke to them all:

"Now the wish-granter,   warlord of Weders,
lies on his death-bed.   The leader of Geats
stays in the slaughter-place,   slain by the worm
sprawled at his side.   Dagger-stricken,   2555
the slayer was felled,   though a sword had failed
to wound the serpent.   Weohstan's son,
Wiglaf is waiting   by Beowulf's body;
a living warrior   watches the lifeless,
sad-heartedly   sitting to guard   2560
the loved and the loathed.   Look now for war
as Franks and Frisians   learn how the king
has fallen in combat.   Few foreigners love us,
for Hygelac angered   the harsh Hugas
when his fleet forayed   to far-off Frisia.   2565
Fierce Hetware   met him with forces

bigger than his.   They broke him in battle;
that mail-clad chieftain   fell with his men.
Hygelac took   no trophies to thanes;
no king of the Meroving[30]   wishes us well.   2570

I also foresee   strife with the Swedes,
feud without end,   for all know Ongentheow
slew Hrethel's son   when Haethcyn first forayed
near Ravenswood[31]   with hot-headed Geats
and raided the realm   of Scylf-land's ruler.   2575
That fearsome old foe,   father of Ohthere,
quickly struck back.   He cut down our king[32]
to rescue the queen   Haethcyn had captured.
Her captors had shorn   the crone of her gold,
dishonored the aged   mother of Onela.[33]   2580
Ongentheow followed   hard on their heels.
Wounded, weary   and fiercely-harried,
those left unslain   by Swedish swords
limped off leaderless,   hid in the holt.
A huge army   beleaguered them there.   2585
All night long   Ongentheow taunted
the wretched raiders.   At daybreak, he swore,
he would slice them to slivers.   Some would swing
slung on his gallows,   sport for the ravens.[34]
But gladness came   again to grim Geats   2590
hearing Hygelac's   horns[35] in the morning,
the trumpet calls   of the troop that tracked them.
Haethcyn's brother,   bold with his band,
had rallied for battle.
                          A bloody swath
Scylfings and Geats   left on the landscape,   2595
everywhere smeared   with gore from the stricken.
So the two folks   stirred further feuds.
Wise in warfare,   old Ongentheow
grimly stood off,   seeking the safety

---

30 **Meroving** That is, of the Merovingians.   31 **Ravenswood** The forest in Sweden
where the Swedish king Ongentheow killed Haethcyn. See notes 13 and 14.   32 **king**
That is, Ongentheow killed Haethcyn.   33 **mother of Onela** Onela's mother, queen of
King Ongentheow, is not named.   34 **ravens** The reference may be to Ongentheow's
threat to sacrifice Geatish warriors to the god of war, in a ritual similar to that possibly
alluded to elsewhere in the poem; see note 11.   35 **horns** The horns signal Hygelac and
his men arriving after the battle had begun.

of higher ground.   He had heard of Hygelac's   2600
strength in struggles,   his pride and prowess.
Mistrusting his force   to fend off the foray,
he feared for his family   and fell back to guard
the hoard hidden   behind his earthworks.
Then Hrethel's people   pressed the pursuit: 2605
the standards of Hygelac   stormed the stronghold.
There the Swede   was snared between swords.
Eofor humbled   that hoary-haired leader,
though Wulf[36] struck first,   fierce with his weapon,
and a cut vein colored   the king's white head.   2610
Undaunted, Ongentheow   warded him off;
Wulf was wounded   the worse in return:
Ongentheow's blow   broke open his helm,
hurled him headlong,   helpless and bleeding
though not destined   to die on that day.   2615
Then Eofor faced   the folk-lord alone.
Sternly he stood   when his brother slumped:
Hygelac's soldier[37]   with sword in his hand
and helmet on head,   hoarded smithwork
shaped by old crafts,   shattered the shield-wall.   2620
The king crumpled,   struck to the quick.

Now the Geats gathered   after the slaughter.
Some bound the wound   of Eofor's brother
and bundled him off   the field of battle.
Meanwhile one warrior   plundered the other: 2625
Eofor stripped   the hard-hilted sword,
helm and corselet   from Ongentheow's corpse.
He handed that heap   of armor to Hygelac.
Pleased with his prizes,   the king pledged in turn
to reward war-strokes   as lord of the Weders.   2630
He[38] gave great riches   to Wulf and Eofor.
Once they were home,   he honored each one
with a hundred thousand[39]   in land and linked rings.
No man in middle-earth   ever begrudged them
favor and fortune   bestowed for their feat.   2635

36 **Wulf** A Geat who, along with Eofor, is a son of Wonred. The ferocious sons'
names mean "wolf" and "boar," respectively.   37 **soldier** Eofor, Wulf's brother.
38 **He** Hygelac.   39 **a hundred thousand** A reference to the value of the land and the
rings in coins of an unknown monetary unit.

Yet a further honor was offered Eofor:
the king's only daughter[40] adorned his house,
awarded in wedlock to Wonred's son.

Full of this feud, this festering hatred,
the Swedes,[41] I am certain, will swiftly beset us,   2640
as soon as they learn our lord lies lifeless
who held his hoard, his hall and his realm
against all foes when heroes had fallen,
who fostered his folk with fair kingship.
Now must we hasten, behold our sovereign,   2645
and bear him for burial. The brave one shall not
be beggared of booty to melt on his bier.
Let funeral flames greedily fasten
on gold beyond measure, grimly gotten,
lucre our leader bought with his life.   2650
No thane shall take tokens to treasure
nor maiden be made fairer with finery
strung at her throat. Stripped of their wealth,
they shall wander woefully all their lives long,
lordless and landless now that their king   2655
has laid aside laughter, sport and song.
Their hands shall heft many a spear-haft,
cold in the morning. No call of the harp
shall waken warriors after their battles;
but the black raven shall boast to the eagle,   2660
crowing how finely he fed on the fated
when, with the wolf, he went rending the slain."[42]

Thus the terrible tidings were told,
and the teller had not mistaken the truth.
The warriors all rose and woefully went   2665
to look on the wonder with welling tears.
They found on the sand under Earnanaess[43]
their lifeless lord laid there to rest,

---

40 **daughter** Hygelac and Hygd's daughter is unnamed in the poem. 41 **Swedes** The manuscript reads "Scyldingas," perhaps in error for "Scylfingas" or Swedes. (Compare Mitchell and Robinson 1998, p. 155, note to line 3005, who do not emend this line; thus, in their reading, the herald refers to Beowulf's fights with Grendel and Grendel's mother.) 42 **slain** The raven, eagle, and wolf form the so-called "beasts of battle," a recurrent motif in Old English poetry, who rejoice in anticipation of the feast that battle will bring them. 43 **Earnanaess** A Geatish place-name meaning "eagles' cape," near the location of the dragon fight.

beloved giver   of gifts and gold rings,
the war-king come   at the close of his days   2670
to a marvelous death.   At first the monster
commanded their gaze: grim on the ground
across from the king,   the creature had crumpled,
scaly and scorched,   a fearsome fire-drake
fifty feet long.   He would fly no more,   2675
free in the darkness,   nor drop to his den
at the break of dawn.   Death held the dragon;
he never would coil   in his cavern again.
Beyond the serpent   stood flagons and jars,
plated flatware   and priceless swords   2680
rotting in ruin,   etched out with rust.
These riches had rested   in Earth's embrace
for a thousand winters,   the heritage held
by warders of old,   spell-enwoven
and toilfully tombed   that none might touch them,   2685
unless God Himself,   granter of grace,
true Lord of glory,   allotted release
to one of His choosing   and opened the hoard.

It little profited   him[44] who had wrongfully
hidden the hand-wrought   wealth within walls.   2690
He payment was scant   for slaying the one
with courage to claim it: the kill was quickly
and harshly requited.   So the kingly
may come to strange ends   when their strength is spent
and time meted out.   They may not remain   2695
as men among kin,   mirthful with mead.
Beowulf goaded   the gold's guardian,
raised up the wrath,   not reckoning whether
his death-day had dawned,   not knowing the doom
solemnly sworn   by princes who placed   2700
their hoard in that hollow: the thief who held it
would fall before idols,   forge himself hell-bonds,
waste in torment   for touching the treasure.[45]

---

44 him The dragon.   **45 treasure** This difficult passage certainly suggests that the treasure was cursed and that only God can remove this spell (cf. lines 2682–88), but it does
not make clear in what way, if at all, Beowulf failed in desiring the hoard or if he is
damned for that. As Orchard (2003, p. 154) states, the "idols" and "hell-bonds" (as
translated here) of this speech mark it as a "set-piece, and [it] certainly seems to owe
much to the Christian language of anathema and condemnation."

He failed to consider   more fully and sooner
who rightfully owned   such awesome riches.   2705

So spoke Wiglaf,   son of Weohstan:
"By the whim of one man,   many warriors
sometimes may suffer,   as here has happened.
No means were at hand   to move my master;
no counsel could sway   the kingdom's keeper   2710
never to trouble   the treasure's taker,
but leave him lying   where long he had hidden,
walled with his wealth   until the world's ending.
He kept to his course,   uncovered the hoard.
Fate was too strongly   forcing him hither.   2715
I have entered that hall,   beheld everything
golden within,   though none too glad
for the opening offered   under its archway.
In haste I heaved   much from the hoard;
a mighty burden   I bore from the barrow   2720
straight to my sovereign.   He still was alive.
His wits were clear;   his words came quickly.
In anguish, the Ancient   asked that I say
he bade you to build   a barrow for him
befitting the deeds   of a fallen friend.   2725
You shall heap it high   over his ashes,
since he was the world's   worthiest warrior,
famed far and wide   for the wealth of his fortress.

Now let us hurry   hence to the hoard.
For a second time   I shall see that splendor   2730
under the cliff-wall,   those wonders of craftwork.
Come, I shall take you   close to the trove,
where you may behold   heaps of broad gold.
Then let a bier   be readied to bear
our beloved lord   to his long dwelling   2735
under the watch   of the World's Warden."

Then Weohstan's heir[46]   ordered the earls,
heads of houses   and fief holders,

---

46 Weohstan's heir Wiglaf.

to fetch firewood   fit for the folk-leader's
funeral pyre: "Flames shall now flare,   2740
feed on the flesh   and fade into darkness,
an ending for him   who often endured
the iron showers   shot over shield-walls
when string-driven storms   of arrows arose
with feathered fins   to steer them in flight   2745
and barbed arrowheads   eager to bite."

Wisely Wiglaf,   son of Weohstan,
summoned the seven   most steadfast thanes.
They went in together,   eight earls entering
under the evil   arch of the earth-house   2750
with one man bearing   a blazing torch.
No lot was cast   to learn which liege-man
would plunder the loot   lying unguarded,
as each searcher   could see for himself;
yet none was unhappy   to hurry that hoard   2755
out into daylight.   They heaved the dragon
over the sea-cliff   where surges seized him:
the treasure's keeper   was caught by the tide.
Then they filled a wain   with filigreed gold
and untold treasures;   and they carried the king,   2760
their hoary-haired warlord,   to Hronesnaess.

There the king's kinsmen   piled him a pyre,
wide and well-made   just as he willed it.
They hung it with helmets,   shields and mail-shirts,
then laid in its midst   their beloved lord,   2765
renowned among men.   Lamenting their loss,
his warriors woke   the most woeful fire
to flare on the bluff.   Fierce was the burning,
woven with weeping,   and wood-smoke rose
black over the blaze,   blown with a roar.   2770
The fire-wind faltered   and flames dwindled,
hot at their heart   the broken bone-house.[47]
Sunken in spirit   at Beowulf's slaying,
the Geats gathered   grieving together.

---

47 **bone-house** A kenning for "body."

Her hair wound up,[48]   a woebegone woman[49]   2775
sang and resang   her dirge[50] of dread,
foretelling a future   fraught with warfare,
kinfolk sundered,   slaughter and slavery
even as heaven   swallowed the smoke.

High on the headland   they heaped his grave-mound   2780
which seafaring sailors   would spy from afar.
Ten days they toiled   on the scorched hilltop,
the cleverest men   skillfully crafting
a long-home built   for the bold in battle.
They walled with timbers   the trove they had taken,   2785
sealing in stone   the circlets and gems,
wealth of the worm-hoard   gotten with grief,
gold from the ground   gone back to Earth
as worthless to men   as when it was won.
Then sorrowing swordsmen   circled the barrow,   2790
twelve of his earls   telling their tales,
the sons of nobles   sadly saluting
deeds of the dead.   So dutiful thanes
in liege to their lord   mourn him with lays
praising his peerless   prowess in battle   2795
as it is fitting   when life leaves the flesh.
Heavy-hearted   his hearth-companions
grieved for Beowulf,   great among kings,
mild in his mien,   most gentle of men,
kindest to kinfolk   and keenest for fame.   2800

---

48 wound up The first letter of this compound is unreadable in the manuscript, suggesting a woman either with hair "bound up" or "wound-haired." Clover (2002, p. 32) in her discussion of the woman's role in ceremonial mourning, argues that the Geatish woman's hair must be "wound" or wavy and not "bound" for "mourning women, married or otherwise, . . . are widely described, even emblematized, as having unbound or disheveled hair." **49 woman** Playing the woman's role in the mourning ritual, this unnamed Geatish woman's lament expresses sorrow for the dead hero and fear for the future of the Geatish nation in his absence. As has been pointed out frequently, Andromache, when mourning Hector, bewails the fate that will await her nation with its hero dead (see *Iliad*, xxiv). **50 dirge** Note that the mourning woman composes a dirge. See Clover (2002) for an exploration of women as composers of funeral laments.

CONTEXTS

From the Latin

The Holy Bible
from *Genesis*

Grendel and Grendel's mother are associated in Beowulf *with the biblical figure of Cain, who, according to the account from Genesis, committed the world's first homicide by murdering his brother, Abel. For the* Beowulf*-poet, Cain's act of the fratricide is thus a symbol of social disharmony, and Grendel and his mother are also exiled from all that makes men human—from music, companionship, the structure of the hall—and live in a place that resembles hell. But as* Beowulf *offers a critique of its own social values and heroes, one notes that the monstrous Grendel and Grendel's mother also share violence and vengeance with the heroic warriors of the poem. The treatment of social practice and values in* Beowulf *is nuanced, and the genealogy of the "Grendel–kin" alluded to in the poem relates the creatures both to Cain (Genesis 4) and to the monsters born from the miscegenation of giants and "the daughters of men" (Genesis 6), giving the reader two potent references that cause one also to ponder those inside Heorot. The source of these excerpts is the Douay–Rheims version of the Bible (1582–1610), an English translation from the Latin Vulgate text of Jerome, which is what would have been known in the Anglo-Saxon period.*[1]

---

[1] Jerome (c. 347–420) was commissioned by Pope Damasus in 382 to translate the Bible into Latin, a task at which Jerome labored for some twenty years, never finishing the New Testament. What Jerome did finish is known as the *versio vulgata*; hence Vulgate. For a brief survey of the use of scripture in *Beowulf*, see Andersson (1997, pp. 142–3).

91

Genesis 4:1–16—*The Kin of Cain*

1. And Adam knew Eve his wife, who conceived and brought forth Cain, saying: I have gotten a man through God. 2. And again she brought forth his brother Abel. And Abel was a shepherd, and Cain a husbandman. 3. And it came to pass after many days, that Cain offered, of the fruits of the earth, gifts to the Lord. 4. Abel also offered of the firstlings of his flock, and of their fat: and the Lord had respect to Abel, and to his offerings. 5. But to Cain and his offerings he had no respect: and Cain was exceeding angry, and his countenance fell. 6. And the Lord said to him: Why art thou angry? and why is thy countenance fallen? 7. If thou do well, shalt thou not receive? but if ill, shall not sin forthwith be present at the door? but the lust thereof shall be under thee, and thou shalt have dominion over it. 8. And Cain said to Abel his brother: Let us go forth abroad. And when they were in the field, Cain rose up against his brother Abel, and slew him. 9. And the Lord said to Cain: Where is thy brother Abel? And he answered: I know not: am I my brother's keeper? 10. And he said to him: What hast thou done? the voice of thy brother's blood crieth to me from the earth. 11. Now therefore cursed shalt thou be upon the earth, which hath opened her mouth and received the blood of thy brother at thy hand. 12. When thou shalt till it, it shall not yield to thee its fruit: a fugitive and a vagabond shalt thou be upon the earth. 13. And Cain said to the Lord: My iniquity is greater than that I may deserve pardon. 14. Behold thou dost cast me out this day from the face of the earth, and from thy face I shall be hid, and I shall be a vagabond and a fugitive on the earth: every one therefore that findeth me, shall kill me. 15. And the Lord said to him: No, it shall not so be: but whosoever shall kill Cain, shall be punished sevenfold. And the Lord set a mark upon Cain, that whosoever found him should not kill him. 16. And Cain went out from the face of the Lord, and dwelt as a fugitive on the earth at the east side of Eden.

Genesis 6:1–17—*The Race of Giants*

1. And after that men began to be multiplied upon the earth, and daughters were born to them. 2. The sons of God seeing the daughters of men, that they were fair, took to themselves wives of all which they chose. 3. And God said: My spirit shall not remain in man for ever, because he is flesh, and his days shall be

a hundred and twenty years. 4. Now giants were upon the earth in those days. For after the sons of God went in to the daughters of men, and they brought forth children, these are the mighty men of old, men of renown. 5. And God seeing that the wickedness of men was great on the earth, and that all the thought of their heart was bent upon evil at all times, 6. it repented him that he had made man on the earth. And being touched inwardly with sorrow of heart, 7. he said: I will destroy man, whom I have created, from the face of the earth, from man even to beasts, from the creeping thing even to the fowls of the air, for it repenteth me that I have made them. 8. But Noe found grace before the Lord. 9. These are the generations of Noe: Noe was a just and perfect man in his generations; he walked with God. 10. And he begot three sons, Sem, Cham, and Japheth. 11. And the earth was corrupted before God, and was filled with iniquity. 12. And when God had seen that the earth was corrupted (for all flesh had corrupted its way upon the earth), 13. he said to Noe: The end of all flesh is come before me, the earth is filled with iniquity through them, and I will destroy them with the earth. 14. Make thee an ark of timber planks: thou shalt make little rooms in the ark, and thou shalt pitch it within and without. 15. And thus shalt thou make it. The length of the ark shall be three hundred cubits: the breadth of it fifty cubits, and the height of it thirty cubits. 16. Thou shalt make a window in the ark, and in a cubit shalt thou finish the top of it: and the door of the ark thou shalt set in the side: with lower, middle chambers, and third stories shalt thou make it. 17. Behold, I will bring the waters of a great flood upon the earth, to destroy all flesh, wherein is the breath of life under heaven. All things that are in the earth shall be consumed.

Publius Cornelius Tacitus
from *Germania*

> *Publius Cornelius Tacitus (c. 54–c. 117) served as a senator, consul, and governor of Asia. Tacitus finished* Germania *in about 98 and wrote two major historical works later in his life: the* Annals *and the* Histories, *which together cover the history of Rome*

from the death of Augustus to 96, though each of these works is now incomplete. Germania *contrasts the virtues of the barbarian Germans—including a love of freedom and honor, the observance of social hierarchy, and the practice of a pure and "natural" masculinity and of marital chastity—with the decadence of the Roman Empire.* Tacitus *uses the contemporary interest in the German provinces not only to moralize, but also to supply a vivid account of the Germanic tribes in their continental homeland, an account that offers tantalizing analogies to speculations about Germanic practices. Traces of these practices may be observed in* Beowulf, *which emphasizes honor, courage, and loyalty to one's chief and war-band and underscores the importance of songs and funerary rites.*

Chapter 3

The Germani, like many other people, have a tradition that Hercules is said to have visited their country, and him above all other heroes they extol in their songs when they advance into battle. Amongst them too are found that well-known kind of verse which they call *baritus*. By their chanting of this, they not only inspire bravery, but also by listening to the sound, they divine the success of the approaching fight. For, according to the different din on the battlefield, they either attack furiously or shrink fearfully. Nor do they regard it as many voices chanting together, but as the single voice of valor. They chiefly aim to produce a harsh, discontinuous roar, and therefore they apply their shields to their mouths, whence the voice may by reverberating be amplified more deeply and loudly. Besides there are some of the opinion, that Ulysses, while he wandered about in his long and fabulous voyages, was carried into this ocean and entered German lands, and that by him Asciburgium was founded and named, a city to this day standing inhabited on the bank of the Rhine. They add that in the same place was formerly found an altar consecrated by Ulysses, with the name of his father Laertes added to his own, and that on the borders of Germany and Raetia are still extant certain monuments on barrows inscribed with Greek characters. I do not intend either to confirm with arguments of my own or to refute these traditions. Let every one believe or deny the same according to his own bent.

Chapter 13

There is rank even in these retinues [that follow the chiefs], at the discretion of the chief whom they follow, and there is a great rivalry, both among the followers to excel in the estimation of their chiefs and among the chiefs for the size and the strength of their retinues. To be surrounded by a large force of hand-picked young warriors is their glory in peace and their defense in war. Nor is it only among a chief's own nation, but also among neighboring ones, that the superior number and quality of a chief's retinue brings him great renown and name. For neighboring nations court them with embassies and compliment them with gifts, and very often the fame of such men will alone decide a war.

Chapter 14

On the day of battle, it is a disgrace to the chief to be surpassed in feats of bravery by his followers, and to his followers to fail in matching the bravery of the chief. But it is infamy during life, and an indelible shame, to return alive from a battle where their chief was slain. To preserve their chief, to defend him, and to credit to him all their own heroic deeds, is the sum and most sacred part of their obligation. The chiefs fight for victory; for the chief, his followers fight. Many young noblemen, when their own land languishes in its vigor by long periods of peace and inactivity, deliberately seek out other tribes which have some war at issue. For the Germani have no taste for peace; besides, by perilous adventures they more quickly blazon their fame, and they cannot otherwise than by violence and war support their huge body of retainers.

Chapter 27

In their funerals, they show no vainglory. This only is carefully observed: that with the corpses of their famous men, certain woods be burned. Upon the funeral pyre, they heap neither garments nor spices. Into the fire are always thrown the arms of the dead, and sometimes his horse. With a mound of turf only is the tomb raised. They condemn the pomp of tedious and elaborate stone monuments, which would only lie heavily on the dead. Weeping and wailing they soon abandon; their sorrow and woe they long retain. In women, it is reckoned appropriate to bewail their grief; in men, to remember it.

Jordanes
from *On the Origin and Deeds of the Goths (De origine actibusque Getarum)*

The historian Jordanes, fl. c. 550, wrote his history of the Goths, generally referred to by the short title Getica, *as an abridgment of the much longer, but now lost account by Cassiodorus (c. 490–c. 585) on the same subject. The following excerpt relates the death and funeral of Attila, the king of the Huns from 445–453. Compare the elaborate funeral rituals for Attila detailed here with the funerary customs found in* Beowulf, *and, most spectacularly, with the ceremonies of cremating Beowulf and raising his burial mound which end the poem.*

Chapter 49

Shortly before he [Attila] died, as the historian Priscus[1] relates, he took in marriage a very beautiful girl named Ildico, after countless other wives, as was the custom of his race. He had given himself up to excessive joy at his wedding, and as he lay on his back, heavy with wine and sleep, a rush of superfluous blood, which would ordinarily have flowed from his nose, streamed in a deadly course down his throat and killed him, since it was hindered in the usual passages. Thus did drunkenness put a disgraceful end to a king renowned in war. On the following day, when a great part of the morning was spent, the royal attendants suspected some ill and, after a great uproar, broke in the doors. There they found the death of Attila accomplished by an effusion of blood, without any wound, and the girl with downcast face weeping beneath her veil. Then, as is the custom of that race, they plucked out the hair of their heads and made their faces hideous with deep wounds, that the renowned warrior might be mourned, not by effeminate wailings and tears, but by the blood of men. Moreover a wondrous thing took place in connection with Attila's death. For in a dream some god stood at the side of Marcian, Emperor of the East,[2] while

---

[1]Priscus, born in Thrace in the early fifth century, wrote a history in eight books, of which only fragments are extant. Sent by the Roman government with a message for Attila in 448, Priscus relates meeting and talking with Attila in his court, a remarkable account that survives.

[2]Marcian, the Eastern emperor (396–457), had refused to give Attila the tribute he had demanded in 450, thus precipitating the Huns' invasion of the Roman Empire.

he was disquieted about his fierce foe, and showed him the bow of Attila broken in that same night, as if to intimate that the race of Huns owed much to that weapon. This account the historian Priscus says he accepts upon truthful evidence. For so terrible was Attila thought to be to great empires that the gods announced his death to rulers as a special boon. We shall not omit to say a few words about the many ways in which his shade was honored by his race. His body was placed in the midst of a plain and lay in state in a silken tent as a sight for men's admiration. The best horsemen of the entire tribe of the Huns rode around in circles, after the manner of circus games, in the place to which he had been brought and told of his deeds in a funeral dirge in the following manner: "The chief of the Huns, King Attila, born of his sire Mundiuch, lord of bravest tribes, sole possessor of the Scythian and German realms—powers unknown before—captured cities and terrified both empires of the Roman world and, appeased by their prayers, took annual tribute to save the rest from plunder. And when he had accomplished all this by the favor of fortune, he fell, not by wound of the foe, nor by treachery of friends, but in the midst of his nation at peace, happy in his joy and without sense of pain. Who can rate this as death, when none believes it calls for vengeance?" When they had mourned him with such lamentations, a *strava*, as they call it, was celebrated over his tomb with great reveling. They gave way in turn to the extremes of feeling and displayed funereal grief alternating with joy. Then in the secrecy of night they buried his body in the earth. They bound his coffins, the first with gold, the second with silver and the third with the strength of iron, showing by such means that these three things suited the mightiest of kings: iron because he subdued the nations, gold and silver because he received the honors of both empires. They also added the arms of foemen won in the fight, trappings of rare worth, sparkling with various gems, and ornaments of all sorts whereby princely state is maintained. And that so great riches might be kept from human curiosity, they slew those appointed to the work—a dreadful pay for their labor; and thus sudden death was the lot of those who buried him as well as of him who was buried.

Gregory of Tours
from *The History of the Franks (Historia Francorum)*

> *According to his own report, Gregory was born on Saint Andrew's Day (November 30) in 538 or 539, in a city then called Arvernus; he became the nineteenth bishop of Tours on August 20, 573. Sometime after his consecration as bishop, he began writing this universal history and account of his times in ten books, apparently continuing with his work nearly up to his death on November 17, 594. The Danish king cited in the translated excerpt below is the Hygelac found in* Beowulf, *and thus Gregory's history supplies the only dated event (c. 521) that can be attested from a source independent of the poem.*

Book III, Chapter 3

The next thing that happened was that the Danes sent a fleet of ships under their king, named Chlochilaich,[1] and invaded Gaul from the sea. They came ashore and laid waste to one of the regions ruled by Theuderic, and they captured some of the inhabitants. Then they loaded their ships with what they had taken and with the captives, and they sailed back to their country. But their king remained on the shore, waiting until the ships had reached open waters, when he planned to go on board. When Theuderic learned that his land had been invaded by foreigners, he sent his son Theudebert to those parts with a powerful force armed with all the needed equipment. The Danish king was killed, the enemy beaten in a naval battle, and all the plunder returned to land.

from the *Book of Monsters (Liber monstrorum)*

> *Composed by an unknown Anglo-Saxon around the end of the seventh century or the beginning of the eighth century, this Latin work divides monsters into human, animal, and serpentine types, and then treats some 120 examples of them in three books. It*

---

[1]The name in Latin is *Chlochilaichus*, equivalent to the Old English "Hygelac."

*relies on Latin and Christian prose sources and on Virgil, includ-
ing the tradition of commentary on Virgil. The "book of monsters" also uses some of the same sources as do two texts found in
the* Beowulf *manuscript: the* Marvels of the East *and* Alexander's
Letter to Aristotle.[1] *Most of the "book of monsters" has been
traced to known sources, but no source for either excerpt below is
known.[2] The "monster" is a theme deployed throughout*
Beowulf, *as is the monstrous subtype, the giant.[3]*

Part I, Chapter 2

About King Huiglaucus [Hygelac] and his amazing magnitude.

Now there are monsters of remarkable amazing magnitude,
namely King Huiglaucus, who ruled the Geats and was killed by the
Franks. No horse could carry him, even when he was twelve years
old. His bones are preserved on an island in the Rhine River, where
it flows into the ocean, and they are shown as a wonderment to people who come from afar.

Part II, Chapter 23

But that beast is said to be amongst the fiercest of all brutes, in
which they assert that there is such a quantity of venom that lions
fear it, although it is an animal of weaker body, and they reckon
that its poison has such strength that the cutting-edge even of iron,
dipped in it, melts.[4]

---

[1]Lapidge (1982) uses this connection to place and date *Beowulf*'s composition. See
also Whitbread (1974).

[2]Orchard 1997; Orchard 2003, pp. 133–37.

[3]See Orchard (1995) for a reading of the problem of the monsters in *Beowulf* and
both the Latin text and English translation of the *Liber monstrorum*. For the
medieval monster seen through postmodern identity theory, see Cohen (1999). For
two discussions of giants as a thematic problem in *Beowulf*, see Bandy (1973) and
Orchard (1995, pp. 86–115 and pp. 254–320).

[4]Orchard (2003, p. 135) notes that the "creature seems to share this curious quality
with Grendel, whose blood likewise causes the blade of the giant sword to melt, an
image of which the *Beowulf*-poet gives two descriptions, first in his own voice (lines
1605b–1617) and then in Beowulf's (lines 1666b–1668a)." See, in this translation,
lines 1418 ff and 1470 ff.

Bede

from *An Ecclesiastical History of the English People* (*Historia ecclesiastica gentis Anglorum*)

Bede, called by the honorable title "the Venerable," was the most influential writer of Latin in Anglo-Saxon England. He was born about 673 near what is now Newcastle-upon-Tyne and died in 735 at the twin monasteries of Wearmouth (now Monkwearmouth) and Jarrow, where he had served as a monk for most of his life. Besides the history from which these excerpts are taken, more than thirty of Bede's works in Latin survive, including epistles, homilies, Biblical exegesis, accounts of saints' lives, and treatises on computistical and literary matters. Bede was highly regarded for his erudition and his Latinity, and many of his works survive in abundant copies. For example, the Ecclesiastical History *is found in more than 130 complete English and continental manuscripts. Some, like his works on literary figures and meter, became standard pedagogical texts used for instruction for hundreds of years. The single surviving vernacular work by Bede is a five-line poem composed on his deathbed. Bede's* Ecclesiastical History *speaks to many themes, but pertinent here is Roger Ray's statement that "Like Luke, Bede narrated the triumph of the catholic faith over mixed customs among a new people of God destined to preach the Gospel abroad."*[1] *These excerpts illustrate several crucial issues in* Beowulf: *Bede's famous formulation of the three Germanic tribes who invade the British Isles speaks to a shared Germanic past that underwrites the poem; the letter from Pope Gregory and the narrative of King Edwin instance the problems of converting to Christianity the inhabitants of Britain; and finally, the story of the illiterate Caedmon's "miraculous" ability to compose Christian verse in the vernacular is important in understanding oral traditional composition, which* Beowulf *not only depicts, but perhaps exemplifies.*

Book I.15 [449]

In the year of our Lord 449, Martian being made emperor with Valentinian, and the forty-sixth from Augustus, ruled the empire seven years. Then the nation of the Angles, or Saxons, being

---

[1]Roger Ray, "Bede," Lapidge *et al.* (1999, p. 58).

invited by the aforesaid king, arrived in Britain with three long ships, and had a place assigned them to reside in by the same king, in the eastern part of the island, that they might thus appear to be fighting for their country, whilst their real intentions were to enslave it. Accordingly they engaged with the enemy, who were come from the north to give battle, and obtained the victory; which, being known at home in their own country, as also the fertility of the country, and the cowardice of the Britons, a more considerable fleet was quickly sent over, bringing a still greater number of men, which, being added to the former, made up an invincible army. The newcomers received of the Britons a place to inhabit, upon condition that they should wage war against their enemies for the peace and security of the country, whilst the Britons agreed to furnish them with pay. Those who came over were of the three most powerful nations of Germany—Saxons, Angles, and Jutes. From the Jutes are descended the people of Kent, and of the Isle of Wight, and those also in the province of the West Saxons who are to this day called Jutes, seated opposite to the Isle of Wight. From the Saxons, that is, the country which is now called Old Saxony, came the East Saxons, the South Saxons, and the West Saxons. From the Angles, that is, the country which is called Anglia, and which is said, from that time, to remain desert to this day, between the provinces of the Jutes and the Saxons, are descended the East Angles, the Midland Angles, Mercians, all the race of the Northumbrians, that is, of those nations that dwell on the north side of the river Humber, and the other nations of the English. The two first commanders are said to have been Hengist and Horsa. Of whom Horsa, being afterwards slain in battle by the Britons, was buried in the eastern parts of Kent, where a monument, bearing his name, is still in existence. They were the sons of Victgilsus, whose father was Vecta, son of Woden; from whose stock the royal race of many provinces deduce their origin. In a short time, swarms of the aforesaid nations came over into the island, and they began to increase so much that they became terrible to the natives themselves who had invited them.

Book I.30 [601]

The aforesaid messengers being departed, the holy father, Gregory, sent after them letters worthy to be preserved in memory, wherein

he plainly shows what care he took of the salvation of our nation.[2]
The letter was as follows:

"To his most beloved son, the Abbot Mellitus; Gregory, the servant of the servants of God. We have been much concerned, since the departure of our congregation that is with you, because we have received no account of the success of your journey. When, therefore, Almighty God shall bring you to the most reverend Bishop Augustine, our brother, tell him what I have, upon mature deliberation on the affair of the English, determined upon, viz., that the temples of the idols in that nation ought not to be destroyed; but let the idols that are in them be destroyed; let holy water be made and sprinkled in the said temples, let altars be erected, and relics placed. For if those temples are well built, it is requisite that they be converted from the worship of devils to the service of the true God; that the nation, seeing that their temples are not destroyed, may remove error from their hearts, and knowing and adoring the true God, may the more familiarly resort to the places to which they have been accustomed. And because they have been used to slaughter many oxen in the sacrifices to devils, some solemnity must be exchanged for them on this account, as that on the day of the dedication, or the nativities of the holy martyrs, whose relics are there deposited, they may build themselves huts of the boughs of trees, about those churches which have been turned to that use from temples, and celebrate the solemnity with religious feasting, and no more offer beasts to the Devil, but kill cattle to the praise of God in their eating, and return thanks to the Giver of all things for their sustenance; to the end that, whilst some gratifications are outwardly permitted them, they may the more easily consent to the inward consolations of the grace of God. For there is no doubt that it is impossible to efface everything at once from their obdurate minds; because he who endeavors to ascend to the highest place, rises by degrees or steps, and not by leaps. Thus the Lord made Himself known to the people of Israel in Egypt; and yet He allowed them the use of the sacrifices which they were wont to offer to the Devil, in his own worship; so as to command them in his sacrifice to kill beasts, to the end that, changing their hearts, they might lay aside one part of the sacrifice, whilst they retained another; that whilst they offered the same beasts which they were wont to offer,

---

[2]Pope Gregory sent this letter to Abbot Mellitus before the Abbot departed on his mission to Britain in 601.

they should offer them to God, and not to idols; and thus they would no longer be the same sacrifices. This it behooves your affection to communicate to our aforesaid brother, that he, being there present, may consider how he is to order all things. God preserve you in safety, most beloved son."

Book II.15 [627]

Edwin was so zealous for the worship of truth, that he likewise persuaded Eorpwald, king of the East Saxons, and son of Raedwald,[3] to abandon his idolatrous superstitions, and with his whole province to receive the faith and sacraments of Christ. And indeed his father Raedwald had long before been admitted to the sacrament of the Christian faith in Kent, but in vain; for on his return home, he was seduced by his wife and certain perverse teachers, and turned back from the sincerity of the faith; and thus his latter state was worse than the former; so that, like the ancient Samaritans, he seemed at the same time to serve Christ and the gods whom he had served before; and in the same temple he had an altar to sacrifice to Christ, and another small one to offer victims to devils; which temple, Aldwulf, king of that same province, who lived in our time testifies had stood until his time, and that he had seen it when he was a boy. The aforesaid King Raedwald was noble by birth, though ignoble in his actions, being the son of Tytilus, whose father was Uuffa, from whom the kings of the East Angles are called Uuffings.

Book IV.24 [680]

There was in this monastery of Whitby a certain brother, particularly remarkable for the grace of God, who was wont to make pious and religious verses, so that whatever was interpreted to him out of Scripture, he soon after put the same into poetical expressions of much sweetness and humility, in English, which was his native language. By his verses the minds of many were often excited to despise the world, and to aspire to heaven. Others after him attempted, in the English nation, to compose religious poems, but none could ever compare with him, for he did not learn the art of poetry from men, but from God; for which reason he never could compose any trivial or vain poem, but only those which relate to

[3]This is the Raedwald associated with the Sutton Hoo ship burial. See this translation of *Beowulf*, note to line 47 on p. 5.

religion suited his religious tongue; for having lived in a secular habit till he was well advanced in years, he had never learned anything of versifying; for which reason being sometimes at entertainments, when it was agreed for the sake of mirth that all present should sing in their turns, when he saw the instrument come towards him, he rose up from table and returned home.

Having done so at a certain time, and gone out of the house where the entertainment was, to the stable, where he had to take care of the horses that night, he there composed himself to rest at the proper time; a person appeared to him in his sleep, and saluting him by his name, said, "Caedmon, sing some song to me." He answered, "I cannot sing; for that was the reason why I left the entertainment, and retired to this place because I could not sing." The other who talked to him, replied, "However, you shall sing."—"What shall I sing?" rejoined he. "Sing the beginning of created beings," said the other. Hereupon he presently began to sing verses to the praise of God, which he had never heard, the purport whereof was thus: We are now to praise the Maker of the heavenly kingdom, the power of the Creator and his counsel, the deeds of the Father of glory. How He, being the eternal God, became the author of all miracles, who first, as almighty preserver of the human race, created heaven for the sons of men as the roof of the house, and next the earth. This is the sense, but not the words in order as he sang them in his sleep; for verses, though never so well composed, cannot be literally translated out of one language into another, without losing much of their beauty and loftiness. Awaking from his sleep, he remembered all that he had sung in his dream, and soon added much more to the same effect in verse worthy of the Deity.

In the morning he came to the steward, his superior, and having acquainted him with the gift he had received, was conducted to the abbess [Hild], by whom he was ordered, in the presence of many learned men, to tell his dream, and repeat the verses, that they might all give their judgment what it was, and whence his verse proceeded. They all concluded, that heavenly grace had been conferred on him by our Lord. They expounded to him a passage in holy writ, either historical, or doctrinal, ordering him, if he could, to put the same into verse. Having undertaken it, he went away, and returning the next morning, gave it to them composed in most excellent verse; whereupon the abbess, embracing the grace of God in the man, instructed him to quit the secular habit, and take upon him the monastic life; which being accordingly done, she associated him to the rest of the brethren in her monastery, and ordered that he should be taught the whole series of sacred history. Thus Caedmon keeping in mind all he heard, and as it were chewing the cud,[4] converted the same into most harmonious verse; and sweetly repeating the same, made his masters in their turn his hearers. He sang the creation of the world, the origin of man, and all the history of Genesis; and made many verses on the departure of the children of Israel out of Egypt, and their entering into the land of promise, with many other histories from holy writ; the incarnation, passion, resurrection of our Lord, and his ascension into heaven; the coming of the Holy Ghost, and the preaching of the apostles; also the terror of future judgment, the horror of the pains of hell, and the delights of heaven; besides many more about the Divine benefits and judgments, by which he endeavored to turn away all men from the love of vice, and to excite in them the love of, and application to, good actions; for he was a very religious man, humbly submissive to regular discipline, but full of zeal against those who behaved themselves otherwise; for which reason, he ended his life happily.

Alcuin of York

from *Epistle to a Mercian Bishop*

> *Born about 735 to a noble Northumbrian family, Alcuin was raised and educated at York Minster, first by Ecgberht (d. 766), Archbishop of York, and then by Aelberht (d. 780). On an official journey to Rome in 781, Alcuin met Charlemagne at Parma, later joining his royal court. Named "master of the palace school," Alcuin tutored Charlemagne and other members of the royal family. Charlemagne appointed Alcuin abbot of St. Martin's at Tours in 796. Alcuin's forceful intellect and visionary educational reforms are often credited with sparking the Carolingian Renaissance. Alcuin was a prolific writer in Latin on an encyclopedia of topics, including Biblical exegesis, saints' lives, prayers, grammar, statements of royal policy, rhetoric, and astronomy, as well as a composer of Latin poetry. He emended*

---

[4]The pun here is on Caedmon the cowherd who is ruminating about what he ought to sing, which is figured as chewing his cud like a cow, an animal classified as a ruminant.

*the Bible at Charlemagne's request, making Tours an important
center for Bible production, and insisted on both accuracy and
clarity in the scriptorium, resulting in the new Caroline minus-
cule script.*[1] *When Alcuin died on May 19, 804, Tours had one
of the most remarkable libraries and monastic schools in Europe.
Though he never returned to England for good after joining
Charlemagne's court, Alcuin visited on at least two occasions
and corresponded with many acquaintances and students there.
About 270 of his letters survive. Alcuin's warning about Ingeld, a
figure known from* Beowulf, *indicates how well-known was such
legendary material in the eighth century; it also shows no tolera-
tion for the recitation of any such lays (short songs) about heathen
heroes, particularly perhaps during this period, when the British
Isles were subject to Viking attacks.*

Epistle[2]—To a Mercian Bishop:
"What Has Ingeld to Do with Christ?"

. . .Your reverence should often consider the various happenings in
the world and inquire with an alert mind what fortune awaits us.
The whole human race provides examples to teach us how dangerous a day and how fearful a judgment awaits us at a time we know
not. Let us prepare to meet the great king, whom none can escape,
that we may find him gracious. We must think each day what gift
we bring—as Scripture says "Appear not empty-handed in the sight
of the Lord your God."[Ecclesiastes 35:4] No precious metals, no
sparkling gems, no vain dress, no worldly luxury will be acceptable
before that most just of judges; only generous alms and an increase
of good deserts will avail. Whatever is done here will be judged
there. All goodness will be crowned with eternal reward, and all
wickedness damned to eternal torment. Let our hearts hold to this
with wise foresight, that on that day the soul may not mourn its
lack of good deserts, but we must take great care to think how it
may rejoice in the simple fruit of goodness.

Human foresight in worldly affairs is uncertain. Only what is
done by love in this temporal life according to God's command-
ments will not fail him who thinks of the future. Have a hand gen-

---

[1]Alcuin did not himself use this script. The ways in which we write and print some of
our alphabet are based on this Caroline script of Alcuin.

[2]This letter is dated 797. The Latin text is in *Monumenta Germaniae Historica,
Epistolae*, vol. IV, no. 124.

erous in giving, a tongue keen to preach, a sober style of life, a priest's authority in chiding sinners, kindly concern in cherishing the lowly. Be very confident in maintaining truth, judging fairly without personal prejudice. Perform the daily offices of the church reverently. . . . You should certainly have in your company a wise steward to see to the care of the poor with concern. It is better for the poor to eat from your table than actors and voluptuaries. Avoid drunkards as the pit of hell, as St. Jerome says. . . .

Let the word of God be read when the clergy are at their meal. It is seemly to hear a reader there, and not a harper; to hear the sermons of the Fathers of the Church, not the lays of the heathen. For what has Ingeld[3] to do with Christ? The house is narrow; it cannot contain them both. The king of heaven will have no part with so-called kings who are heathen and damned for the one king reigns eternally in heaven, while the other, the heathen, is damned and groans in hell. In your houses the voices of readers should be heard, not the rabble of men making merry in the streets.

Nennius

from *History of the Britons (Historia Brittonum)*

This history was composed c. 830 in an unidentified cultural center in northern Wales; the unknown author was very probably Welsh. The history survives only in later copies, one of which ascribes its authorship to "Nennius" in a preface, an attribution that has stuck. The history extends from the creation of the world into the 680s. Of great importance to those interested in King Arthur because it describes the period in which he may have lived and his military campaigns, the history also includes genealogies and anecdotes relevant to the Anglo-Saxon period. Because of the known sources used to write this history, it is clear that its author could use materials written in Latin and Old English. Notice the nation-founding legend quoted below, for its genealogy of Hors and Hengest provides a comparison with the prologue describing Scyld in Beowulf.

---

[3]Ingeld, the son of Froda, referred to twice in *Beowulf* (lines 2025 ff. and line 2064 in the Old English text); see this translation, lines 1790 ff. Ingeld is also referred to in the Old English poem *Widsith*, lines 45–49; see Contexts, From the Old English, pp. 161.

Section 31

After the above-said war between the Britons and Romans, the assassination of their rulers, and the victory of Maximus, who slew Gratian, and the termination of the Roman power in Britain, they were in alarm for forty years. Vortigern then reigned in Britain. In his time, the natives had cause for dread, not only from the inroads of the Scots and Picts, but also from the Romans, and their apprehensions of Ambrosius.

Meanwhile, there arrived three ships driven into exile from Germany, on board which were Hors and Hengest; these were brothers, and the sons of Guictgils, the son of Guitta, the son of Guectha, the son of Woden, the son of Frealaf, the son of Fredulf, the son of Finn, the son of Folcwald, the son of Geta, who was, as they say, the son of god, not of the omnipotent God and our Lord Jesus Christ, who before the beginning of the world was, with the Father and the Holy Spirit, co-eternal and of the same substance, and who, in compassion to human nature, disdained not to assume the form of a servant, but the offspring of one of their idols, and whom, blinded by some demon, they worshiped according to the custom of the heathen. Vortigern received them as friends, and delivered up to them the island which is in their language called Thanet, and, by the Britons, Ruym.

Asser

from the *Life of Alfred, King of the Anglo-Saxons (Vita Ælfredi regis Angul Saxonum)*[1]

Asser, a name derived from "Asher" in Genesis, *was a monk at St. David's monastery in the kingdom of Dyfed (Wales), from which King Alfred summoned him to Wessex, where they met in c. 885 at the royal estate of Dean (Sussex, England). Asser tutored Alfred in Latin and helped him translate Gregory the Great's* Pastoral Care *as part of Alfred's revival of learning. In*

---

[1]This translation is adapted from Stevenson's *Asser's Life of King Alfred* (1904) and on Jane's *Asser's Life of King Alfred* (1924). See Keynes and Lapidge (1983), which includes a translation of Asser's biography on pp. 66–110, and an introduction and notes by two of the period's foremost historians.

return, Alfred put Asser in charge of the important monastery of Exeter, which had jurisdiction over Wessex and Cornwall, along with granting Asser other marks of favor. Asser wrote the Life of Alfred *in 893, basing the first part of it on the Anglo-Saxon* Chronicle *through 887; Asser's work is the earliest biography of an Anglo-Saxon king. The account of Alfred's reign during the tumultuous period 871–99 is supplemented by many important and unforgettable details about Alfred's personality and age; for example, the place and date of Alfred's birth are found only in Asser. Asser died in 908 or 909. Beowulf often reminds the reader of the qualities a good king should have, and Asser depicts the struggle of Alfred striving to exemplary kingship. Like* Beowulf, *Asser's* Life of Alfred *survived into modern times in a single manuscript of c. 1000*[2] *that was also acquired by Sir Robert Bruce Cotton (1571–1631). But unlike the Cottonian manuscript of* Beowulf *that was only singed in the 1731 fire, the manuscript that contained Asser's* Life of Alfred *burned up. The text of the biography has been reconstructed from two sixteenth-century copies of the Cottonian manuscript. Note Alfred's attempt to be literate both in the vernacular and in Latin.*

1. In the year of our Lord's incarnation 849 was born Alfred, king of the Anglo-Saxons,[3] at the royal estate of Wantage, in Berkshire, which country has its name from the wood of Berroc, where the box-tree grows most abundantly. His genealogy is traced in the following order. King Alfred was the son of King Aethelwulf, who was the son of Egbert, who was the son of Ealhmund, who was the son of Eafa, who was the son of Eoppa, who was the son of Ingild. Ingild, and Ine, the famous king of the West Saxons, were two brothers. Ine went to Rome, and there ending this life honorably, entered the heavenly kingdom, to reign there for ever with Christ. Ingild and Ine were the sons of Cenred, who was the son of Ceol-wald, who was the son of Cutha, who was the son of Cuthwine, who was the son of Ceawlin, who was the son of Cynric, who was

---

[2]The manuscript was designated Otho A. xii. For the Cotton fire and *Beowulf*, see pp. 126–27.

[3]Before Alfred's reign, the West Saxon kings were styled in a much less expansive fashion: charters and coins record phrases such as "king of the West Saxons" or "king of the Saxons" for prior rulers. Asser marks Alfred with a new status in his dedication to the *Life*, calling Alfred "ruler of all of the Christians of the island of Britain, king of the Angles and Saxons."

the son of Creoda, who was the son of Cerdic, who was the son of Elesa, who was the son of Gewis, from whom the Britons name all that nation Gewisse, who was the son of Brand, who was the son of Baeldaeg, who was the son of Woden, who was the son of Frithuwald, who was the son of Frealaf, who was the son of Frithuwulf, who was the son of Finn, who was the son of Godwulf, who was the son of Geat, which Geat the pagans long worshiped as a god. . . . Geat was the son of Taetwa, who was the son of Beaw, who was the son of Sceldwa, who was the son of Heremod, who was the son of Itermon, who was the son of Hathra, who was the son of Hwala, who was the son of Bedwig, who was the son of Seth, who was the son of Noah, who was the son of Lamech, who was the son of Methuselah, who was the son of Enoch, who was the son of Mahalaleel, who was the son of Cainan, who was the son of Enos, who was the son of Seth, who was the son of Adam.

14. There was in Mercia, in recent times, a certain valiant king, who was feared by all the kings and neighboring states around. His name was Offa,[4] and it was he who had the great rampart[5] made from sea to sea between Britain and Mercia. His daughter, named Eadburh, was married to Beorhtric, king of the West Saxons.[6] Immediately upon winning the king's affections and the control of almost all the kingdom, she began to live tyrannically like her father, and to abhor every man whom Beorhtric loved, and to do all things hateful to God and man, and to accuse all those whom she could before the king, and so to deprive them insidiously of their lives or power; and if she could not obtain the king's consent, she used to kill them by poison. This is known to have been the case with a certain young man beloved by the king, whom she poisoned, finding that the king would not listen to any accusation against him. It is said, moreover, that King Beorhtric unwittingly tasted of the poison, though the queen intended to give it to the young man only, and so both of them died.

[4]Offa was the king of Mercia from 757 to 796.

[5]Offa's Dyke, a remarkable earthwork running between Wales and England, can still be seen. For this and other defensive projects of the Mercian kingdom, see Cyril Fox, *Offa's Dyke. A Field Survey of the Western Frontier-Works of Mercia in the Seventh and Eighth Centuries A. D.* (1955).

[6]Keynes and Lapidge (1983, p. 236), note that this 789 marriage was "part of a pact between the kings of Wessex and Mercia."

22. He [Alfred] was loved by his father and mother, and indeed by everyone, and above all, by his brothers, and was educated entirely at the court of the king. As he advanced through the years of infancy and youth, his form appeared more comely than that of his brothers; in manner, in speech, and in behavior, he was more graceful than they. His noble nature implanted in him from the cradle a love of wisdom above all things; but, with shame be it spoken, by the unworthy neglect of his parents and teachers, he remained illiterate until he was twelve years old or more; but, he listened with serious attention to the English poems which he often heard recited, and easily retained them in his memory.[7] He was an avid hunter in all its branches, and hunted with great success; for skill and good fortune in this art, as in all others, are among the gifts of God, as we also have often witnessed.

23. On a certain day, therefore, his mother was showing him and his brother a book of English poetry, which she held in her hand, and she said, "Whichever of you shall learn this book the fastest shall have it for his own." Stimulated by these words, or rather by the divine inspiration, and attracted by the beautifully illuminated letter at the beginning of the book, Alfred spoke before all his brothers, who, though his seniors in age, were not so in ability, and answered, "Will you really give that book to the one of us who can first understand and recite it to you?" At this his mother smiled with pleasure, and reassured him, saying, "Yes, I will." Immediately he took the book out of her hand, and went to his teacher to learn it, and in due time he brought it back to his mother and recited it.

24. After this he learned the daily course, that is, the services of the hours, and then certain psalms, and many prayers. He collected these in a certain book[8] which he kept by him day and night, as we ourselves have seen; amid all the bustle and business of this present life, he took it around with him to assist in prayers

---

[7]From this statement and that in Chapter 23, it seems that Alfred could neither read in the vernacular nor in Latin in 860, but relied on the services of readers.

[8]Asser refers to Alfred's "little book" as an *enchiridion*, or "hand-book," and a *hand boc* of Alfred is mentioned by William of Malmesbury (*Gesta Pontificum*, c. 1125). Unfortunately, this little book, which clearly contained psalms and prayers and probably other sorts of excerpts, does not survive.

and was inseparable from it. But, sad to say, he could not gratify his most ardent wish to learn the liberal arts, because, as he said, there were no good scholars at that time in all the kingdom of the West Saxons.[9]

91. Now King Alfred was pierced by many nails of tribulation, even though he was invested with royal power: for from the twentieth year of his age to the present year, which is his forti-eth-fifth, he has been constantly afflicted with most severe attacks of an unknown disease, so that he has not had even a single hour's peace either from suffering the pain which it causes or from the dread which is cast over him by the fear of its coming. Moreover, the constant invasions of foreign nations, by which he was continually harassed by land and sea, without any interval of quiet, were a just cause of disquiet. What shall I say of his repeated expeditions against the pagans, his wars, and the incessant responsibilities of government? What of his daily involvement with foreign nations, from the Mediterranean sea to the farthest end of Ireland? For we have seen and read letters, accompanied by presents, which were sent to him by Elias, the patriarch of Jerusalem.[10] What shall I say of the cities and towns to be rebuilt and of others which he built, where none had been before? What of the royal halls and chambers, wonderfully erected by his command, of stone and wood? Of the royal residences constructed of masonry, removed from their old position and handsomely rebuilt by the king's command in more fitting places? And what about—besides his own disease—the terrible confusion and disorder of his own people who would undertake on their own little or no work, though it was for the common necessity of the kingdom? Yet he alone, once he had taken the helm of his kingdom, sustained by the divine aid, strove to steer his ship, laden with much wealth, into the safe and much desired

[9]As a result of Alfred's educational reforms, learning was revived in England. Alfred's devotion to learning and to the duties of Christian rulership inspired him to translate (either in whole or in part) from Latin to the vernacular four important texts: Boethius's *Consolation of Philosophy*, Augustine's *Soliloquies*, the first fifty psalms of the Psalter, and Gregory the Great's *Pastoral Care* (in the preface of this work, Alfred lays out his plan for educational reform).

[10]Elias, patriarch of Jerusalem, c. 879–907, sought help from rulers in the West in repairing his churches. Alfred could have received such a letter (see Keynes and Lapidge 1983, p. 270).

harbor of his homeland, though almost all his crew were tired, and suffered them not to faint or hesitate, though sailing amid the roiling whirlpools of this present life. For all his bishops, ealdormen, nobles, and his thegns most dear to him, and his reeves, who, next to God and the king, the control of the kingdom seems to belong by right, he most wisely convinced and bound to his own will by gently instructing, flattering, urging, commanding them and, after long patience, by severely punishing the disobedient and by showing in every way hatred of vulgar folly and obstinacy. But if, among the exhortations of the king, his orders were not carried out because of the slackness of the people or because things begun late in time of need were unfinished and of no use to those who undertook them—for I may tell of fortresses[11] ordered by him and still not begun or begun too late to be completed—and the enemy forces broke in by land or sea or, as often happens, on every side, the opponents of the royal ordinances were ashamed with a vain repentance when on the brink of ruin. For, on the testimony of Scripture, I call that repentance vain by which numberless men sorrow when afflicted with the many evil deeds they have wrought. But though—alas, the pity of it!—they are sadly afflicted through this and moved to tears by the loss of fathers, wives, children, servants, slaves, handmaids, and their labor and all of their goods, what help is hateful repentance, when it cannot succor their slain kinsmen, nor redeem those who are captive from odious captivity, nor even can it help them themselves, who have escaped, seeing that they have nothing with which to sustain their own lives? They, grievously afflicted, then repent when it was too late, and regret that they have neglected the king's commands, and they praise the royal wisdom with one voice, and promise to fulfil what they had before refused, that is, concerning the building of fortresses and other things for the common good of the whole kingdom.

[11]Besides these references in Asser, archaeological evidence indicates that Alfred had built many *burhs* or fortresses south of the Thames. This network of fortifications is also described in a document called the *Burghal Hidage*, which was made during the reign of Edward the Elder, Alfred's son. The fortresses appear to be distributed in such a way that most people in Wessex lived within twenty miles of such a fortress.

Aethelweard
from *Chronicle (Chronicon)*[1]

Aethelweard, an important ealdorman known to have witnessed Anglo-Saxon charters, negotiated for the English side in making peace with Olaf Tryggvason in 994, and sponsored by Aelfric, wrote this Latin history sometime after 975. Largely a translation of the Anglo-Saxon Chronicle, Aethelweard's history shows a pronounced interest in West Saxon royal genealogy. Aethelweard probably died shortly after 998, the last time he is found as a witness. Note the presence of names found in Beowulf, *such as Beow, Scyld, and Sceaf, and the arrival of a nation-founding boy by ship in this family tree of the Anglo-Saxon king Aethelwulf.*

Book III, Chapter 3

. . . And then King Aethelwulf died after a year, and his body lies in the city of Winchester. The abovementioned king was the son of King Ecgberht, and his grandfather was Ealhmund, his great-grandfather Eafa, his great-great grandfather Eoppa, his great-great-great grandfather Ingild, brother of Ine, king of the West Saxons who died in Rome, and these kings originated from Cenred. Cenred was the son of Ceolwald. His grandfather was Cuthwine, his great grandfather Ceawlin, his great-great grandfather Cynric, his great-great-great grandfather Cerdic, who was the first possessor of the western region of Britain after he had overcome the armies of the Britons. His father was Elesa, his grandfather Esla, his great grandfather Gewis, his great-great grandfather Wig, his great-great-great grandfather Freawine, his sixth father Frithogar, his seventh Brond, his eighth Baldr, his ninth Woden, his tenth Frithowald, his eleventh Frealaf, his twelfth Frithowulf, his thirteenth Fin, his fourteenth Godwulf, his fifteenth Geat, his sixteenth Tetwa, his seventeenth Beow, his eighteenth Scyld, his nineteenth Sceaf. And this Sceaf arrived on one light ship in the island of the ocean which is called Skaney, with arms all around him. He was a very young boy and unknown to the people of that land, but he was received by them, and they guarded him with diligent attention as one who belonged to them,

---

[1]This translation is indebted to the scholarship of Alistair Campbell's *Chronicon Æthelweardi: The Chronicle of Æthelweard* (1962).

and they elected him king. From his family King Aethelwulf derived his descent. And the number of fifty-five years had passed since Ecgberht began to reign.

William of Malmesbury
from *About the Deeds of the English Kings (Gesta regum Anglorum)*[1]

William of Malmesbury was a monk at Malmesbury Abbey from the time he was a child until his death in c. 1143. His most famous work is this five-book history, reputedly inspired by Queen Matilda asking him to delineate her relationship to the founder of Malmesbury, Aldhelm (c. 640–c. 710), an Anglo-Latin writer of great power and influence. Though completed in 1126, William revised his history during the 1130s. His plan was to supply an account of English history from the death of Bede in 735 into his own times. Toward the end of his life, William wrote History novella, *which covers the period of English history from the reign of King Stephen through 1142. The genealogy of King Aethelwulf, containing allusions to the story of Scyld told in the prologue to* Beowulf, *may be usefully compared with that recorded by Aethelweard.*

Book II, Section 116

. . . From this king [Aethelwulf], the English chronicles trace the line of the generation of their kings upwards, even to Adam, as we know Luke the evangelist has done with respect to our Lord Jesus; and which, perhaps, it will not be superfluous for me to do, though it is to be apprehended that the utterance of barbarous names may shock the ears of persons unused to them. Aethelwulf was the son of Ecgbert, Ecgbert of Elmund, Elmund of Eafa, Eafa of Eoppa, Eoppa was the son of Ingild, the brother of king Ine, who were both sons of Cenred; Cenred of Ceolwald, Ceolwald of Cutha, Cutha of Cuthwin, Cuthwin of Cealwin, Cealwin of Cynric, Cynric of Cre-

---

[1]This translation into English is adapted from Sharpe's *Chronicle of the Kings of England* (1904).

oding, Creoding of Cerdic, who was the first king of the West Saxons; Cerdic of Elesa, Elesa of Esla, Esla of Gewis, Gewis of Wig, Wig of Freawin, Freawin of Frithogar, Frithogar of Brond, Brond of Beldeg, Beldeg of Woden; and from him, as we have remarked, proceeded the kings of many nations. Woden was the son of Frithowald, Frithowald of Frealaf, Frealaf of Finn, Finn of Godulfus, Godulfus of Geat, Geat of Taetwa, Taetwa of Beow, Beow of Sceld, Sceld of Sceaf. He as a small child, so they say, was driven ashore in a boat without oars on a certain island of Germany called Scandza, of which Jordanes, the historian of the Goths, speaks. He was asleep, and at his head was laid a sheaf of corn. For this reason, he was given the name Sceaf and was received as a miracle by the men of that region and was carefully reared. As an adult, he reigned in the town which was then called Sleswic, but is now in fact called Hedeby.[2] That region is called Old Anglia; from there the Angles came to Britain, and it lay between the Saxons and the Goths. Sceaf was the son of Heremod, Heremod of Itermon, Itermon of Hathra, Hathra of Guala, Guala of Bedwig, Bedwig of Streaf, and he, as they say, was the son of Noah, born in the ark.

Sven Aggesen

from *A Brief History of the Kings of Denmark*
(Brevis historia regum Dacie)[1]

> *Sven Aggesen, who was born about 1140–50, wrote a "brief history" of Denmark's kings that ends in 1185. The work was probably sponsored by Archbishop Absalon (c. 1128–1201) at about the same time his younger Danish contemporary Saxo was writing a longer history. The two historians knew of each other's work. The medieval manuscript of the history has been lost, surviving only in a seventeenth-century copy. This history of the*

---

[2]Formerly in the kingdom of Denmark and mentioned in a work by King Alfred, this important trading center for goods and for slaves was sometimes called the "Baltic bridge" on account of its key commercial position. Hedeby was apparently destroyed by fire in 1050.

[1]In some historical traditions, Denmark is called "Dacia," a result of a medieval geographical misunderstanding.

Danish kings contains many figures present in Beowulf; *please see the footnotes to this excerpt.*

Chapter I: About the First Kings of Denmark

Skiold[2] is said to have been the first one to have ruled the Danes. And, as we have alluded to his name, the reason that he was known by such a name was because he commendably guarded all of the boundaries of the kingdom by the protection which his defense afforded. It was from him that, according to the Icelandic fashion, our kings took the title of Skioldungs. Skiold left behind him two heirs to the kingdom, namely Frothi and Haldanus.[3] In the course of time, these brothers quarreled with each other because of their ambition to rule, and Haldanus, having slain his brother, obtained the kingship. He had begotten a son as heir to his kingdom, namely Helghi,[4] who, because of his exceptional courage and energy, always led the life of a sea-pirate. Since he depopulated the coastal territories of every one of the surrounding kingdoms with his raiding fleet and made them subject to his rule, he was given the title Sea-King. Rolf[5] Kraki attained the kingdom in regnal succession. He was outstanding for his inherited courage; he was slain at Lethra,[6] which at that time existed as a very famous royal residence, but is now barely inhabited, being one of the humblest villages in the neighborhood of the city of Roskilde. After him, there ruled his son Rokil,[7] known by the name Slaghenback. He who succeeded in the kingly line was known, because of his physical agility, as Frothi the Bold. His son and heir Weremundus succeeded to the kingdom. He was so outstanding for the virtue of prudence that he was nicknamed "the Prudent." He begot a son named Uffo.[8]

---

[2] "Skiold" means "shield." Compare Scyld in *Beowulf*.

[3] Healfdene in *Beowulf*.

[4] Halga in *Beowulf*.

[5] Hrothulf in *Beowulf*.

[6] The Latinized version of Old Norse "Hleiðargarðr," a Scandinavian royal hall known from Icelandic sources, located near the Danish town now called Lejre on the island of Sjælland (Zealand). It has been argued that this is where Heorot, if Heorot were an actual place, would have stood. See Klaeber (1950, p. xxxvii).

[7] Hrethric in *Beowulf*.

[8] The story of Uffo, the Latinized version of the name Offa, is then narrated.

Saxo Grammaticus
The Deeds of the Danes (Gesta Danorum)[1]

Like Sven Aggesen's History, *this account of Danish history by Saxo (fl. 1185–1208) was sponsored by Archbishop Absalon, who claims to have known both men. Saxo may have been either a clerk or a canon at Lund, where Absalon was archbishop from 1178 to 1201. Although he mentions his indebtedness to Absalon in his preface, he dedicates* Deeds *to Anders Sunesen, Absalon's successor as archbishop at Lund. Completing his work sometime between 1208 and 1219, Saxo writes his history* ab origine gentis *("from the origin of the nation"), dividing it into three parts: the legendary history of Denmark in Books I–IX; the history of ninth-century Denmark to Saxo's own times through Book XIII; and the nearly eyewitness reportage of his own age in Books XIV–XVI. In addition to using likely sources such as Bede and Paul the Deacon's* History of the Langobards, *Saxo also employs and discusses the vernacular sources he used. These sources are of three broad types: narrative poems in the vernacular (probably Old Danish and West Norse); Icelandic history; and Archbishop Absalon himself. These vernacular sources are of great interest for studying* Beowulf *because they share a narrative and cultural reservoir with the Old English poem. The selections from Saxo's* Deeds *begins with the story of the exemplary king Skiold, the Scyld ("shield") of* Beowulf; *the second excerpt is the tale of the dragon-killing champion Frode; and last is the story of Amleth—the original of Shakespeare's* Hamlet, Prince of Denmark, *whose narrative of rulership bridges Denmark and the British Isles.*

Book I: 11, 12[2]

. . . Skiold, his [Lother's] son, inherited his natural bent, but not his behavior; avoiding his inborn perversity by great discretion in his tender years, and thus escaping all traces of his father's taint. So he

---

[1]This English translation is adopted from O. Elton's *The First Nine Books of the Danish History of Saxo Grammaticus* (1893). A corrected modern translation and commentary is Davidson and Fisher, *Saxo Grammaticus: The History of the Danes, Books I–IX* (1979–80).

[2]These numbers refer to Holder's nineteenth–century edition of Saxo and are retained from the Elton translation.

appropriated what was alike the more excellent and the earlier share of the family character; for he wisely departed from his father's sins, and became a happy counterpart of his grandsire's virtues. This man was famous in his youth among the huntsmen of his father for his conquest of a monstrous beast: a marvelous incident, which augured his future prowess. For he chanced to obtain leave from his guardians, who were rearing him very carefully, to go and see the hunting. A bear of extraordinary size met him; he had no spear, but with the girdle that he commonly wore he contrived to bind it, and gave it to his escort to kill. More than this, many champions of tried prowess were at the same time of his life vanquished by him singly; of these, Attal and Skat were renowned and famous. While but fifteen years of age, he was of unusual bodily size and displayed mortal strength in its perfection, and so mighty were the proofs of his powers that the rest of the kings of the Danes were called after him by a common title, the Skioldungs. Those who were wont to live an abandoned and flaccid life, and to sap their self-control by wantonness, this man vigilantly spurred to the practice of virtue in an active career. Thus the ripeness of Skiold's spirit outstripped the fulness of his strength, and he fought battles at which one of his tender years could scarce look on. And as he thus waxed in years and valor he beheld the perfect beauty of Alfhild, daughter of the King of the Saxons, sued for her hand, and, for her sake, in the sight of the armies of the Teutons and the Danes, challenged and fought with Skat, governor of Allemannia, and a suitor for the same maiden; whom he slew, afterwards crushing the whole nation of the Allemannians, and forcing them to pay tribute, they being subjugated by the death of their captain. Skiold was eminent for patriotism as well as arms. For he annulled unrighteous laws, and most heedfully executed whatsoever made for the amendment of his country's condition. Further, he regained by his virtue the realm that his father's wickedness had lost. He was the first to proclaim the law abolishing manumissions. A slave, to whom he had chanced to grant his freedom, had attempted his life by stealthy treachery, and he exacted a bitter penalty; as though it were just that the guilt of one freedman should be visited upon all. He paid off all men's debts from his own treasury, and contended, so to say, with all other monarchs in courage, bounty, and generous dealing. The sick he used to foster, and charitably gave medicines to those sore stricken; bearing witness that he had taken on him the care of his country and not of himself. He used to enrich his nobles not only with home taxes, but also with plunder taken in war; being wont to aver that the prize-money should flow to the soldiers, and the glory to the general.

Book II: 38–40

Hadding was succeeded by Frode, his son, whose fortunes were many and changeful. When he had passed the years of a stripling, he displayed the fulness of a warrior's prowess; and being loth that this should be spoilt by slothfulness, he sequestered his mind from delights and perseveringly constrained it to arms. Warfare having drained his father's treasury, he lacked a stock of pay to maintain his troops, and cast about diligently for the supplies that he required; and while thus employed, a man of the country met him and roused his hopes by the following strain: "Not far off is an island rising in delicate slopes, hiding treasure in its hills and ware of its rich booty. Here a noble pile is kept by the occupant of the mount, who is a snake wreathed in coils, doubled in many a fold, and with tail drawn out in winding whorls, shaking his manifold spirals and shedding venom. If thou wouldst conquer him, thou must use thy shield and stretch thereon bulls' hides, and cover thy body with the skins of kine, nor let thy limbs lie bare to the sharp poison; his slaver burns up what it bespatters. Though the three-forked tongue flicker and leap out of the gaping mouth, and with awful yawn menace ghastly wounds, remember to keep the daunt-less temper of thy mind; nor let the point of the jagged tooth trouble thee, nor the starkness of the beast, nor the venom spat from the swift throat. Though the force of his scales spurn thy spears, yet know there is a place under his lowest belly whither thou mayst plunge the blade; aim at this with thy sword, and thou shalt probe the snake to his center. Thence go fearless up to the hill, drive the mattock, dig and ransack the holes; soon fill thy pouch with trea-sure, and bring back to the shore thy craft laden."

Frode believed, and crossed alone to the island, loth to attack the beast with any stronger escort than that wherewith it was the custom for champions to attack. When it had drunk water and was repairing to its cave, its rough and sharp hide spurned the blow of Frode's steel. Also the darts that he flung against it rebounded idly, foiling the effort of the thrower. But when the hard back yielded not a whit, he noted the belly heedfully, and its softness gave entrance to the steel. The beast tried to retaliate by biting, but only struck the sharp point of its mouth upon the shield. Then it shot out its flickering tongue again and again, and gasped away life and venom together.

Book IV: 97–101

Amleth, when he had accomplished the slaughter of his stepfather, feared to expose his deed to the fickle judgment of his countrymen, and thought it well to lie in hiding till he had learnt what way the mob of the uncouth populace was tending. So the whole neighborhood, who had watched the blaze during the night, and in the morning desired to know the cause of the fire they had seen, perceived the royal palace fallen in ashes; and, on searching through its ruins, which were yet warm, found only some shapeless remains of burnt corpses. For the devouring flame had consumed everything so utterly that not a single token was left to inform them of the cause of such a disaster. Also they saw the body of Feng lying pierced by the sword, amid his blood-stained raiment. Some were seized with open anger, others with grief, and some with secret delight. One party bewailed the death of their leader, the other gave thanks that the tyranny of the fratricide was now laid at rest. Thus the occurrence of the king's slaughter was greeted by the beholders with diverse minds.

Amleth, finding the people so quiet, made bold to leave his hiding. Summoning those in whom he knew the memory of his father to be fast-rooted, he went to the assembly and there made a speech after this manner. [Here Amleth delivers a lengthy, impassioned speech.]

Every heart had been moved while the young man thus spoke; he affected some to compassion, and some even to tears. When the lamentation ceased, he was appointed king by prompt and general acclaim. For one and all rested their greatest hopes on his wisdom, since he had devised the whole of such an achievement with the deepest cunning, and accomplished it with the most astonishing contrivance. Many could have been seen marvelling how he had concealed so subtle a plan over so long a space of time.

After these deeds in Denmark, Amleth equipped three vessels, and went back to Britain to see his wife and her father. He had also enrolled in his service the flower of the warriors, and arrayed them very choicely, wishing to have everything now magnificently appointed, even as of old he had always worn contemptible gear, and to change all his old devotion to poverty for outlay on luxury.

He also had a shield made for him, whereon the whole series of his exploits, beginning with his earliest youth, was painted in exquisite designs. This he bore as a record of his deeds of prowess, and gained great increase of fame thereby. Here were to be seen depicted the slaying of Horwendil; the fratricide and incest of Feng; the infamous uncle, the whimsical nephew; the shapes of the hooked stakes; the stepfather suspecting, the stepson dissembling; the various temptations offered, and the woman brought to beguile him; the gaping wolf; the finding of the rudder; the passing of the sand; the entering of the wood; the putting of the straw through the gadfly; the warning of the youth by the tokens; and the privy dealings with the maiden after the escort was eluded. And likewise could be seen the picture of the palace; the queen there with her son; the slaying of the eavesdropper; and how, after being killed, he was boiled down, and so dropped into the sewer, and so thrown out to the swine; how his limbs were strewn in the mud, and so left for the beasts to finish. Also it could be seen how Amleth surprised the secret of his sleeping attendants, how he erased the letters, and put new characters in their places; how he disdained the banquet and scorned the drink; how he condemned the king and taxed the Queen with faulty behavior. There was also represented the hanging of the envoys, and the young man's wedding; then the voyage back to Denmark; the festive celebration of the funeral rites; Amleth, in answer to questions, pointing to the sticks in place of his attendants, acting as cupbearer, and purposely drawing his sword and pricking his fingers; the sword riveted through, the swelling cheers of the banquet, the dance growing fast and furious; the hangings flung upon the sleepers, then fastened with the interlacing crooks, and wrapped tightly round them as they slumbered; the brand set to the mansion, the burning of the guests, the royal palace consumed with fire and tottering down; the visit to the sleeping-room of Feng, the theft of his sword, the useless one set in its place; and the king slain with his own sword's point by his stepson's hand. All this was there, painted upon Amleth's battle-shield by a careful craftsman in the choicest of handiwork; he copied truth in his figures, and embodied real deeds in his outlines. Moreover, Amleth's followers, to increase the splendor of their presence, wore shields which were gilt over.

From the Old English

A facsimile of British Library, Cotton Vitellius A xv., fol. 132r

Reading Beowulf

A line-by-line transcription of the poem's first leaf[1]

1 HWÆT WE GARDE
2 na ingear dagum. þeod cyninga
3 þrym ge frunon huða æþelingas elle[n][2]
4 fremedon. oft scyld scefing sceaþe[na]
5 þreatum monegum[3] maegþum meado setla
6 ofteah edsode eorl syððan ærest wear[ð]
7 fea sceaft funden he þæs frofre geba[d]
8 weox under wolcnum weord myndum þah
9 oð þæt him æghwylc þara ymb sittendra
10 ofer hron rade hyran scolde gomban
11 gyldan þæt wæs god cyning. ðæm eafera wæs
12 æfter cenned geong in geardum þone god
13 sende folce tofrofre fyren ðearfe on
14 geat þæt hie ær drugon aldor[le]ase. lange
15 hwile him þæs lif frea wuldres wealdend
16 worold are for geaf. beowulf wæs breme
17 blæd wide sprang scylda[s] eaf[er]a scede
18 landum in. Swa sceal [g]e[ong] [gu]ma gode
19 ge wyrcean fromum feoh [giftu]m on fæ[der]

---

[1] See the facing page facsimile of fol. 132r (formerly numbered fol. 129r) of the *Beowulf* manuscript.

[2] Letters supplied in square brackets are conjectural: they may be partly visible and are filled in based on what word fits the sense of the poem, given the amount of space available to write a letter or letters at that place in the manuscript; or they may represent scholarly emendation of a damaged and occasionally mistaken manuscript copy of the poem.

[3] Abbreviations found in the manuscript are expanded using italics in this transcription.

The Manuscript Context

The only copy of Beowulf *is found in The British Library's Cotton Vitellius A xv., the first leaf of which is reproduced on p. 124. Sir Robert Bruce Cotton (1571–1631), the greatest collector of medieval manuscripts after the dissolution of the monasteries in England, owned the manuscript, which was later donated to The British Museum. The manuscript as it now stands includes within its binding several parts that were not originally conceived of as belonging to a single anthology. The first part of the present manuscript contains twelfth-century material that runs from fols. 4 to 93.[1] The second, older, part of the present manuscript contains five items from fols. 94 to 209, the fourth item of which is the poem* Beowulf.[2] *Two of the five items in this part of the manuscript are incomplete. The five items are: (1) a prose life of St. Christopher in Old English, lacking a beginning; (2) an Old English prose* Marvels of the East, *which includes colored drawings; (3) an Old English prose* Letter of Alexander to Aristotle; *(4) the Old English poem* Beowulf *and (5) the Old English poem* Judith, *which is lacking both a beginning and an ending. Scholars have proposed histories of this second part of the manuscript that strive to understand in what sense it represents a coherent collection.[3] These proposals rest on detailed examinations of the codex itself and on linguistic analysis, but as closely studied as this important problem has been, no single account of the second part of the manuscript has emerged.*

Some questions about Beowulf *and the manuscript in which it has been found may never be settled because of a 1731 fire that severely reduced Sir Robert's collection of manuscripts before they could be safely housed in the British Museum. It is estimated that some 200 manuscripts, about one-quarter of those in Sir Robert's donation to the museum, were either destroyed or damaged. Kevin Kiernan quotes from a contemporary account of*

---

[1]That part of the manuscript, which contains four items in Old English, is sometimes referred to as the Southwick Codex.

[2]In the new foliation, *Beowulf* runs from fol. 132r to 197v; in the old foliation, from fol. 129r to 193v. This part of the manuscript is sometimes referred to as the Nowell Codex after its original owner, Laurence Nowell (1520–76). Kevin Kiernan has argued forcefully that *Beowulf* at one time stood alone as a separate manuscript (see Kiernan 1996, pp. 171–278).

[3]Orchard (1995) sees the second, older part of the Cotton Vitellius A xv. as a collection that coheres in terms of both subject and theme.

this devastating event in his meticulous examination of the manuscript containing Beowulf:

> On *Saturday* Morning *October* 23, 1731. About two o'Clock, a great Smoak [sic] was perceived by Dr. *Bentley*, and the rest of the Family at *Ashburnham-House*, which soon after broke out into a Flame. It began from a wooden Mantle-Tree's taking Fire, which lay across a Stove-Chimney, that was under to Room, where the MSS. of the Royal and *Cottonian* Libraries were lodged, and was communicated to that Room by the Wainscot, and by pieces of Timber, that stood perpendicularly upon each end of the Mantle-Tree. They were in hopes of first to have put a Stop to the Fire by throwing Water upon the Pieces of Timber and Wainscot, where it first broke out, and therefore did not begin to remove the Books as soon as they otherwise would have done. But the Fire prevailing, notwithstanding the Means used to extinguish it, Mr. *Casley* the Deputy-Librarian took Care in the first Place to remove the famous *Alexandrian* MS. and the Books under the Head of *Augustus* in the *Cottonian* Library, as being esteemed as the most valuable amongst the Collection. Several entire Presses with the Books in them were also removed; but the Fire increasing still, and the Engines sent for not coming as soon as could be wished, and several of the Backs of the Presses being already on Fire, they were obliged to be broke open, and the Books, as many as could be, were thrown out of the Windows.[4]

As a result of this fire, which Beowulf *at least survived, many edges of the leaves containing the poem were burnt or singed (see the facsimile of the first leaf of the poem for an example of this damage). Before the manuscript underwent modern conservation, this damage resulted in some of the parchment falling away and with that, some of the letters in the poem crumbling away, too. In the nineteenth century, each of the leaves of the poem was mounted within a paper frame in order to save the poem from further disintegration, but this effort meant that some letters toward the edges of the leaves were covered by the protective paper frames, and these letters have only recently been recovered, thanks to advancements in photographic techniques.*

---

[4]This account is quoted in Kevin Kiernan (1996, p. 68), who derives it from "A Narrative of the Fire which happened at *Ashburnham-House, Oct.* 23, 1731, and of the Methods used for preserving and recovering the Manuscripts of the Royal and *Cottonian* Libraries" (BL MS 24,932, p. 11).

With so many grave uncertainties about what is quite literally present in the poem and with the fragility of it as an object
demonstrated so dramatically, what can scholars say for certain
about Beowulf in its manuscript context? A study of the handwriting in which the poem was copied shows that two scribes
copied Beowulf.[5] A great deal of evidence found in the manuscript itself makes it almost certainly true that these two scribes
were copying from an exemplar that had already been written
and was on the desk before them; the one surviving copy of
Beowulf, then, was not made by the author himself. Study of the
handwriting of the two scribes, the construction of the manuscript itself, and the linguistic habits of these two scribes led the
great scholar Neil Ker to date Beowulf to late in the tenth century
or early in the eleventh. David Dumville limits the date further: to
between c. 997 and 1016, the second half of the reign of Aethelred,
who ruled from 978–1016.

We may know something about how the audience of
Beowulf at the time that it was copied thought about the poem, for
Beowulf is divided into sections which the Anglo-Saxons called
fitts, and these sections are marked in the manuscript, usually by
both a capital letter at the start of the fitt and a roman numeral.
Although the scribes made some errors in applying this system of
division to the poem, Beowulf has forty-three fitts. Although it
seems likely that these divisions say something about the poet's
conception of the narrative, it has also been argued that the divisions were breaks that were put in by the scribes themselves and
thus show nothing whatever about the narrative of Beowulf.

Comparative Translations of the
First Twenty-Five Lines of *Beowulf*

*From the first excerpts translated into English by Sharon Turner in
1805 to the version by Sullivan and Murphy in this* Longman Cultural Edition, Beowulf *has attracted scores of translations in what*

---

[5]The first scribe copied the *Life of St. Christopher,* the *Wonders of the East,* the *Letter of Alexander to Aristotle,* and *Beowulf,* lines 1–1939 (in the Old English text).
The second scribe copied the rest of *Beowulf* and *Judith.*

Marijane Osborn calls a "quest for familiarization."[1] *The passages presented below illustrate nine different translators reading the first twenty-five lines of* Beowulf. *Although nothing in* Beowulf *comes easy for the translator, the first twenty-five lines of the poem—its so-called introduction or prologue—are relatively free of insurmountable cruces. Yet these crucial lines call the reader to attention in particular ways that are both direct and nuanced, set forth the sound of the poem, and establish some of its most compelling themes.*

Each translator has tried to unlock the text in a different way. Turner continued to correct his translated excerpts from Beowulf *through his 1820 history of the Anglo-Saxons, but despite his enthusiasm for that age, his version of the Old English poem is inaccurate. Kemble's prose translation is clear and correct, allowing the first serious study of the poem. A similarly cogent reading of the poem is found in C. L. Wrenn's edition, which includes a forthright prose translation by John R. Clark Hall and, notably, an essay by J. R. R. Tolkien called "On Translating* Beowulf.*"*[2] *Gummere, Lehmann, and Morgan aim for* Beowulf's *aural effect, translating the text into modern English, but imitating its meter in different ways. In a 1965* Saturday Review *(London) article, poet Kenneth Rexroth called Morgan's modern English alliterative four-stress line the most "elegant" of the translations of* Beowulf *to date. Waterhouse uses blank verse to achieve the epic majesty of the poem's pace. In a striking demonstration of neo-medievalism, Morris and Wyatt antique their translation through their choice of archaic and dialectal words; their Kelmscott Press edition also tries in all of the particulars of its construction to achieve the look of a unique hand-produced book—a neo-medieval manuscript. Greenfield emphasizes making* Beowulf *"readable," as the title of his version announces, and his solid scholarship is clearly heard in his translation's strong rhythmic line and in lexical and syntactical choices that underscore the wordplay he finds in the original. Many other excellent and provocative translations of* Beowulf *are now in print; for these, please see the first section of Further Reading, p. 229.*

---

[1]Marijane Osborn in Bjork and Niles (1997, p. 341). See her chapter entitled "Translations, Versions, and Illustrations" in the Bjork and Niles handbook for an excellent review of the most important translations and adaptations of *Beowulf*, including thirteen plates that have been used to illustrate the poem.

[2]This essay, essential reading for its deeply informed statements about translating the poem for the heart and head, is also collected in *The Monsters and the Critics and Other Essays* (Tolkien 1983, pp. 49–71).

Sharon Turner[1]

from *The History of the Manners, Landed Property, Government, Laws, Poetry, Literature, Religion, and Language of the Anglo-Saxons* (1805)

[Book VI, Chapter IV, "History of the Poetry, &c. of the Anglo-Saxons"]

The most interesting remains of the Anglo-Saxon poetry, which time has suffered to reach us, are contained in the Anglo-Saxon poem in the Cotton library, Vitellius, A. 15. Wanley[2] mentions it as a poem in which "seem to be described the wars which one Beowulf, a Dane of the royal race of the Scyldingi waged against the reguli of Sweden." [Here Turner notes, "Wanley Catal. Saxon MS. 218."] But this account of the contents of the MS. is incorrect. It is a composition more curious and important. It is a narration of the attempt of Beowulf to wreck the fæhthe[3] or deadly feud on Hrothgar, for a homicide which he had committed. It may be called an Anglo-Saxon epic poem. It abounds with speeches which Beowulf and Hrothgar and their partisans make to each other, with much occasional description and sentiment.

It begins with a proemium,[4] which introduces its hero Beowulf[5] to our notice:

> BEOWULF was illustrious;
> The fruit wide sprang
> Of the progeny of the Scyldæ;

[1]Sharon Turner (1768–1847), a British historian, was the first to publish a part of *Beowulf*, which appeared in his multivolume survey of Anglo-Saxon England, printed between 1799 and 1805. Although Turner's excerpts from *Beowulf* are deeply flawed, his comprehensive history of the period for which he used the Cotton manuscripts as evidence did a great deal to stimulate interest in Anglo-Saxon England in the nineteenth century.

[2]Humfrey Wanley (1672–1726), whose "catalogue of ancient northern books preserved in the libraries in English," published in 1705 as part of George Hickes's two-volume study, is extremely valuable as a record of all of the Cotton manuscripts, including the one containing *Beowulf*, before the fire of 1731.

[3]The Old English word *fæhð*, meaning enmity, hostility, or feud. Turner quotes the word in its accusative singular form rather than in the nominative.

[4]From the Greek word for an introduction or prologue.

[5]This is Beowulf the Dane, son of Scyld, and not Beowulf the Geat, who is the hero of the poem. The sort of confusion that Turner suffers here is often corrected by emending this "Beowulf" to "Beow." See, in this translation, note 10, p. 4.

> The shade of the lands
> In Swascedi.
>
> HIM in his time again,
> As they were accustomed,
> His voluntary companions,
> His people followed
> When he knew of battle.
> With deeds of praise,
> Every where among the nations
> Shall the hero flourish.[6]

John M. Kemble

from *A Translation of the Anglo-Saxon Poem of Beowulf with a Copious Preface and Philological Notes* (1837)

Lo! we have learned by tradition the majesty of the Gar-Danes, of the mighty kings in days of yore, how the noble men perfected valour. Oft did Scyld the son of Scéf tear the mead-thrones away from the hosts of his foes, from many tribes; the earl terrified them, after he first was found an out-cast. He therefore abode in comfort, he waxed under the welkin, he flourished with dignities, until each one of the surrounding *peoples* over the whale's path must obey him, *must* pay *him* tribute: That was a good king! To him was afterwards offspring born, young in *his* dwelling-places, whom God sent to the people for *their* comfort; he knew the evil-need which they before had suffered for a long while, *when they were* princeless: to him on this account the Lord of life, wielder of glory, gave worldly prosperity. Beówulf was famous; widely spread the glory of Scyld's offspring in the divided lands. So shall a war-prince work with benefits, with prudent gifts of money, *while yet* in his father's support, that to himself in turn, in his old age, welcome comrades may resort, then, when war may come *upon him:* supported by his people, a man shall flourish in any tribe, with praiseworthy deeds.

---

[6]Turner's excerpt covers lines 18 to 25 from the Old English text of the poem.

William Morris and A. J. Wyatt

from *The Tale of Beowulf*[1] (1895)

THE STORY OF BEOWULF

I. And first of the kindred of Hrothgar[2]
What! we of the Spear-Danes of yore days, so was it
That we learn'd of the fair fame of Kings of the folks
And the athelings a-faring in framing of valour.
Oft then Scyld the Sheafson from the hosts of the scathers[,]
from kindreds a many the mead-settles tore[;]
It was then the earl fear'd them, sithence was he first
found bare and all-lacking; so solace he bided[,]
Wax'd under the welkin in worship to thrive[,]
Until it was so that the round-about sitters
All over the whale-road must hearken his will
And yield him the tribute. A good king was that.
By whom then thereafter a son was begotten,
A youngling in garth, whom the great God sent thither
To foster the folk; & their crime-need he felt
The load that lay on them while lordless they lived
for a long while and long. He therefore, the Life-lord[,]
The Wielder of glory, world's worship he gave him:
Brim Beowulf[3] waxed, and wide the weal upsprang

---

[1]The Kelmscott Press was founded in 1891 by William Morris (1834–96) in association with Sir Emery Walker (1851–1933). During its eight years of operation, the Press printed some fifty books, using redesigned Roman types of the fifteenth century and principles of medieval craftsmanship in book design and production. *The Tale of Beowulf* reflects these values and begins with a breathtaking double-page design: an ornate floral title page on the left facing the opening lines of the poem on the right page, which are embellished with floral designs, a rubricated subtitle (a "rubrication," from the Latin *rubrica* for "red," is a heading, often written in red ink), and a decorated initial. The volume is bound in a vellum wrapper fastened with linen tapes. Besides a translation of the poem, the volume contains other aids to studying *Beowulf*: an "Argument" or summary of the poem, an index entitled "Persons and Places," and a glossary entitled "Meanings of Words Not Commonly Used Now." A note on p. 11 says that the book was printed on January 10, 1895. The copy excerpted from here is owned by Princeton University, Rare Books and Manuscripts Division of Firestone Library, and was presented by Mr. J. S. Morgan.

[2]Rubricated as it might have been in a medieval manuscript.

[3]Here Morris and Wyatt add a rubricated note in the left margin: "Beowulf the Scylding, not Beowulf the Geat of whom is told this tale[.]"

Of the offspring of Scyld in the parts of the Scede-lands.
Such wise shall a youngling with wealth be a-working
With goodly fee-gifts toward the friends of his father,
That after in eld-days shall ever bide with him,
Fair fellows well-willing when wendeth the war-tide,
Their lief lord a-serving. By praise-deeds it shall be
That in each and all kindreds a man shall have thriving.

Francis B. Gummere

from *The Oldest English Epic: Beowulf, Finnsburg,*
Waldere, Deor, Widsith, and the German Hildebrand (1909)

BEOWULF
PRELUDE OF THE FOUNDER OF THE DANISH HOUSE

Lo, praise of the prowess of people-kings
of spear-armed Danes, in days long sped,
we have heard, and what honor the athelings won!
Oft Scyld the Scefing from squadroned foes,
from many a tribe, the mead-bench tore,
awing the earls. Since erst he lay
friendless, a foundling, fate repaid him:
for he waxed under welkin, in wealth he throve,
till before him the folk, both far and near,
who house by the whale-path, heard his mandate,
gave him gifts: a good king he!
To him an heir was afterward born,
a son in his halls, whom heaven sent
to favor the folk, feeling their woe
that erst they had lacked an earl for leader
so long a while; the Lord endowed him,
the Wielder of Wonder, with world's renown.
Famed was this Beowulf: far flew the boast of him,
son of Scyld, in the Scandian lands.
So becomes it a youth to quit him well
with his father's friends, by fee and gift,
that to aid him, agéd, in after days,
come warriors willing, should war draw nigh,
liegemen loyal: by lauded deeds
shall an earl have honor in every clan.

C. L. Wrenn (editor)

from *Beowulf and the Finnsburg Fragment: A Translation into Modern English Prose by John R. Clark Hall* (1940)

Lo! We have heard of the glory of the kings of the people of the Spear-Danes in days of yore—how those princes did valorous deeds!

Often Scyld scefing took mead-benches away from troops of foes, from many peoples. He terrified the nobles, after he was first found helpless; he met with consolation for that, increased under the heavens and throve in honour, until each one of those who dwelt around, across the whale's road, had to obey him, and to pay him tribute. A noble king was he!

Later, a son was born to him, a young child in his courts, whom God sent the people for their help; He perceived the deep distress which they, lacking a lord, long had suffered in the past. To him, therefore, the Prince of Life, the glorious Ruler, granted worldly honour; Beowulf the son of Scyld, was renowned, his fame spread widely in the North-lands. So ought a young man to compass by noble deeds, by liberal gifts in his father's possession, that afterwards, in later years, willing companions may stand by him,—that men may do him service when war comes. By commendable deeds a man shall thrive in every people!

Mary E. Waterhouse

from *Beowulf in Modern English: A Translation in Blank Verse* (1949)

Lo, of the Spear Danes' might in days of old
And of the kings of men have we heard tell,
How princes then their deeds of glory wrought.

Often Scyld Scefing from his hosts of foes,
From many clans, captured their banquet halls
And awed their chiefs, since first he was discovered
A helpless child. For that he was consoled,
Throve under heaven, prospered in dignity,
Till the surrounding peoples every one
Beyond leviathan's pathway must obey

And yield him tribute; he was a good king.
To him in course of time a child was born,
A young son in his dwelling, whom God sent
As comfort to the people; He perceived
The urgent need they had for long endured
Without a king. To him the Lord of Life,
Ruler of Glory, granted earthly power;
Renowned was Beowa, the son of Scyld,
And wide his fame was known in Danish lands.
So must a young man by good gifts contrive,
By handsome presents from the ancestral store,
That later in old age his loved companions
Cleave unto him and that when battle comes
His people serve him; for among every race
A man shall prosper by his deeds of praise.

Edwin Morgan

from *Beowulf: A Verse Translation
into Modern English* (1952)

How that glory remains in remembrance,
Of the Danes and their kings in days gone,
The acts and valour of princes of their blood!
   Scyld Scefing: how often he thrust from their feast-halls
The troops of his enemies, tribe after tribe,
Terrifying their warriors: he who had been found
Long since as a waif and awaited his desert
While he grew up and throve in honour among men
Till all the nations neighbouring about him
Sent as his subjects over the whale-fields
Their gifts of tribute: king worth the name!
Then there was born a son to succeed him,
A boy for that house, given by God
As a comfort to the folk for all the wretchedness
He saw they had lived in, from year to year
Lacking an overlord; and the overlord of Life,
Of Glory, gave the man worldly excelling,
Till his fame spread far, the fame of Beowulf

The son of Scyld, on Scandinavian soil.
So should magnanimity be the young man's care,
Rich gifts and royal in his ready companions
Will remain with him still, his people stand by him
When war returns; a man shall flourish
By acts of merit in every land.

Stanley B. Greenfield

from *A Readable Beowulf: The Old English Epic Newly Translated* (1982)

Indeed, we have heard of the Spear-Danes'
glory, and their kings', in days gone by,
how princes displayed their courage then.
    Often Scyld Scefing shattered the hosts,
unsettled many a nation's mead-hall,
terrorized tribes, since first he was found
abandoned; comfort and abundance
later came his way, and worldly fame,
until neighboring nations, near or
far over whale-big seas, obeyed him,
gave tribute: a good king in deed!
To him in his homeland a young heir
soon was born, whom God by His grace sent
for his people's comfort: He perceived
the long distress they'd suffered lordless;
the Lord of life, Ruler of glory,
heaped worldly honors upon Beowulf,
Scyld's son, so that his fame spread widely
in Danish lands in his youthful days.
As he did, every noble youth should do:
spend liberally, give lavish gifts
while with his father, so that in turn,
when he comes of age, companions by choice
will serve him well when war comes; by deeds
worth praise will one prosper everywhere.

Ruth P. M. Lehmann

from *Beowulf:*
An Imitative Translation (1988)

The Dane's Story:
SCYLDINGS SHELTER SCYLD

Now we have heard stories of high valor
in times long past   of tribal monarchs,
lords of Denmark,   how those leaders strove.
    Often Scyld Scefing   by the shock of war
kept both troops and tribes   from treasured meadbench,
filled foes with dread   after first being
discovered uncared for;   a cure for that followed:
he grew hale under heaven,   high in honor,
until no nation   near the borders,
beyond teeming seas   but was taught to obey,
giving tribute.   He was a good ruler.
    To him a boy was born,   a baby in the homestead,
whom God grants us   as gift and comfort
to ease the people.   He apprehended
dire trouble dogged   those destitute people.
But the Lord of life,   Leader of heaven,
offered them honor,   earthly requital.
Beow was famous —   abroad well renowned —
throughout south Sweden,   the successor to Scyld.
Thus should a fine young man   on his father's throne
give generously,   and do good to all
so that when aging,   old companions
stand by him steady   at the stroke of war,
his people serve him.   By praiseworthy deeds
each must prosper   in every tribe.

Old English Elegiac Poetry

The Wanderer[1]

An elegy, similar to The Seafarer *with which it is often connected,*
The Wanderer *is found in the Exeter Book, an anthology of secular
and religious poetry that was copied about 975, perhaps in Exeter,
England. The speaker in* The Wanderer *is exiled from his lord, his
men, and his family and attains a certain tough wisdom through his
solitary suffering. The poem falls into two sections: a first-person
recollection of the exile's gift-bestowing lord, from which the exile
awakens as from a dream, finding his companions to be only sea
birds; and a second section that contains the reflections of a wise
man ("the sage") who, while contemplating a ruin,[2] utters a mov-
ing description of the transitoriness of earthly joys. The wise man's
discourse constitutes a familiar medieval theme, in which a speaker
asks what has become of earthly pleasures; their brevity and loss
are then enumerated and a solution is sought through stoical determination or the hope of heavenly joys. The vivid emotional content
of this poem, accessed in its first part through the "single port" of
memory, parallels both the process and the effect of many of the
discursive recollections found in Beowulf, and the exile's plight as
described underscores the importance of a man belonging within
the company of others—and under the sponsorship of a powerful
leader. Hrothgar's lengthy remarks to Beowulf after the hero's success against Grendel and Grendel's mother, like the sage's in this
elegy, urge a realization and renunciation of the transient glories
found in this world.*

This lonely traveler longs for grace,
For the mercy of God; grief hangs on
His heart and follows the frost-cold foam
He cuts in the sea, sailing endlessly,

[1]Translation by Burton Raffel in Raffel (trans.) and Olsen (ed.), *Poems and Prose
from the Old English*. New Haven and London: Yale University Press, 1998,
pp. 7–10. Reprinted by permission of Yale University Press.
[2]For another recollection inspired by the contemplation of ruined buildings, see *The
Ruin*, pp. 146–48.

Aimlessly, in exile. Fate has opened   5
A single port: memory. He sees
His kinsmen slaughtered again, and cries:
        "I've drunk too many lonely dawns,
Gray with mourning. Once there were men
To whom my heart could hurry, hot   10
With open longing. They're long since dead.
My heart has closed on itself, quietly
Learning that silence is noble and sorrow
Nothing that speech can cure. Sadness
Has never driven sadness off;   15
Fate blows hardest on a bleeding heart.
So those who thirst for glory smother
Secret weakness and longing, neither
Weep nor sigh nor listen to the sickness
In their souls. So I, lost and homeless,   20
Forced to flee the darkness that fell
On the earth and my lord.
                        Leaving everything,
Weary with winter I wandered out
On the frozen waves, hoping to find   25
A place, a people, a lord to replace
My lost ones. No one knew me, now,
No one offered comfort, allowed
Me feasting or joy. How cruel a journey
I've traveled, sharing my bread with sorrow   30
Alone, an exile in every land,
Could only be told by telling my footsteps.
For who can hear: 'friendless and poor,'
And know what I've known since the long cheerful nights
When, young and yearning, with my lord I yet feasted   35
Most welcome of all. That warmth is dead.
He only knows who needs his lord
As I do, eager for long-missing aid;
He only knows who never sleeps
Without the deepest dreams of longing.   40
Sometimes it seems I see my lord,
Kiss and embrace him, bend my hands
And head to his knee, kneeling as though
He still sat enthroned, ruling his thanes.

And I open my eyes, embracing the air, 45
And see the brown sea-billows heave,
See the sea birds bathe, spreading
Their white-feathered wings, watch the frost
And the hail and the snow. And heavy in heart
I long for my lord, alone and unloved. 50
Sometimes it seems I see my kin
And greet them gladly, give them welcome,
The best of friends. They fade away,
Swimming soundlessly out of sight,
Leaving nothing. 55
          How loathsome become
The frozen waves to a weary heart.
       In this brief world I cannot wonder
That my mind is set on melancholy,
Because I never forget the fate 60
Of men, robbed of their riches, suddenly
Looted by death—the doom of earth,
Sent to us all by every rising
Sun. Wisdom is low, and comes
But late. He who has it is patient; 65
He cannot be hasty to hate or speak,
He must be bold and yet not blind,
Nor ever too craven, complacent, or covetous,
Nor ready to gloat before he wins glory.
The man's a fool who flings his boasts 70
Hotly to the heavens, heeding his spleen
And not the better boldness of knowledge.
What knowing man knows not the ghostly,
Wastelike end of worldly wealth:
See, already the wreckage is there, 75
The windswept walls stand far and wide,
The storm-beaten blocks besmeared with frost,
The mead-halls crumbled, the monarchs thrown down
And stripped of their pleasures. The proudest of warriors
Now lie by the wall: some of them war 80
Destroyed; some the monstrous sea bird
Bore over the ocean; to some the old wolf
Dealt out death; and for some dejected
Followers fashioned an earth-cave coffin.

Thus the Maker of men lays waste   85
This earth, crushing our callow mirth,
And the work of old giants stands withered and still.

    He who these ruins rightly sees,
And deeply considers this dark twisted life,
Who sagely remembers the endless slaughters   90
Of a bloody past, is bound to proclaim,
    "Where is the war steed? Where/
                is the warrior? Where is his warlord?
Where now the feasting-places?/
                Where now the mead-hall pleasures?
Alas, bright cup! Alas, brave knight!
Alas, you glorious princes! All gone,   95
Lost in the night, as you never had lived,
And all that survives you a serpentine wall,
Wondrously high, worked in strange ways.
Mighty spears have slain these men,
Greedy weapons have framed their fate.   100
    These rocky slopes are beaten by storms,
This earth pinned down by driving snow,
By the horror of winter, smothering warmth
In the shadows of night. And the north angrily
Hurls its hailstorms at our helpless heads.   105
Everything earthly is evilly born,
Firmly clutched by a fickle Fate.
Fortune vanishes, friendship vanishes,
Man is fleeting, woman is fleeting,
And all this earth rolls into emptiness."   110

    So says the sage in his heart,/
                sitting alone with his thought.
It's good to guard your faith,/
              nor let your grief come forth
Until it cannot call/
            for help, nor help but heed
The path you've placed before it./
              It's good to find your grace
In God, the heavenly rock/   115
           where rests our every hope.

The Seafarer[1]

The Seafarer, *like the elegy entitled* The Wanderer, *is found in the* Exeter Book. *The speaker tells of the physical and mental discomforts he has endured while at sea. Despite the dangers and the cold, the speaker, prompted by signs of Spring, longs to travel to a faraway country. The poem concludes with a recital of the transitory nature of earthly life and its joys. Defects in the meter toward the end of the poem show that several words are missing from the manuscript at this point. Some scholars have noted a change of speaker in the poem, as it shifts from the specific hardships of seafaring to general comments about the human condition, and the problem of understanding the boundaries between speakers and the number of voices in the poem has remained a preoccupation. Some read the poem as concerning, first, the earthly journey, and then the heavenly one. The travails of ocean voyages are unspoken, but implicit, in* Beowulf, *which can be read as a series of adventures that chart a man's spiritual worth in his reactions to mental and physical heroic challenges. In its brilliant contrasts between the warm hall and the chilly ship,* The Seafarer *evokes the short-lived pleasures of this world, a subject in which the* Beowulf-*poet is keenly interested.*

May I for my own self song's truth reckon,
Journey's jargon, how I in harsh days
Hardship endured oft.
Bitter breast-cares have I abided,
Known on my keel many a care's hold,   5
And dire sea-surge, and there I oft spent
Narrow nightwatch nigh the ship's head
While she tossed close to cliffs. Coldly afflicted,
My feet were by frost benumbed.
Chill its chains are; chafing sighs   10
Hew my heart round and hunger begot
Mere-weary mood. Lest man know not
That he on dry land loveliest liveth,
List how I, care-wretched, on ice-cold sea,
Weathered the winter, wretched outcast   15
Deprived of my kinsmen;

Hung with hard ice-flakes, where hail-scur flew,
There I heard naught save the harsh sea
And ice-cold wave, at whiles the swan cries,
Did for my games the gannet's clamour,   20
Sea-fowls' loudness was for me laughter,
The mews' singing all my mead-drink.
Storms, on the stone-cliffs beaten, fell on the stern
In icy feathers; full oft the eagle screamed
With spray on his pinion.   25
                    Not any protector
May make merry man faring needy.
This he little believes, who aye in winsome life
Abides 'mid burghers some heavy business,
Wealthy and wine-flushed, how I weary oft   30
Must bide above brine.
Neareth nightshade, snoweth from north,
Frost froze the land, hail fell on earth then,
Corn of the coldest. Nathless there knocketh now
The heart's thought that I on high streams   35
The salt-wavy tumult traverse alone.
Moaneth alway my mind's lust
That I fare forth, that I afar hence
Seek out a foreign fastness.
For this there's no mood-lofty man over earth's midst,   40
Not though he be given his good, but will have in his youth greed;
Nor his deed to the daring, nor his king to the faithful
But shall have his sorrow for sea-fare
Whatever his lord will.
He hath not heart for harping, nor in ring-having   45
Nor winsomeness to wife, nor world's delight
Nor any whit else save the wave's slash,
Yet longing comes upon him to fare forth on the water.
Bosque taketh blossom, cometh beauty of berries,
Fields to fairness, land fares brisker,   50
All this admonisheth man eager of mood,
The heart turns to travel so that he then thinks
On flood-ways to be far departing.
Cuckoo calleth with gloomy crying,
He singeth summerward, bodeth sorrow,   55
The bitter heart's blood. Burgher knows not—
He the prosperous man—what some perform

Where wandering them widest draweth.
So that but now my heart burst from my breastlock,
My mood 'mid the mere-flood,   60
Over the whale's acre, would wander wide.
On earth's shelter cometh oft to me,
Eager and ready, the crying lone-flyer,
Whets for the whale-path the heart irresistibly,
O'er tracks of ocean; seeing that anyhow   65
My lord deems to me this dead life
On loan and on land, I believe not
That any earth-weal eternal standeth
Save there be somewhat calamitous
That, ere a man's tide go, turn it to twain.   70
Disease or oldness or sword-hate
Beats out the breath from doom-gripped body.
And for this, every earl whatever, for those speaking after—
Laud of the living, boasteth some last word,
That he will work ere he pass onward,   75
Frame on the fair earth 'gainst foes his malice,
Daring ado, . . .
So that all men shall honour him after
And his laud beyond them remain 'mid the English,
Aye, for ever, a lasting life's-blast,   80
Delight 'mid the doughty.
        Days little durable,
And all arrogance of earthen riches,
There come now no kings nor Caesars
Nor gold-giving lords like those gone.   85
Howe'er in mirth most magnified,
Whoe'er lived in life most lordliest,
Drear all this excellence, delights undurable!
Waneth the watch, but the world holdeth.
Tomb hideth trouble. The blade is layed low.   90
Earthly glory ageth and seareth.
No man at all going the earth's gait,
But age fares against him, his face paleth,
Grey-haired he groaneth, knows gone companions,
Lordly men, are to earth o'ergiven,   95
Nor may he then the flesh-cover, whose life ceaseth,
Nor eat the sweet nor feel the sorry,

Nor stir hand nor think in mid heart,
And though he strew the grave with gold,
His born brothers, their buried bodies   100
Be an unlikely treasure hoard.

Deor

Also found in the Exeter Book, Deor is unique among Old English poems in containing a refrain; rare, because it is stanzaic. Deor offers consolation in the form of a series of sorrows surmounted, though with bitterness, as the six examples move from Germanic heroic legend to personal narrative. Because it is a dramatic monologue performed by the subject of the poem, Deor is similar to Widsith, which is a tremendous catalogue of figures from heroic legend. The figures of Weland and of Eormanric are each referred to once in Beowulf, showing the powerful force of allusion to heroic legend that Old English poetry uses. Unfortunately, so little material has survived from this period that many of the references in Deor are opaque to us.

Weland,[1] the stout-hearted warrior, knew about sorrow through
the sword;[2] he suffered hardship, sorrow, and longing for his
companions, ice-cold exile; he often found woes after Niðhad[3]
put compulsion on him, supple bonds of sinew on a better man.
   That passed away, so may this!   5

   In Beadohild's[4] mind, her brothers' death was not as painful as
her own state, when she had clearly seen that she was with child.
She could never think about what would come of that without fear.
   That passed away, so may this!

[1]Weland the smith and famous maker of weapons; found in *Beowulf*, line 404.
[2]The poem says "worm," taken here as a poetic figure for sword, found elsewhere in Old English poetry.
[3]King Niðhad captured Weland and had him hamstrung to prevent his escape.
[4]The daughter of King Niðhad. In revenge for his captivity, Weland kills her brothers and rapes her. She gives birth to a son, Wudga, who is mentioned in *Widsith*, lines 124 and 129, p. 163.

Many of us have heard that the Geat's love for Mæðhild grew   10
boundless, that his anguished passion took all sleep from him.[5]
That passed away, so may this!

Theodoric ruled the stronghold of the Merovingians for
thirty years; that was known to many.
That passed away, so may this!   15

We have heard of Eormanric's[6] wolfish mind; he held wide
sway in the kingdom of the Goths. That was a fierce king. Many
a warrior sat, bound by sorrows, expecting woe, wishing often
that his kingdom would be overcome.
That passed away, so may this!   20

The heavy-hearted man sits deprived of joys; there is gloom
in his mind, and it seems to him that his portion of sadness is
endless. Then he may consider that throughout this world the
wise lord brings many changes: to many a man, he grants honor,
certain fame; to some a sorrowful portion.   25
I will say this of myself: that once I was a poet of the Heoden-
ings, dear to my lord. Deor was my name; for many years I had a
good position, a gracious lord, until now that Heorrenda, a man
skilled in song, has received the land that the protector of warriors formerly gave me.   30
That passed away, so may this!

The Ruin

*The Ruin is the title given to a short elegy imperfectly preserved in
the Exeter Book. The mention of both hot springs and baths in the
poem led nineteenth-century scholars to identify the city described
by the poet as Bath, called Aquae Sulis by the Romans and occu-
pied by the West Saxons in 577, according to the Anglo-Saxon
Chronicle. Concerned with the theme of temporality as is* Beowulf,

---

[5]The source of this third example of suffering has not been identified.
[6]Eormanric is mentioned in *Beowulf*, line 1058.

The Ruin fits two other medieval rhetorical categories: the praise of a beautiful city and the lament for a ruined one. The figure of the ruined city has also been read as depicting spiritual decay. The gaps in the poem, indicated here by periods within square brackets, evoke the poem's own state of ruin as well as the theme of dilapidation.

Wondrous is this stone wall, wrecked by wyrd;[1]
the city's buildings broken, the works of giants fallen to bits.
Roofs have caved in, towers tumbled,
barred gates broken, frost on the mortar,
everything gaping, crumbling, collapsing,   5
undermined by age. The earth's embrace
holds the master-builders
in its hard grip, and a hundred generations
have passed since then. Often this wall,
streaked gray with lichen and stained with red, outlived
   one kingdom after another,   10
withstood storms; but the high wall yielded.
Standing still [. . . . .] heaped up,
Many on [. . . . .]
Ground up grimly [. . . . . .]
[. . . . .] shone they [. .]   15
[. . . . .] cunning work of old [. . .]
[. . . . .] g [. .] with earthen crusts ringed
Resolute men quickly came up with a plan:
bound the roof with metal rings,
the walls wondrously woven round with wire.   20
Bright were the public halls, with many bathhouses,
high the gables, loud the noise of armies,
with many meadhalls full of delights,
until the time that wyrd the mighty overturned it.
Slaughter was widespread, the plague came,   25
death took off every one of the brave men;
their battle stations became waste places,
the city decayed. The builders fell,
the warriors to the earth. Thus these courts crumbled,
and this red arch sheds tiles,   30
the roof decays. The place has fallen into ruin,

---

[1] *Wyrd* is an Old English word that indicates fate or its actions.

broken into mounds, where once many a man,
glad-hearted and gold-bright, gleaming with splendor,
proud and wine-flushed, shining in war-harness,
stared at treasure, on silver, on precious stones,   35
on riches, on possessions, on jewelry,
on this shining city in a broad realm.
Stone houses stood there, a hot stream sprang out
into a wide gush; the wall enclosed all
in its bright interior, there where the baths were,   40
hot at the heart. That was convenient.
They made the water pour [. . .]
over the gray stones in hot streams
until [. . . . .]
[. .] the circular pools were hot [. . . . . . .]   45
[. . . . .] where the baths were.
Then is [. . . . .]
[. . . . .]re; that is a noble thing,
a house [. . . . .] a city [. . . . . . .]

Old English Heroic Poetry

The Battle of Finnsburg[1]

This fragment of a longer heroic poem, now entitled The Battle of
Finnsburg,[2] *is known only from a transcript printed by George
Hickes in 1705. The single leaf from which Hickes made his copy
of what remained of the poem is now lost. This battle is also
recounted by the* Beowulf-*poet, where it is sometimes called "The
Finnesburh Episode." Also alluded to in* Widsith, *no English or
Scandinavian text narrates the story in full, making the reading of
either this heavily damaged poem or the episode in* Beowulf

[1]Translation by Charles W. Kennedy, *An Anthology of Old English Poetry: Translated into Alliterative Verse by Charles W. Kennedy*. New York: Oxford University
Press, 1960, pp. 66–67. Reprinted by permission of the publisher.

[2]The place-name is also written "Finnesburh" or "Finnsburh"; this poem is also
known as *The Finnesburh Fragment*.

extremely difficult. The Battle of Finnsburg *is usually assumed to be contemporary with* Beowulf, *based largely on linguistic and metrical analyses of Hickes's transcript. When complete,* The Battle of Finnsburg *may have been a heroic lay of several hundred lines. Even the surviving fraction of the poem tells a dramatic tale. Beginning in mid-line,* The Battle of Finnsburg *describes a pre-dawn attack by the Frisians (the "men in armor" in this translation) on a hall that Hnæf and his band of Danish warriors occupy. The Danes had come to Frisia in order to visit Hildeburh, who is the wife of the Frisian Finn and the sister of Hnæf the Dane. This poem differs from the account in* Beowulf *in several important respects: the facts of the battle appear to differ,[3] and each poet puts the event to a different use.*

... "are the horns of the hall on fire?"
Then Hnæf made answer,   the battle-young king:
"This is no dawn from the East,   nor flying dragon,
Nor fire burning   the horns of this hall,
But men in armor;   the eagle shall scream,
The gray wolf howl   and the war-wood whistle,
Shield answer shaft.   Now shines the moon
Through scudding cloud.   Dire deeds are come
Bringing hard battle   and bitter strife.
Awake, my warriors,   seize your shields;
Fight like men   in the front of battle;
Be bold of mood,   be mindful of valor!"
    Then sprang up many   a gold-decked thane,
Girding on sword.   The great-hearted warriors,
Sigeferth and Eaha,   drew their swords,
Springing to one door;   Ordlaf and Guthlaf
Guarded the other   while Hengest himself
Followed them close.   Garulf urged Guthere
In the first onset   not so freely
At the door of the hall   to hazard his life,

---

[3]Scholars generally believe that *The Battle of Finnsburg* contains an account of the first fight between the Frisians and the Danes, while the *Beowulf*-poet—who develops other aspects of the Finnsburg battle (for example, the melancholy figure of Hildeburh, whose brother and son are killed, and the frustration of the warrior Hengest, who must serve a lord who caused his own to be killed)—may relate a second engagement that followed a truce in the battle.

Where the bold in battle   would wrench it away.
But the brave-hearted hero,   for all to hear,
Called to know   who was holding the door?
"Sigeferth is my name (said he);   I am prince of the Secgas
A wide-known wanderer;   I have borne many blows
In many fierce battles.   At my hand you can have
Whatever you wish   to have from me."
   Then in the hall   was the sound of slaughter,
Boat-shaped shield   upraised by the brave.
Bucklers burst;   hall-boards resounded;
Till Garulf in fighting   was first to fall,
The son of Guthlaf,   with many a good man,
Bodies of dying.   Swarthy and dark
The ravens were circling.   There was flashing of swords
As if all Finnsburg   were blazing with fire.
   Never have I heard   of worthier warriors
Who bore themselves better   in brunt of war,
Or of finer service   more fitly paid
Than those young heroes   rendered to Hnæf.
Five days they fought   and none of them fell,
His faultless comrades,   and they held the doors.
   Then a wounded warrior   turned him away,
Said his byrny was broken   his war-gear weak,
His helmet pierced.   The prince of the people
Asked how the warriors   survived their wounds,
Or which of the young men. . . .

Waldere[1]

The two remaining leaves of the heroic lay Waldere[2] *were discovered in January 1860 amongst bundles of papers and other parchment leaves by E. C. Werlauff, Head Librarian of the Royal*

---

[1]Translation by Charles W. Kennedy, *An Anthology of Old English Poetry: Translated into Alliterative Verse by Charles W. Kennedy.* New York: Oxford University Press, 1960, pp. 68–69. Reprinted by permission of the publisher.

[2]That is, Walter of Aquitane, a legendary hero kept hostage at the court of Attila the Hun. A different version of this story is found in the tenth-century Latin verse epic *Waltharius.*

Library, Copenhagen. Estimating from the two nonsequential fragments that survive, Waldere *may have been 1,000 lines long. The poem recounts a battle developing among* Waldere *and the two Burgundians Gunther and Hagen, and because so little of* Waldere *survives, it is not completely certain who is speaking or to whom. The speaker of the first fragment is probably Hildegyth, to whom Waldere is betrothed, encouraging Waldere to do brave deeds in battle. Thus, Hildegyth assumes a female role well known from Icelandic sagas. The second fragment consists of a man, probably Waldere, jeering at other warriors. The tones of the speeches preserved in these two fragments are familiar from Old English heroic poetry, and they parallel the voices that incite to bravery or bristle with gibes found in* Beowulf.

Waldere 1

              ... heard him gladly.
"Weland's work surely   can never weaken
For any man   who can hold the hard blade,
Wield the sword, Mimming.   Often in war
Wounded and bloody   man after man
Fell in the fray.   Now let not thy strength,
Soldier of Attila,   or thy valor fail.
    "Now the day has come   when thou shalt accomplish
One of two: either lose thy life,
Or win long fame,   O Ælfhere's son,
Among all mankind.   Not at all, my beloved,
Can I say that ever   in play of swords
I saw you shamefully   shun the battle,
Or turn to the wall   to protect your life,
Though many a hard blade   hacked at your byrny.
But always further   you forced the fighting
Time beyond measure;   I feared for your fate
Lest all too boldly   you pressed to the battle,
The bloody encounter   in clash of war.
    "Now honor your name   with deeds of note
While God is gracious   and grants you strength.
Fear not for the blade!   The best of weapons
Was surely given   to save us both.
With its edge you shall beat down   Guthhere's boast
Who wickedly started   this bitter strife,
Refused the sword,   and the shining casket,

And wealth of jewels.   With never a gem
He shall leave the battle,   return to his lord,
His ancient homeland,   or here shall he sleep
If he . . ."

Waldere 2

Waldere addressed him,   the warrior brave;
He held in his hand   his comfort in battle,
War-blade in his grip,   and uttered these words:
"Lo! grimly you hoped   Burgundian lord,
That the hand of Hagen   would help in the fray
And hinder my fighting;   try and take, if you dare,
Battle-worn though I be,   my good gray byrny.
Here it lies on my shoulders,   shining with gold,
Ælfhere's heirloom   of ample front,
A peerless corselet   for prince's wear
When hand guards body   and frame from the foe!
It fails me not   when the false and unfriendly
Renew their tricks,   and attack me with swords
As ye have done."

The Battle of Brunanburh[1]

> *The longest and arguably the best of the poems recorded in the* Anglo-Saxon Chronicle, The Battle of Brunanburh *occurs as the entry for the year 937. The poem tells how King Æthelstan*[2] *and Edmund,*[3] *his half-brother, leading an army of West Saxons and*

[1]Translation by Alfred, Lord Tennyson, as printed in *Tennyson: A Selected Edition.* Christopher Ricks, ed. Berkeley and Los Angeles: University of California Press, 1989, pp. 621–25. Reprinted by permission of the publisher.

[2]Written here as "Athelstan." Æthelstan succeeded to the kingship after the death of his father, Edward the Elder, in 924 and ruled until 939, when Edmund assumed the throne, perhaps because of Æthelstan's apparent lack of heirs.

[3]Edmund was the first king of all England including Northumbria, reigning from 939 until May 26, 946, when he was stabbed to death while trying to get one of his officials out of a free-for-all. His command over his territory was challenged often throughout his reign, including by the Anlaf in *Brunanburh*, who sometime in 939 regained control of York from Edmund.

Mercians, defeat a mixed force of Vikings, Welsh, and Scots commanded by Anlaf,[4] king of Dublin.[5] The site of this battle may have been at Bromborough, Cheshire, but that is not certain. Æthelstan's victory was a climax of the king's attempt to unite England under his rule. Conventional in its use of heroic imagery, this poem is a straightforward celebration of the English victory, and it is worthwhile to compare this downright handling of the heroic with the more nuanced treatment it is afforded in Beowulf. Tennyson's translation is sometimes credited as the finest one metrically imitative of an Old English poem; as Ricks notes, it is written in unrhymed dactylics and trochees, for, in order to catch the alliterative rhythm of Old English verse, Tennyson said, ". . . I have made free use of the dactylic beat."[6] The poem was first published in 1880.

I.

Athelstan King,
Lord among Earls,
Bracelet–bestower and
Baron of Barons,
He with his brother,
Edmund Atheling,[7]
Gaining a lifelong
Glory in battle,
Slew with the sword–edge
There by Brunanburh,
Brake the shield–wall,
Hewed the lindenwood,
Hacked the battleshield,
Sons of Edward with hammered brands.

II.

Theirs was a greatness
Got from their Grandsires—

---

[4]Anlaf (or "Olaf") Guthfrithson was the Viking king of Dublin, Ireland, who died while on a raid in 941.

[5]The battle may have been a challenge to Æthelstan's supremacy over Northumbria, a position never before held by a ruler from the south of England.

[6]As quoted in Ricks (1989, p. 621).

[7]"Atheling" (Old English, *ætheling*) is a word designating a prince or noble.

Theirs that so often in
Strife with their enemies
Struck for their hoards and their hearths and their homes.
>   III.
Bowed the spoiler,
Bent the Scotsman,
Fell the shipcrews
Doomed to the death.
All the field with blood of the fighters
Flowed, from when first the great
Sun–star of morningtide,
Lamp of the Lord God
Lord everlasting,
Glode over earth till the glorious creature
Sank to his setting.
>   IV.
There lay many a man
Marred by the javelin,
Men of the Northland
Shot over shield.
There was the Scotsman
Weary of war.
>   V.
We the West–Saxons,
Long as the daylight
Lasted, in companies
Troubled the track of the host that we hated,
Grimly with swords that were sharp from the grindstone,
Fiercely we hacked at the flyers before us.
>   VI.
Mighty the Mercian,
Hard was his hand–play,
Sparing not any of
Those that with Anlaf,
Warriors over the
Weltering waters
Borne in the bark's–bosom,
Drew to this island:
Doomed to the death.
>   VII.
Five young kings put asleep by the sword–stroke,

Seven strong Earls of the army of Anlaf
Fell on the war–field, numberless numbers,
Shipmen and Scotsmen.
                    VIII.
            Then the Norse leader,
            Dire was his need of it,
            Few were his following,
            Fled to his warship:
Fleeted his vessel to sea with the king in it,
Saving his life on the fallow flood.
                    IX.
            Also the crafty one,
            Constantinus,[8]
            Crept to his North again,
            Hoar–headed hero!
                    X.
            Slender warrant had
            He to be proud of
            The welcome of war–knives—
            He that was reft of his
            Folk and his friends that had
            Fallen in conflict,
            Leaving his son too
            Lost in the carnage,
            Mangled to morsels,
            A youngster in war!
                    XI.
            Slender reason had
            He to be glad of
            The clash of the war–glaive—
            Traitor and trickster
            And spurner of treaties—
            He nor had Anlaf
            With armies so broken
            A reason for bragging
            That they had the better
            In perils of battle
            On places of slaughter—
            The struggle of standards,

[8]Constantine was the king of the Scots, whose son died in this battle.

The rush of the javelins,
The crash of the charges,
The wielding of weapons—
The play that they played with
The children of Edward.
   XII.
Then with their nailed prows
Parted the Norsemen, a
Blood–reddened relic of
Javelins over
The jarring breaker, the deep-sea billow,
Shaping their way toward Dyflen[9] again,
Shamed in their souls.
   XIII.
Also the brethren,
King and Atheling,
Each in his glory,
Went to his own in his own West-Saxonland,
  Glad of the war.
   XIV.
Many a carcase they left to be carrion,
Many a livid one, many a sallow–skin—
Left for the white–tailed eagle to tear it, and
Left for the horny–nibbed raven to rend it, and
Gave to the garbaging war–hawk to gorge it, and
That gray beast, the wolf of the weald.[10]
   XV.
Never had huger
Slaughter of heroes
Slain by the sword–edge—
Such as old writers
Have writ of in histories—
Hapt in this isle, since
Up from the East hither
Saxon and Angle from
Over the broad billow

---

[9]Dublin.

[10]A recital of the "beasts of battle" typescene in which animals, usually the raven, eagle, and wolf, rejoice in the carrion on the battlefield. *Beowulf* and *The Battle of Maldon* use variations of this typescene.

Broke into Britain with
Haughty war–workers who
Harried the Welshman, when
Earls that were lured by the
Hunger of glory gat
Hold of the land.

Old English Wisdom Poetry

Vainglory[1]

Found in the Exeter Book, Vainglory *begins with an exclamation designed to get our attention—as do* Beowulf *and* Andreas. *This homiletic poem contrasts the spiritual values of a proud man and a humble one. The jarring metrics of the poem when describing the haughty have been read as part of the poet's design for expressing the quality of sinfulness. Like the elegies* The Wanderer *and* The Seafarer, Vainglory *contains the advice of a wise man ("the prophet"), who expresses a reasoned and temperate position, as against the examples of the disordered behavior of the arrogant man. Readers of* Beowulf *will note the knowing description of the results of drunkenness in the hall, including the soused boasts of the warrior; the description of the hall's liveliness and noise; and the use of the arrow to make concrete the powerful attacks of sin.*

Listen, long ago I was told many extraordinary and astonishing things by someone both learned and experienced, a wise man with a message. Through the prophet's teaching this man, expert with books, brought to light a treasure of words, spoken in the past by a preacher, so that as a result of his solemn song, I could afterwards recognize God's own son, a welcome guest wherever men live; and in the same way discern that weaker spirit, who was deprived of authority for his offences.

[1]Translation by T. A. Shippey, *Poems of Wisdom and Learning in Old English.* Cambridge: D. S. Brewer, 1976, pp. 55 and 57. Reprinted by permission of the publisher.

This can be easily grasped by anybody who does not show spiritual wantonness, during this brief existence, to pervert his intellect; and during his lifetime, does not allow drunkenness to get control of him, where there are many men holding a meeting, proud war-makers in the mead-halls. They sit at the feast, composing true songs, exchanging words. They try hard to find out what battlefield may remain among men inside the hall, when wine makes a man's heart excited. Noise increases, the hubbub of the company, and voices ring out competing with each other. In the same way, minds are divided into types, for men are not all alike.

One sort presses on violently in his pride, an immoderate spirit swells within him; of these there are too many. He is filled by the devil's flying arrows of envy, by deceitful temptations. He yells and shouts, boasts about himself far more than does the better man, thinks that his behavior must seem absolutely irreproachable to everybody. But there will be another outcome of it all, when he sees the result of his offence. He tricks and cheats, he thinks of many barbed devices, he lets fly with premeditated shafts, he snipes continuously. He does not realize the guilt he has brought into being by his enmity; and, out of spite, he hates his superior, allowing treacherous arrows to break through the stronghold's wall, the fortress his ruler had commanded him to defend. Sitting proudly at the feast, overcome by wine, he lets his words stream out maliciously, pushing for a quarrel, swollen with violence, inflamed by spite and hostility and tricks to cause trouble, full of pride. Now you can be sure: if you meet a man of this kind living among other people, know from these few plain statements that he is a child of the devil enclosed in flesh, that he lives his life perversely, has a soul destined for hell and worthless to God, the king of glory. The prophet sang this, a man of ready speech; he made this song:

"Whoever sets himself up through pride in time of cruelty and raises himself up arrogantly, will have to be humbled miserably after his death-journey, brought down to live fixed in torments, surrounded by thronging worms. It was long ago in the kingdom of God that arrogance arose among the angels, a famous struggle; they instigated the quarrel, started a violent attack. They polluted heaven and despised their superior, when they meant—as was not right—to turn traitor and deprive the noble and mighty king of his lordly throne, and then live in the happy land of glory, on their own terms. The father of creation denied them that by force: the fight turned out to be too fierce for them."

But there is a different fate for the other man, who lives humbly here on earth and always keeps on friendly terms with every member of his family and with people generally and who loves his enemy, even though he has often been deliberately provoked by him in this world. The humble man can rise from here to happiness and glory, the hope of the saints, the land of the angels. It will not be so for the other one, who lives among his sins, proud of his disgraceful deeds. Their rewards will not be the same from the king of glory.

Recognise from these words: if you happen to meet a humble person, a man among the people, God's own son will always be his closest associate—a guest to be wished for in this world—if the prophet did not deceive me.

So we must always and on every occasion—considering what is necessary for salvation—remember in our hearts that greatest ruler of victories. Amen.

Widsith

Widsith, the "far traveler,"[1] is found in the Exeter Book. Introduced in a brief preface, the speaker then tells of his travels, enumerating the rulers and regions of the world he has visited. Many of the personal and place names mentioned are found in Beowulf,[2] *but* Widsith *is largely a list of Germanic legends during the age of tribal migration (the fourth to the sixth centuries), rather than a nuanced use of these allusions.* Widsith *concludes with remarks about the life of a minstrel and the nature of fame. The poem not only displays the speaker's skills as a poet but also develops the figure of the poet as one having great knowledge of geography, history, and cus-*

---

[1]Mitchell and Robinson (1998, p. 196n), note that *widsith* means "far journey" in Old English, "but since in other Germanic languages a nickname 'far traveller' occurs (e.g., the Old Norse epithet *inn viðförli* 'the far traveller' is affixed to various men's names), *Widsith* is usually taken to mean 'far traveller'."

[2]Mitchell and Robinson (1998, p. 197), cite ten passages in *Widsith* that are relevant to *Beowulf*. Please note that the spelling of names in *Widsith* differs from *Beowulf*.

toms. The speaker's catalogue of centuries of history invites his audience into this erudition, as does the Beowulf-*poet when he opens the poem with what "we have heard." Even with our slender knowledge of many allusions in* Widsith, *the poet's recital is mesmeric, and the speaker's fictive autobiography vivid.*

Widsith spoke, unlocked his word-hoard,
he who of men traveled most through races and peoples
over the earth and often had received in the hall
precious treasure. From the Myrging race
he descended. He with Ealhhild,   5
fair weaver of peace,
from the east out of Angle, sought first
the home of Eormanric the Gothic king,
fierce breaker of oaths. Then he began to speak of many things:
"I have heard much from men, those ruling over people: 10
every prince must live by fit customs;
one man after the other rules the land,
he who wishes his princely throne to prosper.
Of these was Hwala best for a time
and Alexander the most powerful   15
of all the race of men,
and he prospered most of those of whom I have heard tell
    throughout the earth.
Attila ruled the Huns, Eormanric the Goths,
Becca the Banings, Gifica the Burgundians.
Caesar ruled the Greeks and Caelic the Finns,   20
Hagena the Holmrugians and Heoden the Glommas.
Witta ruled the Swabians, Wada the Haelsings,
Meaca the Myrgings, Mearchealf the Hundings.
Theodric ruled the Franks, Thyle the Rondings,
Breoca the Brondings, Billing the Waernas.   25
Oswine ruled the Eowan, and Gefwulf the Jutes,
Fin Folcwalding the Frisian race.
Sigehere ruled the Sea-Danes for a very long time,
Hnaef the Hocings, Helm the Wulfings,
Wald the Woingas, Wod the Thuringians,   30
Saeferth the Secgan, Ongendtheow the Swedes,
Sceafthere the Ymbras, Sceafa the Longobards,
Hun the Haetwere and Holen the Wrosnas.

Hringweald was called the king of the pirates.
Offa ruled the Angles, Alewih the Danes: 35
he was the bravest of all these men,
yet he did not surpass Offa in courage,
for Offa gained,—first among all men,
when he was still young,—the greatest of kingdoms.
No one of his age was mightier in battle   40
than he was. With his sword alone
he fixed the border with the Myrgings
at Fifeldor. Afterwards his territory was held
by Angles and Swabians, as Offa had won it.
Hrothwulf and Hrothgar held peace together   45
for a very long time, uncle and nephew,
after they had repulsed the Viking-kin
and Ingeld's army crushed,
hewn to pieces at Heorot the Heathobeard's host.
Thus I traveled through many foreign lands   50
in this wide world; good and evil
I suffered there, separated from family,
cut off from noble kin, served far and wide.
Therefore, I may sing and tell my tale,
before this illustrious company in the meadhall,   55
recite how my noble patrons chose to reward me so generously.
I was with the Huns and with the Ostrogoths,
with Swedes and with Geats and with South-Danes.
With the Wendlas was I, and with Waernas and with Vikings.
With the Gefthas was I, and with Wends and with Gefflegas. 60
With the Angles was I, and with Swabians and with Aenenas.
With the Saxons was I, and with Secgan and with Sweordweras.
With the Hronas was I, and with Danes and with Heathoreamas.
With the Thuringians was I, and with the Throwendas,
and with the Burgundians, where I received an arm-ring: 65
there Guthere gave to me a bright jewel,
to reward my song. No sluggard king was he!
With the Franks was I, and with Frisians and with Frumtings.
With the Rugas was I, and with the Glommas and with the
        Romans.
So too was I in Italy with Aelfwine,   70
he had, I have heard, of all mankind
the quickest hand to win praise,
a heart generous in giving out rings,

brilliant arm-rings, the child of Eadwine.
With the Saracens was I, and with the Serings.   75
With the Greeks was I, and with the Finns and with Caesar,
he who had merry cities in his might,
riches and all that one could want and the kingdom of the Welsh.
With the Scots was I, and with the Picts and with the Scride-Finns.
With the Lidwicings was I, and with the Leonas and with
     the Longobards,   80
with heathens and with heroes and with Hundings.
With the Israelites was I, and with the Assyrians,
with the Hebrews and with the Jews and with the Egyptians.
With the Medes was I, and with the Persians and with the Myrgings
and the Mofdings and against the Myrgings,   85
and with Amothingas. With the East Thuringians was I,
and with Eolas and with Iste and Idumingas.
And I was with Eormanric all this time;
then the king of the Goths was good to me.
He, the founder of cities, gave me an arm-ring   90
in which there was reckoned six hundred pieces of pure refined
     gold,
were the treasure weighed in shillings.
This I gave to Eadgils to keep,
my protecting lord, when I came home,
as a reward to the dear one, because he gave me property,   95
my father's native land, this ruler of the Myrgings.
And then Ealhhild gave me another arm-ring,
that noble queen, daughter of Eadwine.
Her praise was spread through many lands,
whenever I through song should say   100
where, under the sky, I knew best
a woman adorned with gold giving gifts.
When Scilling and I in a clear voice
declared before our victorious lord in song,
—loudly from the harp rang out the melodious sound—   105
then many men of proud minds
spoke words: of all that they knew well,
never had they heard it better expressed in song.
After that I passed through the whole land of the Goths;
I always sought the best companions: 110
such was the household of Eormanric.

Hethca I sought, and Beadeca and the Harlungs.
Emerca I sought, and Fridla and the Ostrogotha,
wise and good, the father of Unwen.
Secca I sought, and Becca, Seafola and Theodric,   115
Heathoric and Sifeca, Hlithe and Incgentheow.
Eadwine I sought, and Elsa, Aegelmund and Hungar,
and that proud band of the With-Myrgings.
Wulfhere I sought, and Wyrmhere; very often war did not stop
    there
when the army of the Goths with their strong swords   120
by the Vistula wood had to defend
their ancient realm from Attila's people.
Raedhere I sought, and Rondhere, Rumstan and Gislhere,
Withergield and Freotheric, Wudga and Hama;
those were not the worst comrades,   125
though I have had to name them last.
Often from that band the spear yelled
at hostile people, hissing in flight.
Wudga and Hama, the wanderers,
ruled over men and women with twisted gold.   130
So I always found it in my travels:
that he who is the most beloved to dwellers in a land
to whom God gives power over men
while he lives there."
Thus, the minstrels of men   135
go wandering through many lands:
they say what they need, they return words of thanks,
traveling south or north they meet someone—
wise in the measures of song, generous with gifts,—
who wishes to recount his wisdom before the company,   140
to perform brave deeds, until everything ends,
light and life together. He who is worthy of praise
has everlasting glory under heaven.

from *The Fortunes of Men*

> *Also known as* The Fates of Men, *this example of wisdom poetry is
> found in the Exeter Book.* The Fortunes of Men *consists of two*

lists: first, the various ways in which a man may die and, second,
the various skills and talents that men may possess.[1] *It has been*
argued that the first list contains a recollection of an initiation rite
for the warrior class. Strikingly similar to lines in Beowulf *are the*
passages here that recount the cursed death of the hanged man
(lines 33–42), who is probably a criminal; the grief of the mother at
her son's funeral pyre (lines 43–47); and the murder of the loud-
mouthed drunk in the hall (lines 48–57).

Often it comes to pass by God's might
that man and woman bring a child into the world,
a child into the lineage, and clothe him with bright colors,
they teach and train him until it happens,
in the course of time, that the young limbs   5
and members quicken, grow strong.
Thus, the father and mother foster and feed him,
give gifts and dress him. God alone
knows what the years will bring to him when he grows up!
    To one it happens in the years of his youth,   10
A woeful ending carries him off.
A wolf shall devour him, the gray heath-stepper;
his mother shall mourn his going hence.
Such things are not in the power of man!
    One hunger shall destroy, one the storm shall harass,   15
One the spear shall slay, one battle defeat.
One shall live his life without the light of the eye,
with only hands for feeling. One, feeble of foot,
sick with sinew wounds, shall lament his pain,
mourning his fate and troubled in spirit.   20
    One in the forest from a tall tree
shall fall, wingless; he shall be in flight,
swinging in the air, until he no longer hangs
like fruit from the branch. Then he shall fall down to the roots,
sunk down in mind, bereft of soul,   25
falling to the earth, his soul on its journey.
    One shall travel over distant paths,
going as necessity demands and bearing his food,

---

[1]This second catalogue is similar to the poem known as *The Gifts of Men*, which is
also found in the Exeter Book.

making his way through foreign lands,
a dangerous track; he has few   30
to welcome him, hated everywhere
because of his misfortune, the friendless man.
      One shall ride the broad gallows,
dangling in death until the soul's ward,
the bloody frame, becomes broken.   35
There the dark-feathered raven picks
at his eyes, at the soul-less one.
Nor can the hands hold back this horror:
they may not defend him from the hostile one,
and the dead one, despairing of life,   40
pale on the gallows, awaits fate,
surrounded by the death mist. May his name be accursed!
      One shall the funeral fire torment,
the terrible flames destroy the body of man;
there his death shall be swift,   45
in the fierce, red burning; the woman weeps
as she sees the blaze envelope her son.
      One on the mead-bench, an ale-angry man,
the sword-edge shall deprive of life,
the wine-besotted man; his words were too hasty.   50
One at the beer-feast by the cupbearer's hand
shall become mead-mad; then he does not curb
his mouth by using his mind,
and he shall miserably leave this life,
deprived of pleasure by great wretchedness   55
and men who describe the drunk's revelry
shall call him a man slain by himself.
      One shall in youth by the grace of God
master the misfortune of his time,
and in his old age be blessed   60
by joyful days and rejoice in gladness,
with wealth and with happy feasts,
to the extent to which man holds such treasures.
      Thus, in diverse ways, almighty God
deals out His gifts to every man throughout the earth: 65
He grants and allots and declares,
giving prosperity to one, to another a share of miseries,
to one joy in youth, to another glory in war,
—might in war-play—, to one a blow or stroke,

—radiant glory—,to one skill at the game-table,   70
success at the board. To one books
to become wise. To one the wondrous work
wrought through the goldsmith;
full often he hardens and adorns well
the warrior of the king of Britain, and he gives him broad   75
land as a reward. He receives it gladly.
      One shall gladden men gathered together,
delight those sitting on the benches with beer;
where the drinkers' joy is great.
One shall sit with a harp at his lord's   80
feet, receive treasure
and ever swiftly sweep the strings,
let sound loudly the plectrum, it which leaps,
the nail sounding melodiously; great is the desire for him.
      One shall tame the wild bird in his pride,   85
the hawk on the hand, until the falcon grows gentle,
becomes mild; he puts foot-rings on it,
feeds it thus in fetters, the proud one in its plumage,
he wearies the swift flier with little food,
until the captive in dress and deeds   90
becomes accustomed to his giver
and used to the young man's hand.
      Thus, wondrously does the God of hosts
decree and decide and rule the fate of everyone,
of mankind on earth.   95
Therefore, let all now give Him thanks,
because he cares for men in His mercy.

from *Maxims I*

These excerpts are taken from a lengthy gnomic poem called Maxims I *found in the Exeter Book. "Gnomic" designates a subgroup that belongs to the Old English poetic genre called wisdom poetry.*[1] *All wisdom poems ambitiously claim to pronounce on every aspect of creation, so gnomic poems such as this one are distinguished by*

---

[1] See Shippey (1976) for an edition of the Old English wisdom poems and a discussion of the genre.

their form: sequences of brief proverbial utterances using a simple grammatical structure. Beowulf, *too, absorbs and responds to the gnomic tradition: it both contains many sentential passages that can be illuminated by comparison with examples from wisdom poetry and uses proverbs whose sources can be traced.*[2] *Gnomic poems are sometimes classified by the Old English verb forms they employ:* sceal *gnomes ("ought to," "shall," or "must") express what is expected or customary; and* bið *gnomes ("is" or "will be") express immutable truths or universals. Many of the lines from* Maxims I *fall into the category of* sceal *gnomes. For examples of* bið *gnomes, see* Maxims II, *lines 5 ff.*

Question me with wise words! Let your thoughts not be hidden,
the mystery that you must know most fully! I will not tell you my
    secret
if you conceal from me your wisdom and the thoughts of your
    heart.
Wise men must exchange proverbs. Man shall first praise God,
our father, because He bestowed on us at the beginning   5
life and transitory will. He will remind us of those gifts.
The lord shall dwell in glory, men live on the earth,
the young grow old. For us, God is eternal,
fate changes Him not, nor does anything trouble Him,
the almighty, neither disease nor age.   10
He does not grow old in spirit, but He is still as He was,
a patient prince. He gives us our thoughts,
differing minds, many languages.
Many an island far and wide contains
many races. The lord, the almighty,   15
has established for mankind
spacious domains, just as many peoples
as customs.

———————————

    20

Frost must freeze, fire melt wood,
earth grow, ice make bridges,

———————————

[2]The definitive analysis of the "traditional utterance" in *Beowulf* is Deskis (1996), whose comprehensive study of thirty-one passages in *Beowulf* not only identifies the analogues or sources for the proverbs, but also seeks to discover by what features these passages are marked as gnomic in the text.

water wear a covering, with wonders enclose
the earth's growth. One shall unbind
the frost's fetters—the almighty God;   25
winter must depart, good weather come—
bright summer hot, the sea not still.
The deep way of death is secret longest;
holly must be burned, from his property must the dead man
be parted. Fame is best.   30
A king must buy a queen with goods,
with drinking cups and with bracelets; both must first
be generous with gifts. Battle-bravery must
grow in the man, and the woman thrive,
beloved by her people, be light-hearted,   35
keep secrets, be generous
with horses and with treasures, at the banquets
ever be and always be before the band of comrades,
—first greeting the protector of nobles,
the first cup into her lord's hand   40
put quickly,—and for them know good advice,
for both of them who live in the hall.

                                                                          45

Feud came about for mankind since the earth
first swallowed Abel's blood. That was not a single day's horror
that sprang far and wide from those drops of discord—
a great wickedness for men, for many people,
a menace mingled with fear. Cain slew his own   50
brother, killing preserved him. It was widely known
that eternal strife harmed men, so the city-dwellers felt terror,
the contention of weapons widespread throughout the earth,
the cruel sword devised and tempered.
The shield shall be ready, the dart on the shaft,   55
the edge on the sword, and the point on the spear,
courage in brave men. Helmets for the bold,
and the soul of the base shall be a treasure wasting.

from *Maxims II*

Maxims II, sometimes called the Cotton Maxims to distinguish them from the similar gnomic poem found in the Exeter Book, is contained in the manuscript Cotton Tiberius B. I. The excerpts translated here resemble some of the thematic problems in Beowulf, where the admonition that a "king must guard his kingdom" is in terrible opposition to the ontological status of the dragon, "proud of its treasures." Maxims II contains examples of both sceal *and* bið *gnomes. As Shippey remarks, this gnomic poet "likes the idea of fitness, wholeness,"[1] a comment that suggests a way to come to grips with the initially puzzling sequences in the poem.*

A king must guard his kingdom. Cities can be seen from far away,
the skilled work of giants, which remain in this world,
the wondrous stone-walled forts. Wind in the sky is the swiftest,
thunder at times the loudest. Christ's powers are great.
Fate is the strongest, winter is the coldest,   5
spring the frostiest and cold for the longest,
summer with its sunshine the most beautiful, the sun is the hottest,
the harvest season the most prosperous—it brings men
the year's crops, those which God sends them.
Truth is the most difficult, treasure is the most valuable,   10
as gold is for every man, and an old man the wisest,
a man made sage by distant years, who has experienced a great
    deal.
Grief is very hard to shake off. Clouds glide on.
A young prince must be encouraged in battle
and in gift-giving by good companions.   15
A warrior must have courage, a sword must feel battle
against the helmet.

A ship must have a mast,   20
a spar for the sail. A sword must lie on the lap,
a magnificent iron one. A dragon must be in a barrow,
wise and proud of its treasures.

[1]Shippey (1976, p. 15).

from the Exeter Book Riddles[1]

The Exeter Book contains three riddle sequences, but, because the manuscript is damaged, it is not known how many separate riddles it contains. Williamson (1977) counts ninety riddles in Old English and one in Latin; one riddle occurs twice. Some riddles have been solved in several ways, but none is incredibly difficult, and it seems that at least one of the purposes of these riddles was the poetic contemplation of the thing being described. Thus, as is frequently remarked, the riddle works like the kenning (for example, "whale-road" for ocean, a kenning found in Beowulf*): each offers a condensed poetic description that must be puzzled out one element at a time before the meaning of the whole figure can be grasped. The selection of riddles printed here perhaps gives an impression of how wide might have been their readership among Anglo-Saxons; even King Alfred, for example, is reputed to have enjoyed riddles. Like the conjointure of Latin and vernacular traditions found in other Old English wisdom poems and in* Beowulf*, the riddles of the Exeter Book demonstrate the complex response and absorption of the Latin riddling tradition in the vernacular; several Anglo-Saxon writers are known to have composed Latin riddles, and they may have written others in the vernacular.[2] These riddles have relevance to* Beowulf*; can you work them out before looking at the solution?*

[Riddle 3]

I am the lone wood in the warp of battle,
Wounded by iron, broken by blade,
Weary of war. Often I see
Battle-rush, rage, fierce fight flaring—
I hold no hope for help to come
Before I fall finally with warriors
Or feel the flame. The hard hammer-leavings
Strike me; the bright-edged, battle-sharp
Handiwork of smiths bites in battle.
Always I must await the harder encounter
For I could never find in the world any

---

[1]Translation by Craig Williamson, *A Feast of Creatures: Anglo-Saxon Riddle-Songs*. Philadelphia: University of Pennsylvania Press, 1982, pp. 63, 69, 77, 78, 81, 93, 107, and 126. Reprinted by permission of the author.
[2]These writers include Aldhelm, Tatwine, Alcuin, and Boniface.

Of the race of healers who heal hard wounds
With roots and herbs. So I suffer
Sword-slash and death-wound day and night.

Solution: **shield**

[Riddle 9]

My dress is silver, shimmering gray,
Spun with a blaze of garnets. I craze
Most men: rash fools I run on a road
Of rage, and cage quiet determined men.
Why they love me—lured from mind,
Stripped of strength—remains a riddle.
If they still praise my sinuous power
When they raise high the dearest treasure,
They will find through reckless habit
Dark woe in the dregs of pleasure.

Solution: **cup of wine or other spirits**

[Riddle 17]

I saw the smooth-prancing E S R O
H, high-powered and head-bright,
Sail on the plain. The proud one
Held on its back a battle-power,
N A M. On the nailed creature came
The O R E H. The wide road carried,
Fierce in its flowing, a bold K W
A H. The journey of these was flash
And glint. Let the wise who catch
The drift of this riddle say what I mean.

Solution: **ship**

[Riddle 18]

I am a strange creature shaped for battle,
Coated in colors, dear to my lord.
Bright thread lurks and swings in my mail,

Cradles the death-gem, gift of a lord
Who grips and guides my body forward
Through the wide rush of war. In the clear
Court of day, I bear the glint of gold,
Bright song of smiths. Often I slay
Soul-bearers with thrust and slash.
Sometimes the hall-king decks me in silver
Or garnet praise, raises my power
Where men drink mead, reigns my killing
Or cuts me loose, heart-keen, swing-tired,
Through the broad room of war. Sometimes I sing
Through the throat of a friend—the curse
Of weapons. No son will seek vengeance
On my slayer when battle-foes ring death.
My tribe will not count children of mine
Unless I lordless leave the guardian
Who gave me rings. My fate is strange:
If I follow my lord and wage war,
Sure thrust of a prince's pleasure,
Then I must stroke in brideless play
Without the hope of child-treasure.
I am bound by an ancient craft to lose
That joy—so in sheer celibacy I enjoy
The hoard of heroes. Wrapped with wire
Like a bright fool, I frustrate a woman,
Steal her joy, slake desire. She rants,
Rails, curses, claps hands, chants
Unholy incantations—bladed words
In a bloodless battle I cannot enjoy.

Solution: **sword**

[Riddle 21]

Wob is my name twisted about—
I'm a strange creature shaped for battle.
When I bend and the battle-sting snakes
Through my belly, I am primed to drive off
The death-stroke. When my lord and tormentor
Releases my limbs, I am long again,

As laced with slaughter, I spit out
The death-blend I swallowed before.
What whistles from my belly does not easily pass,
And the man who seizes this sudden cup
Pays with his life for the long, last drink.
Unwound I will not obey any man;
Bound tight, I serve. Say what I am.

Solution: **bow**

[Riddle 33]

The earth was my mother—I was raised
From her cold, wet womb. I know in my mind
I was not woven from hair or wool
By skillful hands. I have no winding
Weft or warp, no thread to sing
Its rushing song; no whirring shuttle
Slides through me, no weaver's sley
Strikes belly or back. No silkworms spin
With inborn skill their subtle gold
For my sides, yet warriors call me
A coat of joy. I do not fear
The quiver's gift, the deadly arrow's flight.
If you are clever and quick with words,
Say what this strange coat is called.

Solution: **coat of mail**

[Riddle 45]

A moth ate songs—wolfed words!
That seemed a weird dish—that a worm
Should swallow, dumb thief in the dark,
The songs of a man, his chants of glory,
Their place of strength. That thief-guest
Was no wiser for having swallowed words.

Solution: **bookworm**

[Riddle 64]

I stretch beyond the bounds of middle-earth,
Shrink down smaller than a hand-worm,
Grow brighter than the moon, and run
Swifter than the sun. I cradle oceans,
Lakes, paths, green plains in my arms.
I dive down under Hell's way and rise up
Over Heaven's home, arced over angels.
I form-fill all earth and ancient worlds,
Fields and sea-streams. Say who I am.

Solution: **creation, nature**

Old English Religious Poetry

from *Exodus*[1]

*One of the great poetic codices of Old English literature, the Junius
manuscript[2] contains a long sequence of Biblical poetry that includes*
Genesis A *and* Genesis B, Exodus, Daniel, *and* Christ and Satan. *The
Old English* Exodus *derives its narrative from* Exodus *13:20–14:31,
which concerns the Israelites departing from Egypt, their crossing of
the Red Sea, and the drowning of the Egyptians due to God's miraculous intervention.* Exodus *reflects Christian exegesis and thus, for
example, not only understands the literal meaning of the tale but also
sees in it a spiritual meaning, casting the "exodus" as the journey of a
Christian through life to one's true homeland in heaven.*

The Biblical book of Exodus *was clearly important to the
Anglo-Saxons: King Alfred begins his law code with an excerpt
from* Exodus, *an act that seeks to put him in the tradition of law-
givers that commences with Moses, and Ælfric, retelling in a prose*

---

[1]Translation by J. R. R. Tolkien, *The Old English* Exodus: *Text, Translation, and
Commentary by J. R. R. Tolkien.* Joan Turville-Petre (ed.). Oxford: Clarendon
Press, 1981. Reprinted by permission of the Tolkien Estate.

[2]The Junius manuscript (Oxford, Bodleian Library, Junius 11) gets its name from its
owner Franciscus Junius (1591–1677), who received the book from the archbishop
of Armagh, James Ussher (1581–1656), around 1651.

treatise the experiences of the Israelites in the desert, suggests a continuity between the Anglo-Saxon church and the Jewish "priesthood." The poem Exodus, *energized by social and poetical structures familiar to the Anglo-Saxons, presents Moses as a mighty war-chief and a wise speaker. These excerpts from* Exodus *show Moses as a military leader who can also talk to his people and emphasizes the heroic preoccupations of the poem, in which weapons and courage are always occasions for comment. In its depiction of war, where none occurs in the Biblical narrative, the Old English* Exodus *would surely appeal to an audience of* Beowulf. *But* Exodus *is also about demonstrating the divine protection of a chosen people, and the Anglo-Saxons here imagine themselves to be like the Israelites. As J. R. R. Tolkien states in the Introduction to his edition and translation of the poem: ". . .* Exodus *has long deservedly been esteemed as a spirited piece of writing, in which a greater harmony between the ancient English style and the biblical subject-matter has been achieved than is usual. This is not due alone to the greater suitability of the warlike matter to the heroic and traditional style, for the poet . . . has shown a narrative skill in the use of his material, and (still more important) a conception of his material which transcends a mere tale of victory."*[3]

In the first excerpt, note the opening call to attention in the first-person plural pronoun. The second excerpt shows Moses leading his troops ("the seafarers") against the Egyptians. The last excerpt begins with an expatiation on wisdom and concludes with an example of this wisdom when Moses addresses his warriors.

Lo! We have heard how near and far over middle-earth Moses declared his ordinances to men, uttering in words wondrous laws to the races of mankind—to all the blessed healing of their life's care in heaven on high after the perilous journey, to all the living enduring counsel: let him hearken who will!

Unsleeping there all that concourse of one race awaited the onset of the mightier power, until at the grey hour of dawn Moses bade men with brazen trumpets summon the people, call up the warriors to arise and put on their mail, turn their minds to valour, bearing their bright harness; bade with signals assemble the companies yet nigher the shore. The chieftains bold

---

[3]Tolkien (1981, p. 33).

heeded the loud call to war, and host was stirred. The seafarers over the slopes, obeying the trumpet, struck their pavilions upon the field; their army was in haste. Then they numbered in the van, their defence against the evil that pursued, twelve battalions of dauntless hearts—their might was set in motion—in each of these were chosen under arms of the power of the people fifty companies of the men of proven valour of that noble race; each company of that renowned host contained ten numbered hundreds of men with spears and trained to war, warriors of fame. A warlike host was that. There the captains of the army summoned no weakling into the fighting force, such as for their youth not yet might amid the serried shields with hands defend the mail upon their manly breasts against the hostile foe, nor yet had suffered the pain of wound that passed the shield's defence or known body's hurt, the scar of the gallant play of spears; and the old, too, men gone grey in war, might not in that battle avail, if their strength among the valiant companies had waned. Nay, rather the warriors they chose by body's power, so that in the ranks of Israel they should with honour fulfil the valour of their hearts, and their mighty strength be addressed to grasping the spear in war. Then was all the army of those men unflinching from the strokes of battle gathered together eager for the advance. The banner rode on high, brightest of emblems. Yet still all men waited until the herald of their journey shining above their shields nigh to the flowing of the sea passed into the courts of the sky. Thereupon there leapt forth before the hosts a crier, a herald bold of voice, and upraised his shield, commanding the captains to still the ranks while the speech of their proud prince should be heard by many. The ruler of their might purposed to speak words with voice inspired amid the assembled companies. Nobly he spoke, the leader of that host: 'Be ye not by this made more afraid, though Pharaoh have brought against you armies vast, a countless multitude of men! To all of these will the mighty Lord this day by my hand deliver the guerdon of their deeds, that no longer may they live to possess in unhappy thraldom the race of Israel. Ye will not fear battalions already dead and bodies doomed to die—the space is at an end of their swift-passing life. The word of God is taken from your hearts. Counsel better do I know: that ye should honour the Prince of Glory and pray to the Lord of Life for His comfort, salvation, and victory, as ye take your road. Lo! it is the everlasting God of Abraham, the Master of Creation, that defendeth this host with mighty hand; in Him is courage, power, and valour.'

Thereupon eternal counsels upon the shores of the sea to Israel Moses the noble spake, with holy speech, their high errand telling. The deeds of that day he did not in silence keep. Even so shall the peoples of men still in scriptures find each solemn word tht God announced to him upon the journey with words of truth. If the interpreter of lifegiving knowledge bright-burning in the breast, the ruler of the body's house, will with spiritual keys unlock the lavish good there stored, then the secrets (of the writing) will be explained, forth shall counsel come. Words of wisdom it embraceth, and earnestly will teach our hearts that we be not destitute of divine instruction and of the mercies of God; Who to us vouchsafeth yet more, now that learned men tell us of a better and a more lasting life of joy. A fading mirth is this, and cursed with evils, permitted to wanderers, a waiting time of unhappy men. Exiles from home, in mourning they possess this hall of passing guests, lamenting in their hearts; they know the house of torment established under earth, where be fire and snake, an open everlasting tomb of all evil things. Thus now the arch-thieves, old age or untimely death, divide the realm; but a destined hour shall after come, and the greatest power and glory above the earth, a day of wrath upon men's deeds. The Lord himself in that place of meeting shall judge many a man. Then shall He lead the souls of the just, the spirits blest, into the heavens above, where shall be light and life, heaven, abounding joys; His court in bliss shall praise the Lord, the glorious King of Hosts for ever.

Thus spake he with loud voice mindful of wise words, man most gracious, with power strengthened. The host silent and still waited on the destined purpose; they observed the marvellous event, and noted the hope of salvation from their valiant leader's mouth. To many there he spake. 'Great is this multitude; trusty the Leader of the host, a succour most mighty He that this march doth guide! He hath vouchsafed to us in the land of Canaan town, and gold, and kingdom broad. Now He will accomplish that which He long ago did promise with sworn oath,

He, the Lord of Angels, in days of yore unto our fathers' race, if
ye will but keep His holy bidding, that ye shall go ever forth in triumph over every foe, shall possess in victory the halls of men's
revelry between the two seas. Great shall your fortune be!'

from *Judith*

Judith *follows* Beowulf *directly in the manuscript Cotton Vitellius
A. xv. Derived from the apocryphal book* Liber Judith, *it describes
how Judith beheads the Assyrian Holofernes, a general of Neb-
uchadnezzar, thus rescuing her people from destruction by the
Assyrian army. Stark and dramatic,* Judith *treats its source freely,
showing the influences both of secular heroic poetry and of Latin
hagiography. Nothing is known of the circumstances that
prompted the poem's composition, although it could be read as a
political tract, urging English resistance of pagan invaders like the
Vikings.[1] The eleventh-century abbot Ælfric imagines* Judith *as
exemplifying resistance and writes: "Judith, the widow who over-
came the Assyrian general, has her own book among the others
concerning her own victory. It is also set down in our manner in
English, as an example to you people that you should defend your
land with weapons against the invading army."[2]
Judith shares with* Beowulf *the theme of overweening pride,
depicted by Holofernes, against a humble, but tough, piety seen in*
Judith. *Both poems employ the effective rhetorical technique of
portraying bad and good examples. In the first excerpt, Holofernes
exemplifies all that a leader should not be: selfish, uncontrolled,
drunken. Here, traditional formulae used to portray a good
leader—like "gold-friend of men"—are deployed ironically. In the
second excerpt,* Judith, *having discovered Holofernes's weakness
for drink and prayed to God to strengthen her, behaves heroically
and saves her people.*

---

[1]Chamberlain (1975).

[2]Quoted in *The Old English Heptateuch.* S. J. Crawford, ed. Early English Text
Society o.s. 160. London: 1922, p. 48. Ælfric wrote these remarks to a landowner
named Sigeweard in order to explain why he had translated and paraphrased certain books of the Old Testament.

Then Holofernes, the gold-friend of men,
rejoiced as wine poured:
he laughed and he shouted, he yelled and he screamed,
so that people from far off could hear
how the stout-hearted one stormed and shrieked,   25
proud and mead-merry, he repeatedly urged
the bench-sitters to feast well.
Thus, that evil one for the whole day
drenched his troops with wine,—
that strong-hearted treasure-giver,—so that they lay swooning,   30
his whole warband dead drunk, so that they lay as if they were
    dead,
drained of all that was good.

Then that highest Judge of us all
filled her at once with perfect courage,   35
as He does for all men on earth who seek
His aid wisely and with true faith. Then her heart rejoiced,
hope was renewed. Then she grabbed the heathen man
firmly by his hair, and with both her hands she drew him
    towards her,
putting him to shame, and then skillfully   40
she laid the hateful man down,
placing the unbeliever where she could manage best
what she had to do. Then the one with curling tresses
struck the hostile foe with his blood-stained sword,
so that she cut his neck halfway through: 45
there he lay in a swoon,
drunk and badly wounded. He was not dead yet,
wholly lifeless. Then the undaunted woman,
the noble one, again struck
the heathen hound, so that his head rolled   50
off on the floor. The foul corpse lay
there empty; the spirit turned elsewhere
under the deep cliff,[3] and there it was weighed down,
bound forever in torment,

[3]Fry (1987) suggests that this passage, which moves us suddenly from a desert tent to a hellish venue, is an example of a vernacular poetic typescene called "the cliff of death" which always includes a cliff, serpents, darkness, and deprivation. Fry puts the monsters' mere in *Beowulf* in this group. See also Orchard (1995, pp. 41–42).

encircled by snakes, fettered by agonies,   55
held fast in hell-fire
after its departure. Nor need he have any hope,
engulfed by gloom, that he might leave
that hall of serpents, but there he must dwell,
forever and without end,   60
in that dark dwelling, empty of joy.

from *Christ III*

> Christ III *is the final section of the first item found in the Exeter*
> Book; *some scholars have argued that this final section was*
> *intended as a single unified poem about Christ some 1,664 lines*
> *long. Divisions in the Exeter Book manuscript have led others to*
> *believe this item to be three separate poems, hence the title* Christ
> III. Christ III *powerfully expresses the theme of "Judgment Day."*
> *The excerpt included here contains a grim and effective series of*
> *apocalyptic images, notable because they call up the frightening*
> *paradox of a burning sea. This image of "fire and flood" occurs in*
> Beowulf *when Beowulf finds himself in the underwater but eerily*
> *fire-lit hall of the Grendel-kin, as well as later when Hrothgar*
> *warns Beowulf of the transitoriness of earthly life and its pleasures.*
> *Discussing the potency of the "fire and flood" image, Orchard*
> *(1995, pp. 42–44), emphasizes the link between the punishing flood*
> *that swept through the earth in Noah's time and the destructive fire*
> *that will come when the world ends.*

Thus the greedy spirit sweeps through the depths;
the fierce flame fells the high timbered houses
to the ground. The far-famed fire,
hot and hungry, will destroy the whole world
through the terror of burning. City walls   5
will collapse, shattered. Mountains will melt,
and high cliffs, which kept the land
always safe from floods,
barriers fixed and firm against water,
the breaking waves. Then the deadly flame   10

shall kill all beasts and birds,
a wrathful warrior walking the world.
Just as the water flowed,
stirred the floods, then in a sea of fire,
the fish of the sea will sear, stop from swimming;   15
every sea-creature will die miserably.
The water will burn like wax. There shall be more marvels
than any man can conceive of in his mind:
how the din and the storm and the driving gust
shall shatter creation. The warriors shall wail,   20
weep and moan with wretched voices,
hapless, disheartened, troubled by sorrows.
The glaring flame shall blaze upon those befouled by sin,
and the fires shall devour the gold-worked treasures,
all the ancient inheritance of the kings of the land.   25
There shall be din and distress, and the travail of the living,
wailing and loud weeping, the pitiful lament of men,
because of the tumult from heaven. No one guilty of evil deeds
may seek shelter from that, win free
from the fire anywhere in the land: 30
for in every region, the fire shall stretch forth its grasp,
shall fiercely seek, greedily search,
within and without, to the corners of the earth,
until the flash of the flame has wholly consumed
in its surge the foulness of earth's corruption.   35

from *Andreas*

Andreas *is the first poem found in the Vercelli Book.*[1] *This lengthy
account of the life of St.* Andrew *is ultimately derived from the
Greek apocryphal* Acts of Andrew and Matthias, *though the
poem's immediate source is a now-lost Latin version of the Greek*

[1]The Vercelli Book (Vercelli, Biblioteca capitolare CXVII), dated to the second half of
the tenth century, is one of the four great Old English poetic manuscripts. Written in
England, it contains twenty-three items in prose and six in verse. The manuscript was
rediscovered in the early nineteenth century by the German jurist Friedrich Blume,
who recognized the importance of its contents. Vercelli, Italy, was a stopping point on
the pilgrimage route to Rome, but why the manuscript was left there is unknown.

text. In Andreas, *God directs Andrew to rescue Matthew from the land of the fierce and cannibalistic Mermedonians.*[2] *Embarking with a chosen retinue, Andrew and his men survive a storm while on shipboard, captivity, and many other trials, before converting the cannibals and returning home. Similarities to* Beowulf *led some scholars to believe that* Andreas *was consciously modeled on it, but current thinking is that the two poems use common poetic resources. The first excerpt shares with* Beowulf *an opening formula, including a command to attention and the use of the first-person plural pronoun. In the second, Andrew recalls his frightened men to their holy purpose by reminding them of the example of Jesus stilling the tempest at sea. That excerpt concludes with a proverb familiar from* Beowulf's *speech to Unferth at lines 508–10.*

Listen! We have heard in days gone by,
of twelve rich in glory who dwelt beneath the stars,
thegns of the Lord. Their courage in the fight
failed never, even when banners crashed in war,
from that time when they each were apportioned a place,
as God Himself declared to them,
the High King of heaven above.
     Famous men were they, known throughout the earth,
bold leaders and brave in battle,
warriors of might, when shield and hand
guarded the head upon the field of battle, the place of war.

Then wisely with words he [Andrew] began
to cheer his disciples, the glorious men:
"When you set out on the sea,
it was your purpose to hazard your lives among foes
and to suffer death for the love of the Lord,
in the kingdom of the Africans,
to surrender your souls. I myself know
that the maker of angels,

----

[2]The Anglo-Saxons perhaps thought that the fantastic tribe called "Mermedonians" lived in Africa or Ethiopia, places in which great marvels were situated.

the lord of hosts, protects us. The terror of the water
shall be rebuked and vanquished through the king of glory,
the tossing flood grow calmer.
So did it happen before this that we,
in a ship on the surf, made trial of the waves,
riding on the surge. The dread waterways
seemed dangerous, the ocean streams
beat on the cordage, the sea often spoke,
wave upon wave. At times a terror
towered up out of the ocean's breast
over the ship into the hold of the vessel. There the Almighty,
the Lord of mankind, abode in the ship,
in his glory. Men became fearful in heart,
they desired safety, mercy from the Glorious One.
Then the company upon the ship began
to cry out. Straightway the King,
the Lord of angels, rose up. He stilled the waves,
the seething water, He rebuked the winds;
the sea sank down, the size of the ocean floods
became moderate. Then our hearts leaped up
when we beheld under the course of the sky
winds and waves and the water terror
frightened in awe of the Lord.
Wherefore, I wish to tell you truly
that the living God never forsakes
a man on the earth, if his courage is good."

Old English Historical Prose

from the Anglo-Saxon Chronicle

*The term "Anglo-Saxon Chronicle" applies to a set of anonymous
Old English annals providing much of the historical information
known about preconquest England. It is crucial for English literature because it was written in the vernacular and not in Latin, as
were most early European histories. Following the example of the*

*historian Bede, the Anglo-Saxon Chronicle is the first English his-
tory to reckon years from the incarnation of Jesus Christ, that is,
anno Domini. The original compilation, now called the "common
stock," was probably begun in the late ninth century under the
patronage of King Alfred and took its information from many
sources of history, including Kentish, Mercian, South Saxon, and
West Saxon annals and Bede's Latin* Ecclesiastical History of the
English People. *Copies of the Anglo-Saxon Chronicle were probably
distributed from King Alfred's capital, Winchester, to important
regional centers in the West Saxon kingdom where they were maintained systematically with royal and local matters of significance;
both laymen and clerics may have contributed entries. Each manuscript of the Anglo-Saxon Chronicle thus differs in what it records,
but each surviving example begins with Julius Caesar's conquest of
the British Isles; the latest entry made is for 1154. The Anglo-Saxon
Chronicle may have begun as a project for the writing down of an
emerging comprehensive "English" history from Roman Britain
through King Alfred's struggle against Scandinavian invaders, drawing together many peoples into a common resistance. The Anglo-
Saxon Chronicle itself became an authoritative source beginning
with Asser's Latin* Life of Alfred, King of the Anglo-Saxons *down
through the later Anglo-Norman histories. Seven manuscripts and a
fragment of the Anglo-Saxon Chronicle are now extant.[1] As the following selections illustrate, the Anglo-Saxon Chronicle contains
information that exceeds the annalistic, including many passages
central to the study of the cultural milieu of* Beowulf.

793. In this year came terrible portents over Northumbria, frightening the people most miserably: these consisted of immense whirl-
winds and flashes of lightening, and fiery dragons were seen flying
in the air. A great famine immediately followed these signs, and not
long after that, on the eighth of June in the same year, the ravages of
heathen men miserably destroyed God's church on Lindisfarne,[2]
with plunder and slaughter. And Sicga died on February 22.

---

[1]These manuscripts are designated by alphabetic sigla. When possible, the Parker
Chronicle or "A," which is the oldest surviving manuscript of the Anglo-Saxon
Chronicle and which was begun in Winchester, is quoted. It once belonged to Matthew
Parker (1504–75), archbishop of Canterbury from 1559 until his death, who collected
many Anglo-Saxon manuscripts. The Parker Chronicle commences in 891 and ends in
1070. Dates in square brackets represent corrections to the dates recorded in the annal.

[2]The church where the community founded by St. Cuthbert had lived for decades.

827 [829]. In this year the moon grew dark on Christmas night. And in the same year King Ecgberht conquered Mercia and all that was south of the Humber, and he was the eighth king to be bretwalda;[3] the first to rule so great a kingdom was Ælle, king of Sussex; the second was Ceawlin, king of the West Saxons; the third was Æthelberht, king of Kent; the fourth was Rædwald, king of East Anglia;[4] the fifth was Edwin, king of Northumbria; the sixth was Oswald, who reigned after him; the seventh was Oswy, Oswald's brother; the eighth was Ecgberht, king of Wessex. This Ecgberht led an army to Dore against the Northumbrians, where they offered him submission and peace; and after that, they parted.

855. Here the heathen men for the first time settled in Sheppey over the winter. And the same year, King Æthelwulf conveyed by charter the tenth part of his land over all his kingdom to the praise of God and his own eternal salvation. And the same year he traveled to Rome in great state, lived there for twelve months, and then went towards home. And Charles, king of the Franks, gave him his daughter as queen, and after that he came to his people, and they were glad of it. And two years after he came from the Franks he died, and his body lies at Winchester.[5] And he ruled eighteen and a half years. And that Æthelwulf was Ecgberht's son, Ecgberht Ealhmund's son, Ealhmund Eafa's son, Eafa Eoppa's son, Eoppa Ingeld's son; Ingeld was the brother of Ine, king of Wessex, who afterward traveled to St. Peter's and afterwards gave up his life there; and they were the sons of Cenred; Cenred was Ceolwald's son, Ceolwald Cutha's son, Cutha Cuthwine's son, Cuthwine Ceawlin's son, Ceawlin Cynric's son, Cynric Cerdic's son, Cerdic Elesa's son, Elesa Esla's son, Esla Gewis's son, Gewis Wig's son, Wig Freawine's son, Freawine Frealaf's son, Frealaf Frithugar's son, Frithugar Brand's son, Brand Bældæg's son, Bældæg Woden's son, Woden Frithuwald's son, Frithuwald Freawine's son, Freawine Frealaf's son, Frealaf Frithuwulf's son, Frithuwulf's Finn's son, Finn Godwulf's son, Godwulf Geat's son, Geat Tætwa's son, Tætwa Beaw's son, Beaw Sceldwa's son, Sceldwa Heremod's son, Heremod Iter-

---

[3]A term probably signifying "ruler of Britain," first used in the Anglo-Saxon Chronicle (see also Bede's *Ecclesiastical History of the English People*, ii. 5).

[4]For Rædwald's importance to *Beowulf*, see note to line 47 (page 5).

[5]Æthelwulf died in 858. He was first buried at the important minster at Steyning (Sussex, England) and reburied later at Winchester.

mon's son, Itermon Hrathra's son—he was born in the ark; Noah, Lamech, Methuselah, Enoch, Jared, Mahalaleel, Cainan, Enos, Seth, Adam[6] the first man, and our father who is Christ. Amen. And then Æthelwulf's two sons succeeded to the kingdom: Æthelbald to the kingdom of Wessex, and Æthelberht to the kingdom of the inhabitants of Kent and to the kingdom of Essex and to Surrey and to the kingdom of Sussex; and then Æthelbald ruled five years.

865. Here the heathen raiding army stayed in the isle of Thanet, and made peace with the inhabitants of Kent; and the inhabitants of Kent promised them money in return for that peace. And the raiding army stole away by night, and under the cover of that peace and that promise, they raided all eastern Kent.

878. Here in mid-winter, after Twelfth Night, the raiding army stole away to Chippenham, and overran the land of the West Saxons, and drove many of the people across the sea, and the greatest part of the others, they overran, and they submitted to them—except for Alfred the king who with a small band went with difficulty through the woods and into the fastnesses of the swamps. And that same winter a brother of Ivar and Halfdan was in Wessex, in Devonshire, with twenty-three ships, and there he was killed, and eight hundred men with him, and forty of his army.[7] And the Easter after, King Alfred with a small band built a fort at Athelney, and from that fort, with the part of the men of Somerset nearest it, was making war on the raiding army. Then in the seventh week after Easter, he rode to Ecgberht's Stone, east of Selwood, and there all of Somerset and Wiltshire and that part of Hampshire which was on this side of the sea[8] came to join him and were glad to see him. And one day later he went from those camps to Island Wood, and one day to Edington, and there he fought against the whole raiding army and put it to flight, riding after it as far as the fort, where he remained fourteen days. And then the raiding army gave him hostages and great oaths that they would leave his kingdom, and they promised him that their king would receive baptism, and they fulfilled it thus. And

---

[6]See Hill (1987) for the descent from Adam of the royal house of the West Saxons and Bruce (2002), pp. 3–41, for a study of Scyld Scefing in Anglo-Saxon genealogies and poems.

[7]Other versions add that a war-banner called "raven" was taken from the Danes.

[8]Probably those men who had not fled across the English Channel.

three weeks later, King Guthrum, one of thirty of the most honorable men who were in the raiding army, came to him at Aller, which is near Athelney, and there the king sponsored his baptism; and his chrism-loosing[9] was at Wedmore. He was there twelve days with the king, who honored him and his companions with riches.

901 [899]. Here died Alfred, the son of Æthelwulf, six days before the feast of All Hallows [November 1]. He was king over all the English race, except that part that was under the control of the Danes, and he held that kingdom twenty-eight-and-a-half years. Then Edward, his son, succeeded to the kingdom. Then Æthelwold, his father's brother's son, rode out and seized the manor at Wimborne and Twinham, without leave of the king and his council. Then the king rode with his army, and he camped the same night at Badbury near Wimborne. And Æthelwold stayed within the manor with the men that were under him, and he had all the gates barricaded, saying, that he would either live there or die there. Then under cover of that, he stole away in the night, and sought the army in Northumbria. And the king gave orders to ride after him, and he could not be overtaken then. Then they rode after the woman whom he [Æthelwold] had taken without the king's leave and against the command of the bishops, because she was formerly consecrated a nun. And in this year Æthelred, who was ealdorman in Devon, died four weeks before King Alfred.

946. Here King Edmund died on St. Augustine's day [May 26]. It was widely known how he ended his days: that Liofa stabbed him at Pucklechurch. And Æthelflæd of Damerham, daughter of ealdorman Ælfgar, was then his queen. And he had the kingdom for six-and-a-half years; and then after him his brother Eadred the Ætheling succeeded to the kingdom, and he reduced all the land of Northumbria to his rule, and the Scots gave him oaths that they would do all that he wanted.

993 [991]. In this year came Olaf[10] with ninety-three ships to Folkestone, which he raided round about, and then went from there to Sandwich, and so from there to Ipswich, and overran that; and so

---

[9]The white band that is bound about the forehead and anointed with oil is removed about a week after baptism.

[10]Olaf Tryggvason, who was later king of Norway.

to Maldon. And the ealdorman Byrhtnoth came against them there with his army and fought with them; and they killed the ealdorman there, and took possession of the place of slaughter.[11] And afterwards, they made peace with them, and the king received him [Olaf] at the bishop's hands by the advice of Sigeric, bishop of the inhabitants of Kent, and Ælfheah, bishop of Winchester.

Old English Legal Prose

Though no law codes or treaties are mentioned in Beowulf, *which is set in the early sixth century in Scandinavia before vernacular law codes were written, its Anglo-Saxon audience would have known laws and treaties recorded in manuscripts. In these selections, notice the importance of the oath, of civil order, of working out just relationships between the English and the Scandinavians in the British Isles, and of anxiety over reversion to heathen practices.*

from the Laws of Alfred[1]

King Alfred's law code was issued in the late 880s or early 890s, toward the end of his reign. This law code includes a series of quotations from the biblical book of Exodus *and a discussion of how Mosaic law can be applied to Christian nations.*

1. First we direct that which is most necessary: that each man carefully keep his oath and pledge.
7. If anyone fights or draws his weapon in the king's hall, and he is captured, it is to be the king's judgment whether he will grant him life or death.

---

[11] A reference to the famous English defeat at Maldon, for which see the justly famous Old English heroic poem called *The Battle of Maldon.*

[1] Alfred's law code is edited by Felix Liebermann, *Die Gesetze der Angelsachsen.* Vol. I. Halle 1903–16, pp. 15–89; see translations in Whitelock (1979, pp. 407–16); and Keynes and Lapidge (1983, pp. 163–70).

7.1. If he escapes and is afterwards captured, he will pay compensation for the crime, according to what he has done, with his wergeld or a fine.

32. If anyone is guilty of public slander, and it is proved against him, it is to be compensated for with no lighter penalty than the cutting off of his tongue, with the provision that it be redeemed at no lesser rate than it is valued in proportion to the wergeld.

The Treaty between Alfred and Guthrum[2]

Alfred won a victory over the Danish leader Guthrum in 878 (see the Anglo-Saxon Chronicle for that date); this treaty was drawn up about 886, but certainly before 890 when Guthrum, who controlled the Viking population of East Anglia, died. The treaty attempts to clarify the boundary between the part of England that Alfred controlled and that of the Danish settlers in England, regulating conduct between the two groups.

Prologue: This is the peace which King Alfred and King Guthrum and the councillors of all the English race and all the people who are in East Anglia have all agreed on and confirmed with oaths, for themselves and for their subjects, both for the living and those unborn, who care to have God's grace or ours.

1. First, concerning our boundaries: up the Thames [River], and then up the Lea [River], and along the Lea to its source, then in a straight line to Bedford, then up the Ouse [River] to Watling Street.

2. Next: if a man is slain, all of us estimate an Englishman and a Dane at the same amount, at eight half-marks[3] of refined gold, except for the churl who occupies rented land, and their freedmen; these also are estimated at the same amount: both at 200 shillings.

---

[2]Alfred's treaty is edited by Felix Liebermann, *Die Gesetze der Angelsachsen*, Vol. I. Halle: 1903–16, pp. 126–29; see translations in Whitelock (1979, pp. 416–17) and Keynes and Lapidge (1983, pp. 171–72).

[3]The mark is a Scandinavian weight.

3. And if anyone accuses a king's thegn of manslaughter, if he dares to clear himself by oath, he is to do it with twelve thegns of the king. If anyone accuses a man who is less powerful than a king's thegn, he is to clear himself with eleven of his equals and with one thegn of the king. And so in every suit which involves more than four mancuses;[4] and if he dare not clear himself, he is to pay for it with three-fold compensation, according as it is valued.

4. And that each man is to know his warrantor at the purchase of men or horses or oxen.

5. And we all agreed on the day when the oaths were sworn that no slaves nor freemen might go without permission into the army of the Danes, any more than any of theirs to us. But if it happens that from necessity any one of them wishes to have dealings with us, or we with them, for cattle or goods, it is to be permitted on the condition that hostages be given as a pledge of peace and as evidence that anyone may know that no fraud is intended.

Preface to the Laws of Cnut[5]

Cnut, king of England from 1016 to 1035 and king of Denmark from c. 1018 to 1035, was on shipboard when his father, Swein Fork-beard, invaded and conquered England, driving King Æthelred out. Cnut invaded England himself in 1015, defeating Æthelred and Edmund Ironside at the battle of Assandun (Essex, England) on October 18, 1016. The kingdom was divided between the two sides, but when Edmund died in 1016, Cnut secured recognition as the king of all England. This law code is part of a political settlement that enabled him to rule England until his death in 1035. Cnut's laws rely heavily on earlier codes and religious prose; this preface is dated to 1018. Following the ecclesiastical laws are the secular laws referred to as II Cnut.

---

[4]The mancus is both a weight of gold and a unit of currency equivalent to thirty silver pennies; it was used in Anglo-Saxon England.

[5]This preface is edited by Felix Liebermann, *Die Gesetze der Angelsachsen*, Vol. I. Halle: 1903–16, p. 278; see translation in Whitelock (1979, p. 452).

This is the ordinance which the councillors determined and devised according to many good precedents, and that took place as soon as King Cnut, with the advice of his councillors, completely established peace and friendship between the Danes and the English and ended all their former strife. In the first place, the councillors determined that above all things they would always honor one God and steadfastly hold one Christian faith, and that they would love King Cnut with due loyalty and observe Edgar's laws. And they agreed that they would, with the help of God, seek to find out, as best they could, what was needed for the nation. Now we wish to make clear what can benefit us in religious and secular matters; let him heed it, who will. Let us very resolutely turn from sins, and eagerly atone for our misdeeds, and duly love and honor one God, and steadfastly hold one Christian faith, and diligently avoid every heathen practice.

From the Laws of Cnut

4. And we command that everyone zealously begin to purify every part of this land and to cease everywhere from sinful deeds. And if witches or sorcerers, murderers or whores, are caught anywhere in this land, drive them from the country immediately or put them away, unless they cease and most fervently amend themselves.

4.1. And we command that traitors and outlaws from God and man depart from this land, unless they submit and readily amend themselves.

4.2. And that thieves and criminals die, unless they cease.

5. And we earnestly forbid every heathen practice.

5.1. It is heathen practice if one worships idols: namely, if one worships heathen gods and the sun or the moon, fire or surges of water, wells or stones or any kind of forest trees; or if one practices witchcraft, or causes death by any means, either by sacrifice or divination, or takes part in delusions of this sort.

Old English Religious Prose

from *Blickling Homily XVI*

The Blickling Homilies *are an anonymous collection of eighteen sermons found in a single late tenth-century manuscript.*[1] *Richard Morris, who edited them in 1880, was the first to write about the similarity between the monsters' mere in* Beowulf *and this passage, which relates St. Paul's vision of hell.*[2] *The ultimate source of this part of the homily is the late antique* Visio S. Pauli, *an Old English version of which is found in an eleventh-century manuscript. Because that version is not identical in all of its details with* Blickling Homily XVI, *it is concluded that a lost common source of the* Visio *must underlie the several texts that drew upon this horrifying imagery. Vision literature, a well-represented genre in the Anglo-Saxon period, serves to aid in contemplation of the "Day of Judgment" and to urge the repentance that should precede it. This homily was delivered on the occasion of the dedication of a church to St. Michael the archangel; it is sometimes entitled the* Michaelmas Sermon.

As St. Paul was looking toward the northern part of this world, where all the waters go down, he also saw there, above the waters, a certain grey stone. And to the north of the stone there had grown very frosty woods, and there were dark mists, and beneath the stone was the dwelling place of water-monsters and wolves. And he saw that on that cliff many black souls bound by their hands were hanging in the icy woods; and their foes in the shape of water-monsters were clutching at them like greedy wolves, and the water under the cliff below was black, and between the cliff and the water it was about twelve miles down. And when the branches broke, the souls which hung on the branches dropped down, and the water-monsters seized them. There were the souls of those who had sinned wickedly in the world and who would not cease from it

---

[1]The manuscript is at Princeton University, Scheide Library M71. Orchard (1995, p. 39, n55) points out that this homily is number XVII in Morris's edition, but the homilies from XVII to XIX have since been renumbered.

[2]See Morris (1880, pp. vi–vii). For a discussion of the monsters' mere in *Beowulf*, see Orchard (1995, pp. 37–41).

before their life's end. But let us now earnestly bid St. Michael to lead our souls into bliss, where they may rejoice in eternity without end. Amen.

Wulfstan
from *On False Gods*[1]

Unknown before he became bishop of London (996–1002), Wulfstan was a notable stylist in both Latin and the vernacular, as well as an advisor to several Anglo-Saxon kings. He was named bishop of Worcester in 1002 and archbishop of York in 1016, dying on May 28, 1023. Twenty-six of his sermons survive, and his hand is apparent in the law codes of Æthelred and Cnut, and in prose works that helped to shape the roles of ecclesiastical and secular institutions in England. Wulfstan here revises a sermon by the scholarly abbot Ælfric (c. 950–c. 1010), whose distinguished vernacular writings were widely circulated.

Now, it was long ago that, because of the devil, many things went wrong and mankind disobeyed God too much and paganism inflicted damage all too widely—and widely inflicts damage still. We do not read anywhere in books, though, that they set up idols anywhere in the world during all the time which was before Noah's flood. But then it happened that after Noah's flood, Nimrod[2] and the giants wrought the marvelous tower.[3] And as the book tells, it came to pass that there were as many languages as there were workmen. Then afterwards they dispersed into distant lands, and then mankind soon greatly increased. And then at last they were deceived by that old devil who had long betrayed Adam, so that

[1]An edition of the only copy of this sermon is found in Bethurum (1957, pp. 221–24).

[2]For a discussion of Nimrod, described as a great builder of cities and hunter in *Genesis* 10–11, and the "kin of Cain" in *Beowulf*, see Orchard (1995, pp. 77–78 and 82–84). Wulfstan follows a medieval tradition that Nimrod is the founder of Babylon and a rebel.

[3]The Tower of Babel; see *Genesis* 11:1–9. The tradition that the Tower was made by giants is apocryphal; compare the ascription of great desolate buildings to the "work of giants" in *Beowulf* and *The Ruin*.

they perversely and heretically made pagan gods for themselves and scorned the true God and their own Creator who created and fashioned them as men.

Moreover, through the teaching of the devil, they took it for wisdom to worship the sun and the moon as gods on account of their shining brightness. And then at last, through the teaching of the devil, they offered them sacrifices and forsook their lord who had created and fashioned them. Some men also said that the shining stars were gods and began to worship them earnestly. And some believed in fire on account of its sudden heat, some also in water, and some believed in the earth because it nourished all things.[4] But they might have readily discerned, if they had the power of reason, who the true God is who created all things for the enjoyment and the use of us men, which he granted mankind because of His great goodness. . . .

Yet the heathen would not be satisfied with as few gods as they had previously, but in the end, they took to worshiping various giants and violent men of the earth who became strong in worldly power and were awe-inspiring while they lived and foully followed their own lusts. . . .

Wulfstan

from *Sermon of the "Wolf" to the English*[1]

Wulfstan wrote under the alias "Lupus," or "wolf." This sermon is his most well-known work, a beautifully sustained piece of impassioned writing in the vernacular, vividly depicting the sense of assault and peril present during the last years of Æthelred's reign. Its recital of evils, especially the types of disloyalty that Wulfstan lists, recall the actions criticized by the Beowulf-*poet. This sermon survives in five manuscript copies that represent three different versions of the text. It has a long history in print too, having first been edited and published by William Elstob in 1701.*

---

[4]The laws of Cnut prohibit the worship of elements like fire and water (see 5.1).
[1]Edited in Bethurum (1957, pp. 261–75); also translated in Whitelock (1979, pp. 929–34).

The sermon of the Wolf to the English, when the Danes persecuted them most, which was in the year 1014 from the incarnation of our Lord Jesus Christ.

Beloved men, recognize what is true: this world is in haste and draws near its end, and therefore, in the world, things go from bad to worse, and so it must be that because of the sins of the people, things will get very much worse before the coming of the Antichrist—and then it will be terrible and cruel widely throughout the world.

Understand well too that for many years now the devil has led this nation too greatly astray, and there has been little loyalty among men, though they might speak well enough, and too many wrongs have prevailed in the land, and there were never many men who sought after a remedy as diligently as they should. But daily they added one evil to another, and committed wrongs and many lawless acts too widely throughout this land. And on that account, we have also suffered many injuries and insults, and if we are to expect any improvement, we must then deserve better of God than we have previously done. . . .

Among heathen people one dare not withhold little or much of what is pledged in the worship of false gods, and we everywhere withhold God's dues all too often. And among heathen people one dare not diminish, within the temple or outside it, any of the things which are brought to the false gods and given as offerings. And we have utterly stripped God's houses inside and out, and the servants of God are everywhere deprived of respect and protection, while among heathen peoples, one dare not in any way abuse the servants of the false gods, just as one now does widely the servants of God, where Christians ought to keep God's law and protect God's servants. . . .

It is no wonder that things go wrong for us, because we all know full well that for many years now men have too often not cared what they did in word or deed. But this people, as it may seem, has become thoroughly corrupt through manifold sins and many misdeeds, through murders and crimes, through avarice and through greed, through theft and robbery, through the selling of men and through heathen vices, through betrayals and plots, through breaches of law and through deceit, through attacks on kinsmen and through manslaughter, through injury of clergy and through adultery, through incest and through various fornications. And also, far and wide, as we have said before, by the breaking of oaths and of pledges and through various falsehoods, many more than should be are lost and betrayed, and the failure to observe fasts and feasts widely occurs again and again. . . .

And let us do as is necessary for us: turn to justice and in some measure leave wrong-doing, and repair very carefully what we have broken. And let us love God and follow God's laws, and perform earnestly what we promised when we received baptism or those who were our sponsors at baptism. And let us order our words and deeds rightly, and cleanse our thoughts thoroughly, and keep carefully our oaths and pledges, and have some loyalty between ourselves without deceit. And let us often consider the great judgment to which we all must come, and save ourselves from the surging fires of hell's torment, and earn for ourselves the glories and the joys which God has prepared for those who do His will in the world. God help us. Amen.

From the Old Norse

Old Norse Poetry

from the *Elder Edda*
Sayings of the High One and *The Lay of Thrym*[1]

The poems called Sayings of the High One *and* The Lay of Thrym
*are found in the collection of Old Norse poems on traditional sub-
ject matter now entitled the* Elder Edda *(or the* Poetic Edda*). The
word* edda, *of uncertain meaning and etymology, was first applied
to the* Prose *or* Younger Edda, *a four-part work on skaldic poetry
collected and written by Snorri Sturluson (1178/9–1241). The
verse comprising the core of the* Elder Edda *is found in two Icelandic manuscripts: the* Codex Regius[2] *(before 1270), which contains twenty-nine poems, and the related fragmentary manuscript
AM 748 4to (c. 1300), which contains a thirtieth poem. A
"greater"* Elder Edda *includes a second group belonging to a sort*

---

[1]English translation by Patricia Terry, *Poems of the Elder Edda*. Philadelphia: University of Pennsylvania Press, 1990, pp. 11, 12, 16, 21, and 22. Copyright 1990 by
the University of Pennsylvania Press. Reprinted by permission of the University of
Pennsylvania Press. The stanzas translated are numbered 1, 5, 12, 41, 76, 77, 87,
and 88.

[2]The manuscript received its "king's book" after Brynjólfur Sveinsson presented it
to the king of Denmark in 1662.

of "eddic appendix" and a third group of poems of the eddic type (the "eddica minora"). The core verses of the Elder Edda *are distinct from these other two groups because, thanks to the nearly complete state of the Codex Regius, it is clear that the poems are presented in carefully conceived order: the first ten poems cover mythological subjects, and the remainder, including some prose links, heroic ones.*

Both of the selections here come from the mythological part of the Elder Edda. Sayings of the High One *belongs to the genre of "wisdom literature" and contains didactic utterances by the Norse god Odin (Woden), called here by the alias "the High One." The 164 stanzas of this poem are similar, then, to the Old English poems entitled* Maxims I *and* Maxims II. *The selections from* Sayings of the High One *encapsulate adages about behavior: the need for caution, a warning against drunkenness, the value of honor, and a caution about valorizing one's own reputation. Such sharply observed insights would have been as useful in Heorot as they seem to have been in Scandinavian halls.*

The Lay of Thrym, *which is charged by the ironies of dressing up the mighty god Thor as a blushing bride for an eager giant, is thought to be one of the more recent of the eddic poems. When Thor awakens to find that his hammer has been stolen, the trickster god Loki discovers that the giant Thrym has taken the hammer and will return it only if the goddess Freyja becomes his bride. Freyja's angry refusal cites the famous Brising necklace, called "Freya's necklace," in* Beowulf *at line 1056. When Loki later develops a plan to dress Thor as the goddess, it is clear that Thor must wear the necklace as part of his disguise, so strongly is it associated with Freyja. Along with an Old English variation on Freyja's name ("Freya"), these two references show that the* Beowulf-*poet and the composer of the* Elder Edda *shared some of the same mythological traditions.*

Sayings of the High One (Hávamál)

At every doorway   what you have to do
    is look around you
    and look out;
never forget: no matter where you are,
    you might find a foe.

It takes sharp wits   to travel in the world—
      they're not so hard on you at home;
in the flicker of an eye   the fool is found
      who wanders among the wise.

Beer isn't such   a blessing to men
      as it's supposed to be;
the more you swallow,   the less you stay
      the master of your mind.

Give your friends gifts—   they're as glad as you are
      to wear new clothes and weapons;
frequent giving makes friendships last,
      if the exchange is equal.

Cattle die, kinsmen die,
      one day you die yourself;
but words of praise   will not perish
      when a man wins fair fame.

Cattle die,   kinsmen die,
      one day you die yourself;
I know one thing   that never dies—
      the dead man's reputation.

A creaking bow,   a burning flame,
a yawning wolf,   a crow crying,
squealing swine,   a rootless tree,
billows rising,   a kettle boiling,
a dart flying,   falling seas,
new ice,   a serpent coiled,
a bride's bed-talk,   a broken sword,
a bear at play   or a king's boy,
a sick calf,   a willful slave,
sweet words from witches,   the newly slain,
your brother's murder,   though met on the road,
a half-burned house   or a horse too swift
(if he breaks his leg   you've lost your mount)—
a man's too trusting   who takes a chance on these.

The Lay of Thrym (þrymskviða)

Then Freyja was angry and snorted
so that the hall of the Æsir[3] shook
and the mighty Brising necklace broke . . .
[*the gods disguise Thor as a bride*]
They clad Thor in a bride's linen
and gave him the great Brising necklace,
they hung a ring of keys[4] around his waist,
and let womanly dress fall around his knees;
upon his chest were bright gems
and a bridal veil neatly bound his head.

Old Norse Prose

From *Grettir's Saga (Grettis saga Ásmundarsonar)*[1]

The similarity between Grettir's Saga *and* Beowulf *was first noticed in 1878 by Guðbrandur Vigfússon, who called the saga "a late version of the famous Beowulf Legend."*[2] *Scandinavian narrative parallels may be expected, given the setting of* Beowulf *in the kingdoms of the Geats and the Danes. Indeed, striking analogies to* Beowulf *have been located in Icelandic sagas of several genres, including similarities in names, in narratives describing a fight between a hero and a humanoid creature, and in the construction of the heroic character and the heroic*

---

[3]The great gods of Norse mythology.

[4]A sign of a woman's occupation as housekeeper was her ring of keys.

[1]English translation by Denton Fox and Hermann Pálsson, *Grettir's Saga*. Toronto: University of Toronto Press, 1974, pp. 69–80 and 135–40. Copyright 1974 by the University of Toronto Press. Reprinted with permission of the publisher. The title of the saga means "the saga of Grettir, the son of Asmund."

[2]Guðbrandur Vigfússon. "Prolegomena." *Sturlunga saga*. 2 vols. Oxford: Clarendon Press, vol. 1, p. xlix.

society.[3] *These two episodes from* Grettir's Saga *show how powerful and detailed are such similarities.*

Composed between 1310 and 1320, the anonymous Grettir's Saga *may be the latest of the great Icelandic genre of "family sagas"* (Íslendingasögur). *Much of the saga is a biography of Grettir, who, like Beowulf in Hrothgar's kingdom, is a "cleanser" of the land, destroying trolls and other supernatural creatures. But "good luck and great ability are two different things"*[4] *here as in the Old English poem, and Grettir's arc of heroism flames out in tragic circumstances.*

[Because his farmstead is haunted by something that destroys every living creature on it, the farmer Thorhall has difficulty hiring a shepherd. When a wolfish-looking Swede named Glam shows up, Thorhall hires him, only to find himself in a worse predicament. Grettir comes to Thorhall's aid, but the incident changes Grettir's life.]

Chapter 32

There was a man called Thorhall who lived at Thorhallsstead in Forsæludale, which runs from Vatnsdale. He was a rich man, particularly in livestock; he had more animals than anyone else. He was not a chieftain, but nevertheless he was a very notable farmer.

Thorhall's farm was haunted, which made it very difficult for him to get a satisfactory shepherd. He consulted many wise men and asked them what he should do about it, but no one could solve the problem.

Thorhall, who had many excellent horses, used to ride to the Althing every summer. One summer, when he was at the Althing, Thorhall went to the booth of Skapti Thoroddsson the Lawspeaker

---

[3]For a survey of Scandinavian parallels, see Andersson's "Sources and Analogues" in Bjork and Niles (1997, pp. 125–34). For a discussion of the monster, see Orchard (1995, pp. 140–68). A striking lexical similarity is the Old Norse *hepti-sax*, found in Chapter 66 of the saga; this word is unique to *Grettir's Saga*, but a similarly unusual compound *hæft-mece* occurs in *Beowulf* to describe the sword Hrunting that Unferth lends Beowulf.

[4]As says his uncle Jokul to Grettir in Chapter 34.

who was an exceptionally shrewd man and gave good advice whenever he was consulted. (There was this difference between Skapti and his father Thorodd: in spite of the fact that Thorodd was a prescient man he was considered by some to be deceitful, whereas Skapti used to give everyone the advice which he thought would be the most useful, if it were followed; that is why he was called Father-Betterer.) Thorhall went into the booth, and Skapti, who knew what a wealthy man he was, welcomed him and asked him for the news.

'I would like to get some advice from you,' said Thorhall.

'I'm not very good at that,' said Skapti. 'But what is your trouble?'

Thorhall said, 'This is the situation: I'm having much difficulty in keeping shepherds, for some of them have suffered certain injuries, and others have left before their contracts were up, and now no one who knows the circumstances is willing to take on the job.'

'Some evil creature must be at the root of this,' said Skapti, 'and that is why the shepherds are so much more reluctant to work for you than for other farmers. Now that you have sought my advice, I will get you as a shepherd, a man called Glam, who is from the Sylgisdales in Sweden; he came to Iceland last summer. Glam is a big and powerful man, but few people find him very likeable.'

Thorhall said he did not mind that as long as the man could take proper care of the sheep. Skapti said that if Glam, with all his strength and courage, failed, other men would not find it an easy job. At that Thorhall left the booth. This was just before the Althing broke up.

Thorhall missed two pale-dun horses and went himself in search of them; because of this people believe that he was not an important man. He went up to Sleda Ridge and south along the mountain known as Armannsfell, and then he saw a man coming down from Goda Wood and leading a horse with a load of faggots. Soon the two men met; Thorhall asked the other his name, and he said he was called Glam. He was a huge man and very strange looking, with glaring grey eyes and a head of wolf-grey hair. Thorhall was somewhat taken aback at the sight of Glam, but he realized that this must be the man he had been told about.

'For what kind of work are you best suited?' said Thorhall. Glam said he was well suited for herding sheep in winter.

'Will you herd my sheep, then?' said Thorhall. 'Skapti has entrusted you to me.'

'You'll find me most useful,' said Glam, 'if I'm left free to do things my own way, for I become angry when I'm crossed.'

'That won't do me any harm,' said Thorhall. 'I want you to work for me.'

'I might do that,' said Glam. 'But are there any problems?'

'The place is thought to be haunted,' said Thorhall.

'Spooks will never frighten me,' said Glam. 'They could only make life less dull.'

'You may find that attitude useful,' said Thorhall. 'It's certainly no place for a coward.'

They soon reached an agreement, and Glam was to come at the beginning of winter. Then they parted, and Thorhall found his horses in a place that he had just searched. He rode back and thanked Skapti for the favour he had done him.

The summer passed, and Thorhall heard nothing from the shepherd, nor did anyone seem to know anything about him, but at the arranged time he turned up at Thorhallsstead. Thorhall treated him well, but the rest of the household disliked him, Thorhall's wife in particular.

Glam took charge of the sheep, and it was an easy task for him, since he had a powerful bass voice and the sheep used to gather together whenever he shouted. There was a church at Thorhallsstead, but Glam never went there, for he hated the chants and had absolutely no faith. He was rough and repulsive, and everyone found him thoroughly obnoxious.

Time passed until the day before Christmas. Glam got up early in the morning and demanded his food. The housewife said, 'It's not the custom of Christians to eat today, for tomorrow is the first day of Christmas, and so it's our duty to fast all day.'

He answered, 'You have many superstitions which I consider quite pointless. I can't see that people are any better off nowadays than they were before when they didn't bother with such nonsense. I liked the old customs better when people were still heathens. I want my food now, and I'll have none of this quibbling.'

The housewife said, 'I know for certain that this will be a sorry day for you, since you take this evil course.'

Glam told her to bring his food at once, and said that otherwise it would be the worse for her. She didn't dare refuse, and when he had finished his meal he went out in an ugly mood.

It was very dark outside, with fluttering snowflakes and a howling wind. The weather grew worse and worse as the day wore on.

During the morning the people could hear the shepherd clearly, but less so in the afternoon. Then the snow began to drift, and in the evening the weather turned into a blizzard.

People went to church for mass, and so time passed until nightfall, but Glam did not come home. There was some discussion of whether or not he should be searched for, but because of the snowstorm and the darkness nothing came of it.

Glam did not come home Christmas Eve. The people waited until mass was over, and when it was broad daylight several men set out in search of him, and found the sheep scattered about in snowdrifts, beaten down by the storm or straying up on the mountain. Then they came upon a large area of trampled snow high up in the valley; it seemed to them as if a violent struggle had taken place there, for in many places stones as well as earth had been torn up. When they searched more carefully they saw Glam lying near by; he was dead, and his body was dark-blue in colour and swollen up to the size of an ox. They were horrified and shrank back from the corpse. However, they tried to carry it down to the church, but they could drag it no farther than down to the edge of a ravine a little distance away.

So they went back home and told Thorhall what had happened. He asked them what could have brought about Glam's death, and they told him they had traced some footprints so huge that they were just as if the bottom of a cask had been thrown down, and that they led right up to the cliffs at the head of the valley—there had been large splashes of blood all along the track. Because of this people thought that the monster which had been there before must have killed Glam, and also that he must have wounded the monster fatally, for there has never been any sign of it since.

On the second day of Christmas another attempt was made to take Glam's body to church. Oxen were used to haul it along, but they could not move it at all when the slope stopped and they came to level ground. And so they had to give up.

On the third day of Christmas a priest came along with them, and they searched for Glam the whole day without finding him. The priest refused to go again, but Glam was found at once when the priest was not among the searchers. Eventually they abandoned the attempt to bring Glam to church, and buried him in a cairn just where he was.

A little later the people found that Glam was not lying quiet. Terrible things happened; many men fell unconscious at the sight of him, and others lost their sanity. Soon after Christmas, people began to see him walking about the farmhouse and were terrified by him; many of them fled away. Then Glam began to sit astride the roof at night and beat it so furiously with his heels that the house came near to breaking. Soon he was walking about day and night, and men hardly found the courage to go up the valley, even on urgent business. All this was a great calamity for the people in the district.

Chapter 33

In the spring Thorhall engaged new servants and started farming again. The hauntings diminished as the days grew longer, and so time passed until midsummer.

That summer a ship from abroad put in at Hunavatn, and on board was a foreigner called Thorgaut. He was tall and powerful, with the strength of two men. He was on his own, without a job, and he needed to find some employment, since he had no money. Thorhall rode to the ship, saw Thorgaut, and asked if he were willing to work for him. Thorgaut said he was, and added that he was not very particular.

'I must warn you,' said Thorhall, 'that it is no place for weaklings, since the farm has been haunted for some time. I have no wish to deceive you in any way.'

'I can't see myself giving up, even though I should meet some spooks,' said Thorgaut. 'Other men will certainly find it hard to put up with, if it frightens me, and I'm not going to back out on that account.'

They soon came to an agreement, and Thorgaut was to be in charge of the sheep the following winter. The summer passed, and at the beginning of winter Thorgaut began herding the sheep. Everyone liked him.

Glam used to come to the house and sit astride the roof. Thorgaut thought this very amusing, and said the rascal would have to come closer before he was frightened by him. Thorhall warned him to be careful, 'It would be better if you were not to confront him.'

'It is obvious that every trace of courage has been shaken out of all of you,' said Thorgaut, 'but this nonsense is not going to frighten me out of my wits just yet.'

Winter passed until it was Christmas, and on the day before Christmas, when the shepherd was leaving the house to herd the sheep, the housewife said to him, 'I very much hope that the old story will not repeat itself now.'

'Have no fear of that, woman,' said Thorgaut. 'Something worth telling will have to happen before I fail to come back.'

Then he went to his sheep. It was a cold day, and snowing heavily. Thorgaut usually returned home at twilight, but that day he did not come back. People went to church as usual, and it seemed to them that the turn of events was not unfamiliar. Thorhall wanted to organize a search for the shepherd, but the church-goers were unwilling and said they were not going to expose themselves to trolls in the night. The farmer did not have the courage to go by himself, so nothing came of the search.

After breakfast on Christmas Day several men set out in search of the shepherd. First they went to Glam's cairn, for they thought he must have been responsible for the shepherd's disappearance. As they approached the cairn they saw that something remarkable must have happened, and indeed the shepherd was found there with his neck broken and every bone in his body crushed. They brought him back to church, and no one suffered any harm from him afterwards.

Glam began asserting himself even more than ever before, and now he committed so many outrages that the entire household fled away from Thorhallsstead, except for the farmer and his wife. The same cowherd had been there for a long time, and Thorhall did not want him to leave, for the cowherd was a kind man and good at his job. He was getting on in years and very loath to leave; he realized that everything the farmer owned would soon be destroyed if there was no one there to look after the farm.

One morning after midwinter the farmer's wife went to the cowshed to milk the cows at the usual time. It was broad daylight by then, for no one risked going out earlier, except for the cowherd, who used to go out at dawn. The woman heard a crashing noise and a terrible bellowing from the cowshed, so she ran screaming back into the house and said she didn't know what horrible things were happening there.

The farmer went out, and when he came to the cows he found them all goring one another. He didn't like the look of this at all, and went inside. Then he saw where the cowherd was lying on his back with his head in one stall and his feet in another. The farmer went up to him, felt him, and found that he was dead, with his back broken. It had been broken on the edge of the raised slab of stone which separated the two stalls.

The farmer realized that it was impossible for him to stay then any longer, so he fled, taking away with him as many possessions as he could. Every single beast which he left behind was killed by Glam. Then Glam started going through the entire valley, and he laid waste all the farms up from Tongue. Thorhall stayed with friends for the rest of the winter. No one could go to the upper reaches of the valley with a horse or a dog, for it was sure to be killed at once.

In the spring when the days became longer, the hauntings lessened somewhat, and Thorhall wanted to get back to his farm. He had great difficulty in engaging servants, yet he started farming again at Thorhallsstead. Everything happened just as before: when the autumn set in, the hauntings grew worse again. This time it was the farmer's daughter who suffered the most, and eventually she died as the result. Many remedies were tried, but they were all in vain. It seemed obvious to everyone that Vatnsdale would be all laid waste unless some solution could be found.

Chapter 34

Now the story goes back to Grettir Asmundarson, who stayed home at Bjarg through the autumn after his encounter with Bardi at Thoreyjargnup. Just before the beginning of winter Grettir set out from home and rode north across the ridges over to Vididale, and stayed at Audunarstead overnight. He and Audun were fully reconciled; Grettir gave him a fine axe as a present, and they agreed to remain friends.

Grettir rode north to Vatnsdale and paid a visit at Tongue, where his uncle Jokul Bardarson was living at the time. Jokul was a tall strong man, and exceptionally arrogant. He was a seafarer, very difficult to deal with, but a man of considerable importance. Jokul gave Grettir a good welcome, and he stayed there for three days. By this time Glam's reappearances were so much discussed that people talked about hardly anything else. Grettir enquired closely about all that had happened, and Jokul said that the stories did not exaggerate the facts. 'Do you want to pry into matters there, kinsman?' he asked.

Grettir said he did, but Jokul warned him not to go. 'That would be tempting fate,' he said. 'Your kinsmen have much at stake where you are concerned, for we feel that now there is no young man to compare with you. From evil beings like Glam only evil can be gained, and it is always better to deal with human beings than with monsters of his kind.'

Grettir said he still wanted very much to go to Thorhallsstead and see what had been going on.

Jokul said, 'I see that there is no point in trying to discourage you. The old saying is certainly true that "Good luck and ability are two different things."'

'"Disaster is close to your own house once it has entered neighbour's." So you should rather be thinking about what will happen to you in the end,' said Grettir.

Jokul replied, 'It might be that both of us are able to see into the future, and also that neither of us can do anything about it.'

With that they parted, and neither of them liked the other's predictions.

Chapter 35

Grettir rode over to Thorhallsstead and the farmer welcomed him warmly. He asked Grettir where he was going, and Grettir said he would like to spend the night there, if the farmer didn't mind. Thorhall said he would be very grateful if Grettir stayed. 'But lately few people have found it desirable to spend any time here. You must have heard about our trouble, and I shouldn't like you to come to grief because of me. Even if you can manage to get safely away yourself, I know for certain that you will lose your horse, for no one who comes here can keep his horse safe.'

Grettir said that horses were easy enough to get, if anything should happen to his. Thorhall was delighted that Grettir was staying and received him with open arms. They stabled Grettir's horse and put a strong lock on the door, and then they went to bed. The night passed and Glam did not come to the house.

Thorhall said, 'Your visit has certainly brought about an improvement here, for Glam has been in the habit of straddling the roof or breaking the doors every night, as indeed you can see clearly for yourself.'

Grettir said, 'This can mean only one of two things: either Glam will resume his old habit very soon, or else he will give it up for more than one night. So I'm going to stay another night and see what happens.'

Then they went to Grettir's horse, and he had not been tampered with. The farmer thought that every sign was pointing the same way. Grettir stayed for the second night, and the thrall did not come to the house. The farmer thought this very promising, and went to look at Grettir's horse, but this time the stable had been broken into, the horse dragged out through the door, and every bone in its body broken apart.

Thorhall told Grettir what had happened, and said that he should save his own life. 'You are sure to die if you wait for Glam,' he said.

Grettir answered, 'The very least I can have in return for my horse is to get a glimpse of the thrall.'

The farmer said that it would do him no good to see Glam. 'For he does not look like any human being,' he said. 'But every hour that you are willing to spend here is a great comfort for me.'

The day passed, and when the people went to bed, Grettir did not take off his clothes, but lay down on the bench opposite the farmer's bedcloset. He covered himself with a shaggy fur cloak, wrapping one end of it around his feet and the other around his head in such a way that he could see out through the neck-hole. The front benchboard was strong, and Grettir put his feet against it. The entire frame of the outer door had been broken away, and a crude hurdle tied carelessly in its place. The wooden partition which before had separated the hall from the entrance passage was also broken away, both below and above the crossbeam. All the beds had been moved out of place, and the house seemed rather uninviting. A light was kept burning in the hall throughout the night.

When about a third of the night had passed, Grettir heard a great noise outside. Someone seemed to be climbing the house and then straddling the roof-top above the hall, and beating his heels against the roof so that every beam in the house was cracking. This went on for a long time, and then it was as if someone was climbing down from the roof, and coming to the door. Then the door was opened, and Grettir saw the thrall stretching his head through it, and the head was hideously huge, with enormous features.

Glam moved slowly, and when he was inside the door he stretched himself up to his full height so that he towered up to the rafters. He turned towards the hall, laid his arms on the cross beam, and stretched his head into the hall. The farmer did not utter a single sound, for he thought that the noise outside had been quite enough. Grettir lay still and did not move at all.

Glam noticed a heap lying on the bench, so he crossed the hall and pulled hard at the cloak, but Grettir braced his feet against the beam and did not budge. Glam pulled at the cloak a second time, and much harder, but the cloak did not move at all. The third time Glam seized hold of the cloak with both hands and pulled at it so violently that Grettir was forced up from the bench, and then they tore the cloak in two between them.

Glam looked at the torn piece he held in his hand and wondered who could have pulled so hard against him. At that moment Grettir leapt under his arms, grasped him around the waist, and clasped him as hard as he could, hoping to bring him down. But the thrall gripped his arms so tightly that he was forced to break away. Grettir kept retreating from one bench to the other, and they started breaking up the beams and smashing everything that was in their way. Glam wanted to get outside, but Grettir braced his feet against anything he could, and yet Glam succeeded in dragging him out of the hall. Then they had a fierce struggle, for the thrall wanted to force Grettir out of the house, but Grettir realized that, difficult as it was to deal with Glam inside, it would be even worse in the open, and so he struggled with all his might against being dragged outside.

Glam was now using all his power, and when he reached the vestibule he pulled Grettir towards him. Grettir realized that he could resist no longer, and so he flung himself violently into the thrall's arms and at the same time braced his feet against a half-sunken boulder that stood in the entrance. Glam had been striving hard to pull Grettir his way, so he was unprepared for this. He fell backwards and crashed out through the door, his shoulders catching the lintel so that the roof was torn apart, both the rafters and the frozen roof-sods, and as he fell on his back out of the house, Grettir landed on top of him.

Outside the moonlight was bright but intermittent, for there were dark clouds which passed before the moon and then went away. At the very moment when Glam fell, the clouds cleared away, and Glam glared up at the moon. Grettir himself once said that that was the only sight he ever saw which frightened him. Then, because of exhaustion and the sight of Glam rolling his eyes so fiercely, Grettir was overcome by such a faintness that he could not draw his short sword, and so he remained there lying closer to death than to life.

Glam, who was endowed with more power for evil than any other revenant, then spoke the following words:

'You have been very determined to meet me, Grettir, but it will hardly surprise you if you do not get much luck from me. I will tell you this: you have acquired by now only half of the strength and vigour which you were destined to get if you had not met me. I cannot take away from you what you already have, but I can see to it that you will never be stronger than you are now, and yet you are strong enough, as many will find to their cost. Up until now your deeds have brought you fame, but from now on outlawry and slaughter will come your way, and most of your acts will bring you ill luck and misfortune. You will be made an outlaw and forced to live by yourself. I also lay this curse on you: you will always see before you these eyes of mine, and they will make your solitude unbearable, and this shall drag you to your death.'

As soon as Glam had spoken these words the faintness that had come over Grettir left him. He drew his short sword, cut off Glam's head, and placed it against his buttocks.

Then the farmer came outside. He had put on his clothes while Glam was making his speech, but had not dared to come anywhere near until Glam was laid low. Thorhall praised God and thanked Grettir warmly for vanquishing this unclean spirit. Then they set to work and burned Glam to ashes, gathered them into a skin bag, and buried them at a place far away from all paths of men and pastures of animals. After that they went back home. It was about daybreak, and Grettir lay down to rest, for he was very stiff.

Thorhall sent for men from the neighbouring farms, and showed them and told them what had happened. All who heard about this deed were greatly impressed by it, and said that no man in the entire country was Grettir Asmundarson's equal in strength, in courage, or in accomplishments. Thorhall gave him fine gifts when he left, a good horse, and splendid clothes, for the ones he had been wearing were torn into tatters. They parted the best of friends.

From there Grettir rode over to As in Vatnsdale. Thorvald gave him a good welcome, and questioned him closely about his encounter with Glam. Grettir told him all about their dealings and said that this long struggle had been the greatest test of his strength he had ever experienced. Thorvald warned Grettir to restrain himself. 'If you do that, all will go well with you, but otherwise you will have much bad luck.'

Grettir said that this incident had done little to improve his temper, and that he had now much less control over himself than before, and found it more difficult to put up with any offences. He also said that he could notice one change: he had become so frightened of the dark that he did not dare go anywhere alone after nightfall, because all kinds of phantoms appeared to him then. It has since become a common saying that people who suffer hallucinations have Glam's vision, or that Glam has lent them his eyes.

Afterwards Grettir rode back home to Bjarg, and he stayed there for the rest of the winter.

[*A farmstead called Sandhaugar is haunted by trolls who attack twice at Christmastime, making off with a man each time. Although he has been outlawed, Grettir comes to help, disguised as "Gest," which is another name for Odin.*]

Chapter 64

There was a priest called Stein who lived at Eyjardaleriver in Bardardale; he was a good farmer and owned a lot of livestock. He had a son, Kjartan, who was a vigorous young man. A man called Thorstein the White was living at Sandhaugar, south of Eyjardaleriver. He had a wife called Steinvor, who was young and cheerful; their children were still small. The farm at Sandhaugar was said to be haunted by trolls. Two years before Grettir came to the north it happened that Steinvor had gone to the Christmas mass at Eyjardaleriver, as was her custom, but her husband stayed home. In the evening the household went to bed, and during the night they heard a great noise in the hall, as something moved towards the farmer's bed. No one had the courage to get up and see what was happening, for there were only a few people on the farm. When the housewife came home in the morning her husband had vanished, and no one knew what had become of him.

Twelve months passed, and the next Christmas the housewife again wished to go to mass. She asked her servant to stay home; he was unwilling, but told her she could have her own way. Everything happened just as before, and the servant disappeared. This was thought a great marvel. When some spatterings of blood were discovered in the outer doorway, people realized monsters must have taken both men.

The news of this spread far and wide. Grettir got to hear of it, and since he was so good at putting an end to hauntings and ghosts, he set off for Bardardale and arrived at Sandhaugar on the day before Christmas. He concealed his identity and called himself Gest. The housewife thought that he was an exceptionally big man, but the rest of the household were frightened by him. He asked if he could stay for the night, and the housewife said he was welcome. 'But you must look after your own safety.'

He said that so it should be. 'I will stay here,' he said, 'but you go to mass, if you want.'

She said, 'I think you must be a very brave man, if you dare to stay here at home.'

'I'm always willing to try something new,' he said.

'I don't want to stay at home,' she said, 'but I can't get across the river.'

'I will help you across,' he said.

Then she made herself ready to go to church, and took along her small daughter. There had been a great thaw, and the river was in flood, and filled with broken ice.

The housewife said, 'Neither men nor horses can cross the river now.'

'There must be fords in it,' said Grettir, 'and don't be frightened.'

'Take the girl first,' said the housewife. 'She is lighter.'

'I can't be bothered to make two trips for this,' said Grettir. 'I will carry you on my arm.'

She crossed herself and said, 'This is impossible. And what are you going to do with the girl?'

'I'll think of something,' he said.

He picked them both up and put the girl on her mother's knee, and carried them on his left arm; he had his right arm free, and in this way he waded into the water. The women were so frightened they did not dare to scream. The river immediately crashed against his chest, and a huge ice-floe was driven at him, but he pushed his free hand against it, and fended it off. Then the water became so deep that the river was surging on his shoulder, but he waded through it strongly until he reached the bank on the other side, and tossed the women onto dry land.

Then he turned back, and it was already dusk when he reached Sandhaugar. He asked for food, and when he had eaten he told the household to go to the back of the hall. Then he took the table and other available timber and built a bulwark across the hall; it was so high that none of the household could get over it. No one dared to contradict him or to murmur in any way. The door in the hall was on the sidewall, close to the gable, and by the door there was a raised wooden floor. He lay down on it, but did not take off his clothes. There was a light burning in the hall near the door.

The housewife arrived at Eyjardaleriver for mass, and everyone wondered how she could have crossed the river. She said she did not know whether it was a man or a troll who had carried her across. The priest said that it certainly must have been a man. 'But there will be few men who are his equal,' he said, 'and we should keep silent about it, for it may be that this man is meant to put an end to your troubles.' She spent the night there.

Chapter 65

Now to tell of Grettir: as midnight was approaching he heard a loud noise outside, and then a great she-troll came into the hall. She carried a trough in one hand and a big cleaver in the other. She looked around when she came inside, saw where Grettir was lying, and rushed at him. He got up to meet her; they started grappling fiercely with each other, and fought for a long time in the hall. She was the stronger, but he eluded her skillfully, and everything that came in their way was smashed, even the partition. She dragged him out through the door and into the entryway, but there he stood firm. She wanted to drag him out of the house, but could not do it until they had broken away the whole frame of the outer door and carried it out on their shoulders. The ogress shoved him down to the river and all the way to the edge of the gorge. Although he was exceedingly weary, he had to fight even harder than before, or else let her throw him down into the gorge. They kept fighting all night, and he thought he had never come up against so powerful a monster before. She held him so tightly to herself that he could not use either of his hands, and was forced to clasp his arms around the woman's waist. When they reached the gorge, he gave the ogress a swing, so that his right hand was freed. At once he seized the short sword at his waist, drew it, and struck at her shoulder, slicing off her right arm. With that he was freed, and she dived down into the gorge and vanished under the waterfall.

Grettir was stiff and worn out, and he lay for a long time at the top of the cliff. When the dawn broke he went back to the house and lay down on his bed, all bruised and swollen. When the housewife came home from church, she thought her house had been terribly disarranged. She went up to Grettir and asked him what had happened and why everything was broken and smashed. He told her the whole story; she was greatly impressed, and asked who he was. He gave her his true name, and asked her to send for a priest, because he wanted to see one. She did this, and when the priest Stein came over to Sandhaugar he soon found out that it was Grettir Asmundarson who had been calling himself Gest. The priest asked him what he thought had happened to the men who had disappeared. Grettir said he thought they must have disappeared into the gorge, but the priest answered that he could not believe that story without some evidence. Grettir said they would soon find out, and with that the priest went back home. Grettir lay in bed for many days, and the housewife took good care of him. And so the Christmas season passed.

Grettir said that the she-troll dived down into the gorge when she received the wound, but the men of Bardardale claim that the day dawned upon her as they were wrestling, and that she died when he cut off her arm—and she still stands there on the cliff, turned into stone.

The people in the valley sheltered Grettir secretly for the rest of the winter.

It happened one day after the Christmas season that Grettir went to Eyjardaleriver, and when he met the priest there he said, 'I know, priest, that you put little belief in what I say. I want you to come with me to the river and see for yourself whether there is any evidence.'

The priest agreed, and when they came to the waterfall they saw there was a cave down under the cliff. The cliff was so sheer that it could not be climbed, and it was almost ten fathoms down to the water. They had brought a rope with them.

The priest said, 'It is utterly impossible for you to get down there.'

Grettir replied, 'It is certainly possible, and especially for those who are men of courage. I am going to find out what there is in the waterfall, and you must look after the rope.'

The priest told him to have it his own way, and he drove a peg into the top of the cliff, piled stones around it, and sat down.

Chapter 66

Now to tell of Grettir: he tied a stone to a loop at the end of the rope, and dropped it down to the water.

'How do you intend to get down?' asked the priest.

'I have a feeling that I don't want to be tied up when I reach the waterfall,' said Grettir.

After that he got ready for the descent: he wore few clothes, and girded himself with a short sword, but had no other weapon. Then he plunged down from the cliff and into the waterfall. The priest glimpsed the soles of his feet, but had no idea what happened to him after that. Grettir dived under the waterfall; this was a difficult thing to do, because the eddy was so strong that he had to dive down to the riverbed before he could get behind the waterfall. Inside, there was a ledge, and he climbed up on it. Above it, and behind the waterfall, there was a huge cave under the cliff edge where the river came crashing down. He went into the cave, where a great log-fire was burning. Grettir saw sitting there an immensely huge giant of terrifying appearance. When Grettir approached him the giant jumped up, seized a pike, and struck with it at his visitor. This pike, which had a wooden shaft, could be used both for striking and thrusting; such a weapon was called a hepti-sax. Grettir parried the blow with his short sword, and hit the shaft, cutting it in two. Then the giant tried to reach back to get a sword which hung there in the cave, but at that moment Grettir struck him in the chest and sliced away his front ribs and belly, so that his entrails gushed out of him and into the river, which swept them downstream. The priest, who was sitting by the rope, noticed some bloodstained shreds of flesh being swept down the river. He assumed that Grettir must be dead, and thought there was no reason to stay, so he ran home, leaving the rope unattended. It was evening by then, and the priest reported that Grettir was certainly dead. He added that such a man was a great loss.

But meanwhile, Grettir kept striking the giant furiously until he was dead. Then he went farther back in the cave, lit a light, and made a search. It is not known how much treasure he found in the cave, but people think it was a fair amount. He stayed there into the night, and found the bones of two men, which he put into a bag. Then he made his way out of the cave and swam to the rope, thinking to find the priest there. When he realized that the priest had gone home, he had to climb up the rope, hand over hand, but he managed to get to the top of the cliff. Then he went back to Eyjardaleriver and left the bag containing the bones on the church-porch. Beside it he left a staff on which these verses were beautifully carved in runes:

Alone I made my way
into the gloomy gorge.
The rock-splitting cascade
gave me a cold wet greeting.
The crushing waterfall
embraced me forcibly.
In this ogre-infested place,
the eddy slapped my shoulder.

The ugly giant came out
to welcome me;
he grappled with me
in a long hard struggle.
I cut the shaft of his hepti-sax,
and then my gleaming sword
ripped the breast and belly open
of this black monster.

In the runes Grettir also said that these bones had been taken by him from the cave. Next morning when the priest came to church he found the staff and the bones, and he read the runes. Grettir had gone back to Sandhaugar.

Snorri Sturluson
from the *Saga of the Ynglings* (*Ynglinga saga*)[1]

Constituting the first part of Snorri's great history known as Heim-skringla *("the orb of the world"), the* Saga of the Ynglings *gives an*

[1]Adapted from the translation by Samuel Laing, *The Heimskringla Or, The Chronicle of the Kings of Norway. Translated from the Icelandic of Snorro Sturleson* [sic], *with a Preliminary Dissertation.* 3 vols. London: Longman Brown, 1844.

account of the legendary kings of Sweden, a dynasty believed to have been founded by Odin, after he led the gods from Asia to Scandinavia. Snorri's history extends into the ninth century. After Odin's death, the kingdom was ruled first by Njörð, and then by Yngvi-Frey, after whom the dynasty is named. This saga was probably written c. 1223–35, but certainly before Snorri died in 1241. In the excerpts below, funerary customs similar to those in Beowulf *are recounted.*

Chapter 8

Odin established the same law in his land that had been in force in Asaland: that all dead men should be burned, and their belongings laid with them upon the pyre, and the ashes be cast into the sea or buried in the earth. Thus, said he, every one will come to Valhalla with the riches he had with him upon the pyre; and he would also enjoy whatever he himself had buried in the earth. For men of consequence a mound should be raised to their memory, and for all other warriors who had been distinguished for manhood a standing stone; which custom remained long after Odin's time.

Chapter 10

Odin died in his bed in Swithiod; and when he was near his death he made himself be marked with the point of a spear, and said he was going to Godheim, and would give a welcome there to all his friends, and all brave warriors should be dedicated to him; and the Swedes believed that he was gone to the ancient Asgard, and would live there eternally. Then began the belief in Odin, and the calling upon him. The Swedes believed that he often showed himself to them before any great battle. To some he gave victory; others he invited to himself; and they reckoned both of these to be fortunate. Odin was burnt, and at his pyre there was great splendor. It was their belief that the higher the smoke rose in the air, the higher would rise he whose pyre it was; and the richer he would be, the more wealth that was destroyed with him.

Chapter 27

. . . There was a great battle, in which King Hake [of Sweden] went forward so bravely that he killed all who were nearest to him, and at last killed King Eric, and cut down the banner of the two brothers.

King Jorund with all his men fled to their ships. King Hake had been so grievously wounded that he saw his days could not be long; so he ordered a warship which he had to be loaded with his dead men and their weapons and to be taken out to the sea; the tiller to be shipped, and the sails hoisted. Then he set fire to some tar-wood, and ordered a pile to be made over it in the ship. Hake was almost if not quite dead, when he was laid upon his pyre. The wind was blowing off the land—the ship flew, burning in bright flame, out between the isles, and into the ocean. Great was the fame of this deed afterwards.

From the *Saga of King Hrolf Kraki* (*Hrólfs saga kraka*)[1]

This anonymous, fourteenth-century Icelandic saga of the "mythic heroic" or "legendary" genre has often been compared to Beowulf.[2] *The saga's subject is King Hrolf and his twelve champions at the Danish court of Hleiðargarðar, a court linked to Hrothgar's at Heorot. Several Danish legendary histories[3] derive Hrolf's descent from Odin through Skjöld, the eponymous founder of the Danish royal line alluded to in the preface to* Beowulf. *One of the most intriguing—and contested—links is that between "Beowulf" (understood as bee-wolf, a kenning for bear)[4] and the bear-warrior Bodvar in this saga. A rich instance of the problem is found in the story of the champion's birth. The son of Bjorn (bear) and Bera (she-bear), Bodvar is nicknamed* bjarki *(little bear), and this child*

---

[1]English translation by Jesse L. Byock, *The Saga of King Hrolf Kraki*. New York: Penguin Books, 1998, pp. 36–41. Copyright 1998 by Penguin Books. Reproduced by permission of Penguin Books Ltd. A convenient summary of the positive case for associating *Beowulf* and this saga is made by Byock in the introduction to his translation, pp. xxv–xxviii.

[2]Hrolf is also found in line 45 of the Old English poem *Widsith* as "Hrothwulf." *Beowulf* shares many other Danish personal names with the saga, including Healfdene/Hálfdan, Hrothgar/Hróar, Halga/Helgi, and Heoroward/Hjörvarð.

[3]These include *Langfedgatal*, a twelfth-century genealogical list; Sven Aggesen's late-twelfth-century history of the Danish kings; an abstract of the now-lost *Skjöldunga saga*, which presumably narrated the history of the Danish dynasty; and Saxo's Danish history written about 1200.

[4]In an essay called "Beowulf's Name," R. D. Fulk and Joseph Harris make a persuasive and elegant case for accepting another etymology for "Beowulf" (in Heaney 2002, pp. 98–100).

becomes the ferocious hero who will free the Danish kingdom from
the ravages of a flying creature.

Chapter 19. Bjorn Rejects Queen Hvit's Advances: The Curse

Bjorn went back to his quarters after arguing with his father, each
thinking the other to be wrong. Bjorn, downcast and angry, his face
as red as blood, then took to his bed. The queen, wanting to lift his
spirits, spoke tenderly to him. He asked her to go away, which she
did for a time.

The queen often spoke with Bjorn, telling him that, while the
king was away, they had an opportunity to share one bed. She said
that their living together would be much better than her experience
with a man as old as King Hring.

Bjorn, taking this proposal badly, gave the queen a hard slap.
He told her to leave him alone and then threw her out. She said that
she was unaccustomed to being rejected or beaten. 'And it seems
that you, Bjorn, think it preferable to embrace a commoner's
daughter. You deserve a punishment, something far more disgraceful than enjoyment of my love and my tenderness. It would not
come as a surprise if something should happen to make you suffer
for your stubbornness and your stupidity.'

She then struck him with her wolfskin gloves, telling him to
become a cave bear, grim, and savage: 'You will eat no food other
than your own father's livestock and, in feeding yourself, you will
kill more than has ever been observed before. You will never be
released from the spell, and your awareness of this disgrace will be
more dreadful to you than no remembrance at all.'

Chapter 20. Bjorn's Transformation into a Bear
and the Birth of Bodvar

Then Bjorn disappeared, and no one knew what had become of
him. When people realized that Bjorn was missing, they searched
for him. As might have been expected, he was not to be found.

Next to be told is that the king's cattle were being killed in large
numbers by a grey bear, large and fierce. One evening it happened
that Bera, the freeman's daughter, saw the savage bear. It
approached her unthreateningly. She thought she recognized in the
bear the eyes of Bjorn, the king's son, and so she did not try to run
away. The beast then moved away from her, but she followed it all
the way until it came to a cave.

When she entered the cave, a man was standing there. He greeted Bera, the freeman's daughter, and she recognized that he was Bjorn, Hring's son. Theirs was a joyful reunion. For a time they stayed together in the cave, because she did not want to part from him while she still had a choice. He told her it was not right for her to be there with him, because he was a beast by day, even if he again became a man at night.

King Hring, when he returned home from the wars, was told everything that had happened while he was away. He learned about the disappearance of his son Bjorn. He was also told about the huge creature that had arrived in the land, attacking mostly the king's own livestock. The queen strongly urged killing the animal, but this was delayed for a time. The king expressed no opinion, even though he thought the events most unusual.

One night, while Bera and the prince lay in their bed, Bjorn began to speak, 'I suspect that tomorrow will be my death's day, for they will hunt and trap me. In truth, I find no pleasure in living because of the curse that lies upon me. You are my only delight, but that too will now cease. I want to give you the ring that is under my left arm. Tomorrow you will see the men stalking me. When I am dead, go to the king and ask him to give you whatever is under the beast's left shoulder; he will grant you this request.'

'The queen,' Bjorn continued, 'will be suspicious of you when you want to leave. She will try to make you eat some of the bear's meat, but you must not eat it, because, as you well know, you are pregnant and will give birth to three boys. They are ours, and it will be obvious from their appearance if you have eaten any of the bear's meat. This queen is a great troll. Then go home to your father, where you will give birth to the boys, one of whom will seem best to you. If you are not able to raise them at home, because of their strange and uncontrollable natures, bring them here to the cave. You will find here a chest with three bottoms. Runes are carved on it, and they will tell what each of the boys should receive as his inheritance. Three weapons are imbedded in the rock, and each of our sons shall have the one intended for him. Our firstborn will be called Elk-Frodi, the second son, Thorir, and the third, Bodvar. It seems to me most likely that they will not be weaklings and that their names will long be remembered.'

Bjorn foretold many things to her, and afterwards the bear-shape came over him. Then the bear went out, and she followed him.

When she looked around, she saw a great company of men circling the side of the mountain. A large pack of hounds raced in front of the men, and now the bear began to run. Turning away from the cave, he ran along the slope of the mountain. The hounds and the king's men gave chase, but the bear proved difficult for them to catch. Before he was overtaken he maimed many men and killed all the dogs.

At last the men formed a ring around him. The bear ranged about inside the ring, but understood the situation and knew that he would not be able to escape. Then he attacked in the direction of the king. Grabbing the man who stood next to the king, he ripped the man apart while still alive. By then the bear was so exhausted that he threw himself down on the ground. The men seized their opportunity and quickly killed him.

The freeman's daughter saw these events. She went up to the king and said, 'Sire, will you give me what is under the beast's left shoulder?'

The king granted her request, saying that nothing there could be unsuitable to give to her. By then, the king's men were well along in flaying the bear. Bera went to the carcass and took the ring, hiding it carefully. The men did not see what she took, but then no one was paying much attention.

The king asked who Bera was, because he did not recognize her. She gave whatever answer she thought best, although it was not the truth.

The king then returned home and Bera found herself swept along among his followers. The queen, now very cheerful, made Bera welcome, inquiring who she was. As before, Bera concealed the truth.

The queen prepared a great feast and had the bear meat readied for the men's enjoyment. The freeman's daughter was in the queen's chamber, unable to get away because the queen was suspicious about her identity. Sooner than expected, the queen entered the room with a plate of bear meat. She told Bera to eat, but Bera did not want to eat.

'How uncommonly rude,' said the queen, 'that you reject the hospitality that the queen herself has chosen to offer you. Eat it quickly, otherwise something worse will be prepared for you.'

The queen cut a small piece of the meat for Bera, and in the end Bera ate it. The queen then cut another piece and put it into Bera's mouth. Bera swallowed a small morsel of it, then spat the rest out of her mouth. She declared that she would not eat any more, even if she were to be tortured or killed. 'It may be,' said the queen, 'that this bit will be enough,' and she burst out laughing.

Bera then escaped and went home to her father. She had a very difficult pregnancy. She told her father the whole story relating to her condition and the reasons for what had happened. A little while later she fell ill and gave birth to a boy, though of an extraordinary kind. He was a man above the navel, but an elk below that. He was named Elk-Frodi. She bore another son, who was named Thorir. He had dog's feet from his insteps down. Because of this, he was called Thorir Hound's Foot; otherwise, he was the most handsome of men. A third boy was born, and this one was the most promising. He was named Bodvar, and there was no blemish on him. Bera loved Bodvar the most.

The boys shot up like weeds. When they were at the games with other men, they were fierce and unyielding in everything. Men received rough treatment at their hands. Frodi maimed many of the king's men, and some of them he killed. So matters continued until the boys were twelve years old. By then, because they were so strong that none of the king's men could stand up to them, they were no longer permitted to take part in the games. . . .

From the *Saga of Gold-Thorir (Gull-þóris saga)*

Found in a single vellum manuscript dating from around 1400, the Saga of Gold-Thorir *was likely composed a century earlier, after the period of the great Icelandic "family sagas." This excerpt shows the hero, Thorir Oddsson, winning great wealth from a band of Vikings who have now been transformed into dragons. Thorir attacks them in their watery hideout, but the hoard turns out to be cursed as was predicted, and Thorir, now grown greedy and spiteful, vanishes along with his treasure. The saga states that some think that Thorir himself has turned into a dragon. Many have noticed the plentiful similarities between this episode of the saga and that of the descent into the mere in* Beowulf. *The Old Norse saga also shares with the Old English poem a concern about heroic conduct and adventure and an anxiety about the allure of treasure.*

[*Thorir hears about a group of dragons living behind a waterfall in a cave and guarding a great treasure. These dragons had once been human: a Viking named Val and his sons. Relying on the advice of his dead uncle Agnar, Thorir and his companions go off to win the gold.*]

They told Ulf what had happened and asked him to guide them to the cave of Val. Ulf spoke against the journey and offered them money not to go, telling them that no one had returned who had gone there. Also he said that it would grieve him if those men should be lost whom Sigmund his friend had sent to him. But Thorir wanted to go no matter what; and a little later he and his fellows set out on their journey, and went north, past Finnmark until they came north to the foot of Blesaberg: for that is the name of the mountain where the cave of Val was found, and it is in the north by the Arctic Sea. A great river rushes down through a ravine from the mountain there and out into the sea. Then Thorir knew that they had come to the place to which he had been directed.

They went up to the mountain and did as Agnar had told them: they uprooted a huge tree and pushed its branches over the edge of the ravine and heaped rocks around its roots; then they took a rope and fastened it to the branches. Then Thorir offered his companions the chance to go down, and each to have the wealth that he got. But none of them dared to venture as far as the cave, even if that was the only danger, and they begged Thorir to turn back.

Thorir said, "That cannot be now: it looks as if I shall take the risk myself and have the wealth with few others to claim it."

They said they would make no claims on the money, and they said he would have enough to deserve it, if he got it. They found that Thorir was quite another man from what he had been. Thorir took off all his outer clothing in order to be lightly dressed: he had on the tunic, which was Agnar's gift, and the gloves, belt and knife, and slender rope which Agnar had given him, and he also had the spear with a thong which his father had given him. He walked out along the tree and hurled his spear over the river, and it stuck fast in the woods on the other side. After that he let himself down by the rope, letting the line pull him away from the cliff and under the waterfall.

And when Ketilbjorn saw this, he said that he would go with Thorir and share his luck; then he let himself down with the rope. Thorhall Kinnarson also said he would go, and Thrand the Tall said that Sigmund should never learn that he did not dare to help those to whom he had promised his backing. Thorir had reached the cave by now, and he dragged each of the others to him as they came from above. A rocky promontory jutted into the sea in front of the waterfall, and Bjorn Beruson and Hyrning went along it, and so came to the foot of the falls. They pitched a tent there on the point of the promontory, for no one could get nearer the waterfall because of the noise, the falling water, and the spray.

Thorir and his companions kindled a light in the cave and went on until a wind blew towards them, putting out the light. Then Thorir called on Agnar for help, and at once there came a great beam of light from the entrance of the cave, and they went forward for a while by the light until they heard the hissing of the dragons. But as soon as the beam of light reached the dragons, they all fell asleep; and then there was no lack of light for it shone from the dragons and the gold they were lying on. Then they saw where there were some swords with the hilts projecting from the dragons' sides. Then Thorir and his companions quickly grabbed the swords, leapt upon the dragons, and stabbed them under the shoulders to their hearts. Thorir managed to take the helmet from the largest dragon, but at the same moment the largest dragon seized Thrand the Tall and flew out of the cave with him, and then so did the others, one after another, with fire pouring from their mouths along with poison.

Now those who were outside saw a glow coming from the waterfall; they ran out of the tent, just as the dragons flew up from the waterfall, and Bjorn saw that one of the dragons had a man in his mouth. They thought then for certain that all the men who had gone into the cave must be dead. The largest dragon flew ahead, the one who had the man in his mouth; and as they flew up over the promontory, Bjorn rushed up onto the mountain side and stabbed the dragon with an inlaid spear. But as the dragon got the wound, there gushed from it so much blood into Bjorn's face that he was killed very quickly; and the blood and poison touched the foot of Hyrning, and caused him such furious pain that he could scarcely stand.

Now it must be told of Thorir and his companions that they got great wealth in the cave, enough booty for many men in gold and precious treasures; and it is said, that they remained in Val's cave for three days. There Thorir found the sword Hornhjalti, which Val had carried. Afterwards, Thorir hauled himself up first, and then drew up the treasure, and then his fellows.

From an Icelandic Folktale[1]

When Grendel attacks the warriors in Heorot, he grabs his victim with a taloned hand. Beowulf *subsequently emphasizes the creature's horrible grip, which, when Beowulf has detached it from Grendel's body, is displayed as a marvel from the gables of Hrothgar's hall. Thus, the episode in* Beowulf *shares elements with the folktale type called "the hand and the child." Several versions of this tale are found in Iceland.*

[*Five brothers receive names signifying their talents from an old woman, who has asked and received a drink from them.*]

The brothers lived with their parents until they were grown up. Then they said that they would leave the cottage to seek their fortunes elsewhere. Their parents consented. They went away, and nothing is told of their journey until they came to the king. They asked the king to be allowed to stay over the winter, but they said that either they all would stay, or none of them. The king said that they could stay with him over the winter, if they would watch over his daughters during the Yuletide. They agreed to that, and so they all were with the king.

And so it was that the king had had five daughters. For two years past, one had disappeared each night of Yule from the maidens' chamber, although there had been a guard. No one knew how they had vanished, and nowhere could they be found, for all of the searches that the king had caused to be made. As soon as the brothers knew how matters stood, they caused the king to build a new maidens' chamber, standing alone and very strong.

Now Yule came. The three princesses who were left went into the chamber, and all five brothers: they meant to keep watch over the princesses, but they all slept, except Wide-awake. There was a light in the chamber, and it was locked tightly. Early in the night, Wide-Awake saw a shadow on the window, and then a horribly huge hand stretched in over the bed of one of the princesses. Then Wide-Awake roused his brothers quickly, and Hold-Fast seized the paw which was stretched in, so that its owner could not withdraw

[1] Jón Árnason printed this folktale in his 1864 collection of Icelandic folk- and fairy-tales. See the comments and English translation in Chambers (1959, pp. 490–503).

it, though he tried hard to do so. Then came Strong-in-the-Blow, and he struck off the hand on the window-ledge. Then the creature outside leaped away, and the brothers chased after him.

Sharp-Tracker followed the footsteps. At last they came to some steep rocks, which no one could climb, except Good-Climber: he climbed up the rocks and threw a rope down to his brothers, and so dragged them all up. They found themselves by a great mouth of a cave and went in. There they saw a troll who was weeping. They asked what troubled her. She did not wish to tell them, but in the end she said that her man had lost one hand in the night, and therefore it went badly for her. They told her to be comforted, for they would cure the man. "But no one must look at us," said they, "while we are curing him; and we are so cautious about our secrets that we tie up all who are near, so that no one can come to us while we are doing the medicine, for a lot depends upon that." So they offered to cure the troll's man at once, if she would let them tie her up. She did not like the idea, but in the end, she let them. They bound her tightly and then went into the cave to her man. He was a terrible troll, and the brothers did not delay, but killed him on the spot. After that, they went to the she-troll and killed her.

Further Reading

Editions, Translations, and Manuscript Facsimiles

Alexander, Michael, ed. *Beowulf*. London: Penguin, 1995.

Chickering, Howell D., Jr., ed. and trans. *Beowulf: A Dual-Language Edition*. New York: Anchor Books, 1977.

Crossley-Holland, Kevin, trans., and Heather O'Donoghue, ed. *Beowulf: The Fight at Finnsburh*. Oxford: Oxford University Press, 1999.

Davis, Norman, ed. *Beowulf Reproduced in Facsimile, with a Transliteration and Notes by Julius Zupitza*. Early English Text Society o.s. 245. 2nd ed. rev. London: Oxford University Press, 1959.

Dobbie, Elliott van Kirk, ed. *Beowulf* and *Judith*. Anglo-Saxon Poetic Records, vol. 4. New York: Columbia University Press, 1953, pp. 3–98 [text], pp.113–281 [notes].

Donaldson, E. Talbot, trans., and Nicholas Howe, ed. *Beowulf: A Prose Translation*. New York: W. W. Norton & Company, 2002.

Heaney, Seamus, trans., and Daniel Donoghue, ed. *Beowulf: A Verse Translation*. New York: W. W. Norton & Company, 2002.

Jack, George, ed. *Beowulf: A Student Edition*. Oxford: Oxford University Press, 1994.

Klaeber, Friedrich, ed. *Beowulf and the Fight at Finnsburg*. 3rd ed. Boston: D. C. Heath and Company, 1950.

Liuzza, Roy M., trans. *Beowulf: A New Verse Translation*. Peterborough, Ontario: Broadview Press, 2000.

Malone, Kemp, ed. *The Nowell Codex, British Museum Cotton Vitellius A. xv, Second Manuscript*. Early English Manuscripts in Facsimile, 12. Copenhagen: Rosenkilde & Bagger, 1963.

Malone, Kemp, ed. *The Thorkelin Transcripts of Beowulf*. Early English Manuscripts in Facsimile, 1. Copenhagen: Rosenkilde & Bagger, 1951.

Mitchell, Bruce, and Fred C. Robinson, eds. *Beowulf, an Edition with Relevant Shorter Texts*. Oxford: Blackwell Publishers, 1998.

Swanton, Michael J., ed. and trans. *Beowulf. Edited with an Introduction, Notes and New Prose Translation*. Rev. ed. Manchester: Manchester University Press, 1997.

Wrenn, C. L., ed., and John R. Clark Hall, trans. *Beowulf and the Finnsburg Fragment. With Prefatory Remarks by J. R. R. Tolkien*. Rev. ed. London: George Allen & Unwin Ltd., 1940.

Handbooks and Essential Collections

Baker, Peter S., ed. *Beowulf: Basic Readings*. New York: Garland Publishing, 1995.

Bessinger, Jess B., Jr., and Robert F. Yeager. *Approaches to Teaching Beowulf*. New York: Modern Language Association of America, 1984.

Bjork, Robert E., and John D. Niles, eds. *A Beowulf Handbook*. Lincoln: University of Nebraska Press, 1997.

Calder, Daniel G., ed. *Old English Poetry: Essays on Style*. Berkeley: University of California Press, 1979.

Chambers, R. W. *Beowulf: An Introduction to the Study of the Poem with a Discussion of the Stories of Offa and Finn*. 3rd ed., with a supplement by C. L. Wrenn. Cambridge: Cambridge University Press, 1959.

Chase, Colin, ed. *The Dating of Beowulf*. Repr. with a new Afterword. Toronto: University of Toronto Press, 1997.

Damico, Helen, and Alexandra Hennessey Olson, eds. *New Readings on Women in Old English Literature*. Bloomington: Indiana University Press, 1990.

Fulk, R. D., ed. *Interpretations of Beowulf: A Critical Anthology*. Bloomington: Indiana University Press, 1991.

Godden, Malcolm, and Michael Lapidge, eds. *The Cambridge Companion to Old English Literature*. Cambridge: Cambridge University Press, 1991.

Lapidge, Michael, *et al.*, eds. *The Blackwell Encyclopedia of Anglo-Saxon England*. Oxford: Blackwell Publishers, 1999.

Liuzza, Roy M., ed. *Old English Literature: Critical Essays*. New Haven: Yale University Press, 2002.

Nicholson, Lewis E., ed. *An Anthology of Beowulf Criticism*. Notre Dame: University of Notre Dame Press, 1963.

Niles, John D., ed. *Old English Literature in Context: Ten Essays*. Cambridge: D. S. Brewer, 1980.

O'Keeffe, Katherine O'Brien, ed. *Reading Old English Texts*. Cambridge: Cambridge University Press, 1997.

Orchard, Andy. *A Critical Companion to Beowulf*. Cambridge: D. S. Brewer, 2003.

Osborn, Marijane. *Beowulf: A Guide to Study*. Los Angeles: Pentangle Press, 1986.

Robinson, Fred C. *The Tomb of Beowulf and Other Essays on Old English*. Oxford: Blackwell Publishers, 1993.

Shippey, T. A., and Andreas Haarder, eds. *Beowulf: The Critical Heritage*. London: Routledge, 1998.

General Studies and Works Cited

Alexander, Michael. *A History of Old English Literature*. Peterborough, Ontario: Broadview Press, 2002.

Bandy, Stephen C. "Cain, Grendel, and the Giants of *Beowulf*," *Papers on Language and Literature* 9 (1973), 235–49.

Blair, Peter Hunter. *The World of Bede*. Rev. ed. Cambridge: Cambridge University Press, 1990.

Bruce, Alexander M. *Scyld and Scef: Expanding the Analogues*. New York: Routledge, 2002.

Bruce-Mitford, R. L. S. *The Sutton Hoo Ship Burial: A Handbook*, 3rd ed. London: British Museum, 1979.

Cable, Thomas. *The English Alliterative Tradition*. Middle Age Series. Philadelphia: University of Pennsylvania Press, 1991.

Campbell, James, ed. *The Anglo-Saxons*. New York: Penguin, 1991.

Carver, Martin. *Sutton Hoo: Burial Ground of Kings?* Philadelphia: University of Pennsylvania Press, 1998.

Chamberlain, D. "*Judith*: a Fragmentary and Political Poem," in *Anglo-Saxon Poetry: Essays in Appreciation*. L. E. Nicholson and D. W. Frese, eds. Notre Dame: Notre Dame University Press, 1975, pp. 135–59.

Clover, Carol J. "The Germanic Context of the Unferth Episode," *Speculum* 55 (1980), 444–68. [Repr. in Baker 1995; see Handbooks and Essential Collections, p. 230.]

Cohen, Jeffrey Jerome. *Of Giants: Sex, Monsters, and the Middle Ages*. Minneapolis: University of Minnesota Press, 1999.

Davis, Craig R. *Beowulf and the Demise of Germanic Legend in England*. New York: Garland Publishing, 1996.

Deskis, Susan E. *Beowulf and the Medieval Proverb Tradition*. Medieval & Renaissance Texts & Studies, 155. Tempe: Arizona State University, 1996.

Dumville, David. "Kingship, Genealogies and Regnal Lists," in *Early Medieval Kingship*. Peter H. Sawyer and I. N. Wood, eds. Leeds: Leeds University Press, 1977, pp. 72–104.

Earl, James W. *Thinking about Beowulf*. Stanford: Stanford University Press, 1994.

Evans, Angela Care. *The Sutton Hoo Ship Burial*. London: The British Museum Press, 1986.

Fell, Christine. *Women in Anglo-Saxon England*. Oxford: Blackwell Publishers, 1984.

Foster, J. "A Boar Figurine from Guilden Morden, Cambs." *Medieval Archaeology* 21 (1977), 166–7.

Frank, Roberta. "The *Beowulf* Poet's Sense of History," in *The Wisdom of Poetry: Essays in Early English Literature in Honor of Morton W. Bloomfield*. Larry D. Benson and Siegfried Wenzel, eds. Kalamazoo, MI: Medieval Institute Publications, 1982, pp. 53–65.

Frantzen, Allen J., and John D. Niles, eds. *Anglo-Saxonism and the Construction of Social Identity*. Gainesville: University Press of Florida, 1997.

Friis-Jensen, Karsten, ed. *Saxo Grammaticus: A Medieval Author between Norse and Latin Culture*. Copenhagen: Museum Tusculanum, 1981.

Fry, Donald K. "Old English Formulas and Systems." *English Studies* 48 (1967), 193–204.

Georgianna, Linda. "Hrethel's Sorrow and the Limits of Heroic Action in *Beowulf*," *Speculum* 62 (1987), 829–50.

Goffart, Walter A. *The Narrators of Barbarian History (A.D. 550-800): Jordanes, Gregory of Tours, Bede, and Paul the Deacon*. Princeton: Princeton University Press, 1988.

Graham-Campbell, James. *Cultural Atlas of the Viking World*. New York: Facts on File, 1994.

Harris, Joseph. "A Nativist Approach to *Beowulf*: the Case of Germanic Elegy," in Henk Aertsen and Rolf H. Bremmer, Jr., eds. *Companion to Old English Poetry*. Amsterdam: Vrje UP, 1994, pp. 45–62.

Harris, Joseph. "Beowulf's Last Words," *Speculum* 67 (1992), 1–32.

Harrison, Kenneth. *The Framework of Anglo-Saxon History, to A. D. 900*. London: Cambridge University Press, 1976.

Higham, N. J. *An English Empire: Bede and the Early Anglo-Saxon Kings*. Manchester: Manchester University Press, 1995.

Hill, John M. *The Cultural World of Beowulf*. Toronto: University of Toronto Press, 1995.

Hill, Thomas D. "The Myth of the Ark-Born Son of Noe and the West-Saxon Royal Genealogical Tables," *Harvard Theological Review* 80 (1987), 379–83.

Howe, Nicholas. *Migration and Mythmaking in Anglo-Saxon England*. New Haven: Yale University Press, 1989.

Irving, Edward B., Jr. *Rereading Beowulf*. Philadelphia: University of Pennsylvania Press, 1989.

Irving, Edward B., Jr. *A Reading of Beowulf*. New Haven: Yale University Press, 1968.

Kaske, Robert E. "*Sapientia et Fortitudo* as the Controlling Theme of *Beowulf*." *Studies in Philology* 55 (1958), 423–56.

Kiernan, Kevin S. *Beowulf and the Beowulf Manuscript*. Foreword by Katherine O'Brien O'Keeffe. Rev. ed. Ann Arbor: The University of Michigan Press, 1996.

Lapidge, Michael. "*Beowulf*, Aldhelm, the *Liber Monstrorum* and Wessex," *Studi Medievali*, 3rd series, 23 (1982), 151–92.

Leake, Jane. *The Geats of Beowulf: A Study in the Geographical Mythology of the Middle Ages*. Madison: University of Wisconsin Press, 1967.

Mellinkoff, Ruth. "Cain's Monstrous Progeny in *Beowulf*: Part I, Noachic Tradition." *Anglo-Saxon England* 8 (1979), 143–62. "Part II, Post Diluvian Survival," *Anglo-Saxon England* 9 (1981), 183–97.

Mitchell, Bruce. *An Invitation to Old English and Anglo-Saxon England*. Oxford: Blackwell Publishers, 1995.

Newton, Sam. *The Origins of Beowulf and the Pre-Viking Kingdom of East Anglia*. Woodbridge, Suffolk: D. S. Brewer, 1993.

Niles, John D. *Beowulf: The Poem and Its Tradition*. Cambridge: Harvard University Press, 1983.

O'Keeffe, Katherine O'Brien. *Visible Song: Transitional Literacy in Old English Verse*. Cambridge: Cambridge University Press, 1990.

Orchard, Andy. "Oral Tradition," in *Reading Old English Texts*. Katherine O'Brien O'Keeffe, ed. Cambridge: Cambridge University Press, 1997, pp. 101–23.

Orchard, Andy. *Pride and Prodigies: Studies in the Monsters of the Beowulf Manuscript*, Cambridge: D. S. Brewer, 1995.

Overing, Gillian R. *Language, Sign, and Gender in Beowulf*. Carbondale and Edwardsville: Southern Illinois University Press, 1990.

Page, R. I. *Chronicles of the Vikings: Records, Memorials and Myths*. London: The British Museum Press, 1995.

Scowcroft, R. Mark. "The Irish Analogues to *Beowulf*," *Speculum* 74 (1999), 22–64.

Shippey, T. A. *Old English Verse*. London: Hutchison, 1972.

Skovgaard-Petersen, Inge. "Saxo, Historian of the Patria," *Mediæval Scandinavia* 2 (1969), 54–77.

Swanton, Michael J. "The Manuscript Illustrations of a Helmet of Benty Grange Type." *Journal of the Arms and Armour Society* 10 (1980), 1–5.

Tolkien, J. R. R. *The Monsters and the Critics and Other Essays*. Christopher Tolkien, ed. London: George Allen & Unwin, 1983.

Ward, Benedicta. *The Venerable Bede*. London: Geoffrey Chapman, 1990.

Webster, Leslie. "The Iconographic Programme of the Franks Casket," in Jane Hawkes and Susan Mills, eds. *Northumbria's Golden Age*. Stroud: Sutton,1999, pp. 227–46.

Webster, Leslie. "Stylistic Aspects of the Franks Casket," in Robert T. Farrell, ed. *The Vikings*. Chichester: Phillimore, 1982, pp. 20–32.

Webster, Leslie, and Janet Backhouse. *The Making of England: Anglo-Saxon Art and Culture, AD 600–900*. Toronto: University of Toronto Press, 1991.

Whitbread, L. "The *Liber Monstrorum* and *Beowulf*," *Mediaeval Studies* 36 (1974), 434–71.

Whitelock, Dorothy. *The Audience of Beowulf*. Oxford: Clarendon Press, 1951.

Whitelock, Dorothy. "*Beowulf* 2444–71." *Medium Ævum* 8 (1939), 198–204.

Wormald, Patrick. "Bede, *Beowulf*, and the Conversion of the Anglo-Saxon Aristocracy," in *Bede and Anglo-Saxon England: Papers in Honour of the 1300th Anniversary of the Birth of Bede, Given at Cornell University in 1973 and 1974*. Robert T. Farrell, ed. London: British Archaeological Reports, 1978, pp. 32–95.

Wright, Charles D. *The Irish Tradition in Old English Literature*. Cambridge Studies in Anglo-Saxon England, 6. Cambridge: Cambridge University Press, 1993.

Analogues and Related Texts

Aethelweard. *Chronicon Æthelweardi : The Chronicle of Æthelweard*. Alistair Campbell, ed. and trans. London: Thomas Nelson and Sons Ltd., 1962.

Alcuin. *Alcuin of York: His Life and Letters*. Stephen Allott, trans. York: William Sessions Limited, 1974.

Allen, Michael J. B., and Daniel G. Calder. *Sources and Analogues of Old English Poetry: The Major Latin Texts in Translation*. Cambridge: D. S. Brewer, 1976.

Bede. *The Ecclesiastical History of the English People*. Bertram Colgrave and R. A. B. Mynors, ed. and trans. Oxford: Clarendon Press, 1969.

Crossley-Holland, Kevin, trans. *The Anglo-Saxon World: An Anthology*. Oxford World's Classics. Oxford: Oxford University Press, 1984.

Davidson and Fisher 1979–80. *See* Saxo Grammaticus.

Dronke, Ursula, ed. and trans. *The Poetic Edda*. 2 vols. Oxford: Oxford University Press, 1969 and 1997.

Faulkes 1987. *See* Snorri Sturluson.

Fox, Denton, and Hermann Pálsson, trans. *Grettir's Saga*. Toronto: University of Toronto Press, 1974.

Garmonsway, G. N., and Jacqueline Simpson, trans. *Beowulf and Its Analogues*. Including *Archaeology and Beowulf* by Hilda Ellis Davidson. New York: E. P. Dutton & Co., 1968.

Gregory of Tours. *History of the Franks*. Lewis Thorpe, trans. Harmondsworth: Penguin, 1974.

Jordanes. *The Gothic History of Jordanes in English Version*. Charles C. Mierow, trans. Princeton: Princeton University Press, 1915.

Keynes, Simon, and Michael Lapidge, trans., introduction, and notes. *Alfred the Great: Asser's Life of King Alfred and Other Contemporary Sources*. New York: Penguin, 1983.

Morris, John, ed. and trans. *Historia Brittonum: English and Latin*. London: Phillimore, 1980.

Morris, Richard (ed.). *The Blickling Homilies : With a Translation and Index of Words, Together with the Blickling Glosses*. Early English Text Society o.s. 58 [1874], 63 [1876], 73 [1880]. London: Oxford University Press, 1880. [reprinted as one volume, 1967]

The Sagas of the Icelanders: A Selection. Örnólfur Thorsson, general ed. Preface by Jane Smiley. Introduction by Robert Kellogg. New York: Penguin, 2001.

Saxo Grammaticus. *History of the Danes*. Volume I: English Text, Volume 2: Commentary. Peter Fisher, trans., and Hilda R. Ellis Davidson, ed. Cambridge: D. S. Brewer, 1979, 1980.

Shippey, T. A., ed. and trans. *Poems of Wisdom and Learning in Old English*. Cambridge: D. S. Brewer, 1976.

Snorri Sturluson. *Edda*. Anthony Faulkes, ed. and trans. London: J. M. Dent, 1987.

Swanton, Michael J., ed. and trans. *The Anglo-Saxon Chronicle*. New York: Routledge, 1998.

Tacitus. *The Agricola and The Germania*. Harold Mattingly, trans. rev. by S. A. Handford. New York: Penguin, 1970.

Whitelock, Dorothy, ed. *English Historical Documents, c. 550–1042*. 2nd ed. New York: Oxford University Press, 1979.

Williamson, Craig, trans. *A Feast of Creatures: Anglo-Saxon Riddle-Songs*. Philadelphia: University of Pennsylvania Press, 1982.

Williamson, Craig, ed. *The Old English Riddles of the Exeter Book*. Chapel Hill: The University of North Carolina Press, 1977.

Wulfstan. *The Homilies of Wulfstan*. Dorothy Bethurum, ed. Oxford: Clarendon Press, 1957.